Praise for

'"It's done," Anthony Albanese tells his inner circle on election night, after taking the concession call from Scott Morrison. Errington and van Onselen's dissection of Labor's election victory is peppered with insider accounts of the key moments of the 2022 election campaign and the events that culminated in the Labor win after nine years in the wilderness. Tracking the rise of Anthony Albanese from long-time loyal Labor son to Prime Minister of Australia, they reveal his ambitions, his tactics and some very human moments. This engrossing 360-degree account of the 2022 campaign tells the story from all sides, with insights and intel from those making the decisions that won and lost the election'

Fran Kelly, journalist and former host
of Radio National's *Breakfast*

'Through their journalistic and academic lenses, Peter and Wayne help us better understand the motivations, miscalculations and master strokes of the campaign, and how Australian politics changed at this election. The inside stories of Morrison's missteps, the nature of Albanese's power within Labor and the challenges confronting the new Government — it's all there'

David Speers, journalist and host
of ABC's *Insiders*

Peter van Onselen is an academic, author and journalist. He is Network Ten's political editor and contributing editor at *The Australian* newspaper. Dr van Onselen is Winthrop Professor of Politics and Public Policy at The University of Western Australia.

Wayne Errington is Adjunct Associate Professor of Politics and Public Policy and a former Head of Politics and International Relations at the University of Adelaide. Dr Errington has published feature articles and opinion pieces in all the major national newspapers.

Together they have written *John Winston Howard: The Biography* (2007), *Battleground: Why the Liberal Party Shirtfronted Tony Abbott* (2015), *The Turnbull Gamble* (2016), *How Good Is Scott Morrison?* (2021) and *Who Dares Loses: Pariah Policies* (2021).

VICTORY

THE INSIDE STORY OF LABOR'S RETURN TO POWER

PETER VAN ONSELEN
AND WAYNE ERRINGTON

To Virginia + Geoff
I hear this victory will
make you both Very happy!

Paul Kelly.

■ HarperCollins*Publishers*

HarperCollins*Publishers*
Australia • Brazil • Canada • France • Germany • Holland • India
Italy • Japan • Mexico • New Zealand • Poland • Spain • Sweden
Switzerland • United Kingdom • United States of America

HarperCollins acknowledges the Traditional Custodians
of the land upon which we live and work, and pays respect
to Elders past and present.

First published in Australia in 2022
by HarperCollins*Publishers* Australia Pty Limited
Gadigal Country
Level 13, 201 Elizabeth Street, Sydney NSW 2000
ABN 36 009 913 517
harpercollins.com.au

A catalogue record for this book is available from the National Library of Australia

ISBN 978 1 4607 6338 4 (paperback)
ISBN 978 1 4607 1581 9 (ebook)

Cover design by HarperCollins Design Studio
Front cover image by Sam Ruttyn/Newspix
Back cover image by AAP Image/Mick Tsikas
Typeset in Baskerville by Kelli Lonergan
Printed and bound in Australia by McPherson's Printing Group

MIX
Paper from
responsible sources
FSC® C001695

Contents

Contents

The prime minister who almost never was

For thirty years, Anthony Albanese's closest political sounding board had been his wife, Carmel Tebbutt. They met through Young Labor, started dating in 1988 and married in 2000.

Having been deputy premier of New South Wales, Tebbutt had left state politics in 2015 and was forging a career in the not-for-profit sector. On New Year's Day 2019, Tebbutt told Albanese their marriage was over. 'I thought we would spend our life together,' he told us. 'It was a life-changing thing because it wasn't expected.' The break-up was a complete shock to him, a sign perhaps that he had spent too much time in Canberra. To no avail, he offered to quit politics if it would save their marriage. 'When that didn't make a difference,' he told us, 'I was not in a great personal state. I found that very personally traumatic and I was wondering what I was going to do with my life because it was heading in one direction and then it wasn't. It just changed instantly.'

Albanese greatly missed Tebbutt's counsel. 'What I had to come to terms with was I needed to accept it rather than understand it.' He had to think hard about his future. The 2019 election was approaching fast, but he didn't rush his decision about whether to contest his seat of Grayndler.

'Friends outside politics who were helping me through that difficult time counselled me that when you get a shock in your life you don't change other things. I stayed in the house where I was with [my son] Nathan.' Albanese decided to take a holiday overseas to clear his head. 'I went by myself to London and Lisbon. I knew people in London and I've got a lot of Portuguese people in my electorate so I went to Lisbon, met the foreign minister. I had that two weeks just to think about "Am I up to this?" — another election campaign and all that. I had to be certain. I was.'

Anthony Albanese has always been a political animal. Student politics, Young Labor, political staffer and into parliament. There is more to life, though, than just politics.

Part 1

The rebuild

Chapter 1

Three more years hard Labor

Anthony Albanese was booked to appear on Channel Nine's panel on election night, 2019. Karl Stefanovic had lined it up well in advance. There was a Labor message group for anyone on a media panel, but after the polls closed it went quiet. For thirty minutes into the count there wasn't much hard evidence coming in but, after a little more than an hour, Albanese realised Labor was in trouble. Now the messages were coming in thick and fast, but not from the officially sanctioned message group. Albanese had thought Labor would win but, once it was apparent they had lost, he didn't want to answer questions all night about what went wrong and whether he would run for the leadership. He spoke to media adviser Matthew Franklin off camera. The Member for Chifley, Ed Husic, took over, ostensibly so Albanese could address his supporters back in Grayndler.

The priority now was to make sure he would be the next leader of the Australian Labor Party. In 2013, Albanese had taken too long to make it known he would be a candidate, giving Bill Shorten time to lock up factional deals and freeze him out. In 2016, Shorten exceeded expectations in defeat, thwarting any post-election challenge. By the time of the 2019 election, Albanese packed up his office prior to going on the road. After the election, he believed, he would either be in the ministerial wing or the opposition leader's suite. In defeat, Albanese knew Shorten would be finished as leader. He wasn't going to delay announcing his candidature, allowing someone else to move into position as Shorten's natural successor. Shortly after extricating himself from the election panel he went to Petersham RSL. 'I spoke to people that night and confirmed that I was running,' he told us. 'I announced it the next day and had the support of the majority of the caucus that afternoon. Because of my personal situation I was totally focused on it.'

Who else would contest? Shadow Finance Minister Jim Chalmers considered his options. His supporters argued that a Queenslander could win back seats in his home state, and there was a need for a generational handover. In the end, Chalmers didn't contest the leadership, agreeing to serve as Albanese's shadow treasurer, a big promotion. Chris Bowen's ambitions were not great, given his perceived responsibility, as shadow treasurer, for the 2019 election debacle. Albanese's biggest real threat, at least in the eyes of the public, was Tanya Plibersek, Shadow Education Minister and Deputy Leader of the Opposition. Having entered Parliament in 1998, Plibersek had almost as much experience as Albanese. But at seven years his junior, she could also be a bridge between the older generation and the next. They couldn't run on a joint ticket — neighbouring Sydney seats and a joint left-wing leadership tilt was out of the question — so only one could prevail. Besides, Plibersek wasn't interested in being Albanese's deputy, and vice versa.

To gain the all-important support of the right, Albanese linked up with Victorian Richard Marles, who lacked the following to win the membership vote but did carry votes in caucus. Marles realised that his fortunes were tied to Albanese's and settled for running as his deputy. With Marles in the deputy role, Albanese was more confident making Chalmers his shadow treasurer. Marles, Tony Burke, Don Farrell and Joel Fitzgibbon all encouraged fellow right-wingers to support Albanese. Many did. Shorten supported his deputy of the previous six years, but Plibersek would need a big chunk of support from the left in caucus and there wasn't any. In defeat, Shorten's authority was gone. Plibersek quickly found out that Albanese was the left's preferred candidate. Public exposure could overcome a lack of factional support, as Kevin Rudd had shown, and Plibersek sought to borrow from his playbook. But this contest was over before it started. Plibersek promptly declared that she wanted to spend more time with her family.

The right couldn't agree on a single candidate so Bowen's run in fact ended before it started. Years of Albanese compromising with the New South Wales right had paid off, alongside years of factional head counting for other left-wingers within the party. He split the right and held most of the left together. Albanese's competitors melted away and he won the leadership uncontested. The job would be his.

Most wannabe prime ministers telegraph their desire to lead well ahead of time. Albanese is different. 'There are no articles from 1996 saying "this bloke's coming into the parliament and he might lead one day,"' he told us. 'There are some in the media and some on the other side who think I'm not worthy of being prime minister — didn't have the right pedigree, don't pronounce all my words correctly or whatever. I'm gonna show you!' When we asked him when the kid from public housing thought he was worthy of becoming prime minister, he said not until 2013, seventeen years after entering parliament. 'There was a delay in me getting into the field because I wasn't sure. I had to convince myself of two things: that I thought I was the best candidate and I was capable of winning an election. I saw myself being leader of the House. I saw myself being a cabinet minister. Being from the New South Wales left, I didn't think being prime minister was a possibility.' Upset by the leadership ructions under Kevin Rudd and Julia Gillard, he had told Shorten he would never challenge him once he was leader. 'That's just not me.' Over six years of ups and downs in opposition Albanese kept that promise. Now was his time.

A question of authenticity

One of the first things Anthony Albanese did on winning the leadership was to pay tribute to his mother, Maryanne. 'She lived for all of her sixty-five years in the same council house in

Camperdown where she was born,' he said. 'She had a tough life. She made a brave decision in 1963 to keep a child and care for me as a single mother. I owe her everything.'

Albanese's approach to politics remains rooted in the values of his family. He often cites his mother's trifecta of values. 'My mum raised me with three great faiths,' he told us:

> The Catholic Church, the South Sydney Football Club and the Australian Labor Party. She was very loyal to all three. The Catholic Church gave me a lot of my social justice values. Where I grew up, I never met anyone who admitted to voting for anyone but Labor. You went to Mass on Sunday. You went to the footy on Saturday afternoon if South Sydney was playing at home, and you went to the Labor Party branch meeting at Camperdown on the second Wednesday of every month.

This was identity, not convenience. 'Labor's part of who I am. It's not just a sort of belief. It's part of who you are. Like you didn't contemplate going for a team other than South Sydney either.'

The contrast with the chancer Scott Morrison, who didn't just swap teams but rugby codes for political purposes, was notable. Albanese helped South Sydney return to the national competition after they were excluded from it in 1999. The Rabbitohs brought Albanese into a network of characters as diverse as actor Russell Crowe, businessman Mike Cannon-Brookes and one-time Souths Director of Football and conservative broadcaster Alan Jones.

Part of Albanese's identity is avowedly working class. At university, he was hostile to many of the growing number of leftists from Sydney's leafier suburbs whom he met while studying for his economics degree. At the same time, he also found friends from that same milieu who sympathised with the plight of single-parent families, despite their right-wing politics. He retains the toughness and resourcefulness of his difficult childhood. He had to fight for everything and build his own network, so he prizes loyalty. The right's Graham Richardson paid Albanese the highest compliment: 'Whatever happens with Albo, you will never see the white towel thrown in,' he told Albanese's biographer Karen Middleton.

Albanese's social views have evolved just like the suburbs of Sydney's inner west changed during his childhood, with wave after wave of migration. While long a supporter of equal rights, Albanese makes the following distinction: 'One of the things that drives me is that I do think about what my mother would do. That's one way that you avoid some of the woke issues. Mum couldn't care less who people were in terms of gender or sexuality or anything else. She also wouldn't have been distracted from her life and the big issues that drive people.' Shortly before the 2022 election was called, Sydney's *Daily Telegraph* did Albanese the favour of plastering this sentiment over its front page. 'I am not woke,' screamed the headline, along with the useful translation in smaller type, 'Albanese vows to swerve away from the left'. 'Woke' implies a certain fashion and currency attached to one's social views. Albanese can underline the fact that he is no arriviste on social equality and he navigates such issues based on core principles.

There seems to be plenty of political room in this space between the more radical Labor and Greens activists and the religious influence that has overtaken the right of politics in recent decades. On several occasions as a backbencher, Albanese moved private member's bills to provide same-sex couples equal rights to superannuation and spoke passionately about voluntary euthanasia. He approaches these issues through lived experience — Sydney's inner west being a microcosm of Australia's ethnic, sexual and social diversity. There would be no cultural-politics wedge for the conservatives to strike at on Albanese's watch.

Albanese's transition from rabble-rousing student at the University of Sydney to aspiring Labor politician was guided by left stalwart and Hawke government minister Tom Uren, and other left MPs keen to mentor a new generation of leaders. Uren was passionate but pragmatic. Albanese would later say of the former prisoner-of-war: 'I grew up without a dad, but not without a father. Tom Uren was my father figure. When I travelled with him to Hellfire Pass, Vietnam and Singapore in 1987, we became very close.'

Visiting the Thai–Burmese Railway was very emotional for him. He opened up to me. I was more comfortable opening myself up to him. He had two great ethos: you've got to learn something new every day and you've got to grow and be better as a person every day. I didn't have anyone in my life to go through those life lessons until him. That was a really rewarding relationship. He had such a tough life but he had no bitterness about him.

At the railway, other veterans would approach Albanese and say, 'Tommy saved my life.' Albanese admired the fact that Uren had never spoken about those incidents, when Uren had taken a beating from prison guards to save another prisoner's life. 'That experience of him was really important to me,' Albanese continued. 'I was angry about my place in the world and if you had a look at Tom's experiences in life and how he rose above hardship that I can't even imagine, that was pretty inspirational.'

Under Uren's tutelage, Albanese proved to be a dealmaker rather than an ideologue, compromising with the right whenever possible to share the spoils (though often the spoils of defeat rather than victory). From this perspective, his plea for Labor unity during the Rudd–Gillard–Rudd years had resonance. Labor's self-destruction not only wasted their first federal move to government since 1983, it ushered in yet another conservative government to occupy the Treasury benches for a longer period than their predecessors.

Journalist Richard Cooke described Albanese's evolution as the journey 'from combatant into conciliator'. It wasn't a straightforward process, though. Julia Gillard, another Labor leader from the left with a pragmatic streak, found Albanese argumentative when they met through university student union politics and welcomed the change. She told Middleton, 'that mellowing's taken quite a while'.

A broken record

Opposition sucks. Imagine, if you can, sitting on the front bench of the House and Senate opposite the clown show that was Australia's Commonwealth government for nearly nine interminable years between September 2013 and May 2022. With each Coalition victory, the gap further opened between where Australia was and — despite successive election results — where it wanted to be on issues like climate change and social inequality. Harder still if you had a taste of government as a minister — and of good government, under Julia Gillard, at least — only to be thrown out in favour of the three-word slogans and petty prejudices of Tony Abbott.

Those nine years were particularly hard labour for Anthony Albanese. He had entered the House of Representatives in 1996. While the Hawke and Keating governments had established Labor's credentials as election-winners, the Member for Grayndler spent seventeen of twenty-three years in parliament on the losing side before becoming Labor leader. But as a Rabbitohs supporter, he regarded patience as a virtue. Watching Morrison take the top job, however, was particularly galling.

For former senior ministers there was too much of what former Hawke government minister Gareth Evans called 'relevance deprivation syndrome'. To them, Question Time looked less like theatre and more like pantomime. Opposition afforded too much time to reflect on the failures of the previous Labor government: cursing the Greens' opposition to Rudd's Climate Pollution Reduction Scheme, Rudd's failure to call a double dissolution election when talks with the Coalition collapsed, Bill Shorten garrotting a sitting prime minister who was doing well in the opinion polls, and loose talk from Gillard about no carbon tax under her leadership.

There might have been some consolation if the government had been remotely competent. Three prime ministers. Endless policy failures. It's a long list: the LNP created a second-rate National Broadband Network, which proved to be just as costly as the Labor solution that they had campaigned against; embarrassed that the hated industry super funds routinely outperform their private competitors, they tried to disrupt the playing field; they couldn't wait to initiate a pointless Royal Commission into building unions but held out as long as possible into inquiries into finance, aged care and disability services; they dared the vehicle-manufacturing industry to leave, which it promptly did; they smashed records for the number of political appointments to government posts; having stopped the boats, they left refugees languishing in detention as a message, not only to people smugglers, but to voters as well; they designed everything from aged care to compromised carbon and water trading systems in such a way as to maximise returns for the donor class. Morrison's tenure coincided with these issues causing a stench of corruption, so much so that the hitherto esoteric matter of an integrity commission became one of the key issues at the 2022 election.

The hubris was astonishing. The LNP created coffee cups plastered with 'back in the black' to celebrate a budget surplus that never materialised; cut taxes for the wealthy and called it reform; almost broke the Howard government's record for the biggest spending government in Australia's history; spent $5.5 billion dollars on a submarine program which, as Shadow Treasurer Jim Chalmers pointed out, 'didn't produce as much as a canoe'. They had to promise the National Party untold billions in pork-barrelling to finalise an agreement on net zero emissions, after years of embarrassing Australia with climate scepticism. As a final insult, their failure to order vaccines in a timely way may have cost the country thirty billion dollars due to additional lockdowns.

And yet, despite this long list of failures, scraping by politically for three terms of parliament was the Coalition's reward. The economy had recovered from the Global Financial Crisis, even the pandemic, so they thought the 2022 election would be easy. A decisive election win would allow a re-elected Coalition government to balance the budget, reward its friends and punish its enemies. That seems to be what the contemporary Coalition is all about. As it had begun to do under Howard, it gave up any claim to uphold the national interest.

Winning at any cost

The Coalition's abysmal record raises important questions about how they kept winning elections. The answer lies partly in Labor's failings, alongside Liberal cunning. It was the Liberal Party's killer instinct when it comes to its leadership that proved vital. The bloodletting in 2015 and 2018 prompted concern among observers about instability. As Albanese commented, the nation seemed to get diminishing returns from each change of leader but each successive prime minister was able to reset the government's political fortunes. Morrison proved to be a formidable campaigner: relentless, on point, and shameless. Crucial to Morrison's 2019 win was federal director Andrew Hirst, the campaign chief. Experienced, respected and well organised, Hirst had worked as an adviser to four Liberal leaders, rising to deputy chief of staff under Abbott, and as director of communications. He would back up as director for the 2022 campaign. Morrison's Principal Private Secretary, Yaron Finkelstein, was another important player. A former employee of the political strategy firm Crosby Textor, Finkelstein was a trusted Morrison confidant and a conduit between his office, the parliamentary party and the party organisation. When Finkelstein spoke, Liberals listened.

There were plenty of reasons why the 2022 election would be tougher for the government than 2019. Most Liberals assumed that Morrison's 2019 success would usher in more wins, but this time Labor would present a smaller policy target. Having come close to winning the 2016 election, Shorten had seen little reason to change his big-target strategy. Labor's tax policies on negative gearing, trusts and shares had been around for long enough without seeming to drag down their vote. The end to negative gearing for new properties had been part of the 2016 campaign. The plan to end tax rebates for excess franking credits was announced in March 2018 when Turnbull was still prime minister, and Shorten's rhetoric about 'millionaires' welfare' had political resonance with super-wealthy Turnbull as PM. Morrison's prime ministership, though, would present a different sort of challenge.

The 2019 election year had started with the House of Representatives Economics Committee, led by Tim Wilson, inviting anyone with a beef against the proposed franking credits changes to mug for the cameras. It seemed as though Wilson had uncovered every asset-rich but income-poor retiree in the land. Such antics were indulged by the media, and gave the issue a prominence well and truly larger than the revenue Labor expected to reap. There was dissent in shadow cabinet. 'I was concerned about the politics of it, and how it would be received,' Albanese told us. He relays a story of a woman approaching him at Rozelle in Sydney. 'Why are you going to cut my pension?' she asked him. He patiently explained that her pension would not be affected if she didn't own any shares. She was unconvinced. 'It was very complex policy to try to implement from opposition,' he lamented. Shorten's framing of the issue as winding back subsidies, or that the tax rebate being payable even if in the absence of any actual payable tax amounted to a 'gift', was less effective than shorthand Coalition attacks such as 'retirement tax'.

This wasn't the first time Albanese had concerns with Labor's direction under Shorten: 'I was worried about some of the direction of the party in 2018. At the National Conference I was worried that we were agreeing to an agenda that was going to be very hard to deliver. I was wondering what my future would be.'

The conservative side of politics finds it easy enough to recalibrate from presenting too large an electoral target, such as the correction from the 1993 loss to the 1996 victory (although John Howard did take the part-privatisation of Telstra to that election). The debate about election strategy creates more sparks on the left than the right. This is partly a matter of politics as expressive as much as instrumental — we don't want to have to hold our nose as we vote for our preferred party just to keep the other mob out. There is also a concern that we are increasingly being asked in democracies to trust political leaders to do the right thing in government. This reverses the progressive expectation that political representation is more about delegating leaders to enact specified policies on our behalf. On a more practical level, a policy mandate is a powerful weapon to wave at the parliament.

Labor's review of the 2019 loss was conducted by a former Commonwealth cabinet minister, Craig Emerson, and a former South Australian premier, Jay Weatherill. Their report highlighted Labor's 'cluttered' agenda. As an alternative approach, it recommended a smaller number of 'signature policies' woven into a unifying narrative — a 'coherent Labor story'. Who better to tell a coherent Labor story than Albo, a 'broad-brushstrokes politician', as *Guardian* political editor Katharine Murphy called him?

Shadow Finance Minister Katy Gallagher would later describe the new strategy this way: 'What we're trying to do is tailor down into the key areas: renewable energy, childcare, aged care, a future made in Australia,' she said. 'And we have a story to wrap around that about the country we'd like to see, the government we'd like to lead with Anthony.'

'With Anthony' might simply have been garbled rhetoric, but it also speaks to the style of the Labor Party under Albanese's leadership. He is not a dominant political figure in the way some other leaders can be. The temptation is to take such an observation as a criticism — a suggestion that Albanese lacks leadership characteristics, but contemporary politics is the art of the incremental. A leader who likes to crash through but isn't larger than life minimises the risk of crashing if they are incremental with their ambitions. It also helps prevent burnout.

ALP national secretary Paul Erickson has commented that 'leaders who electrify people tend to burn out pretty quickly'. Especially in modern politics. Describing Albanese's leadership aura, Erickson says, 'He presents as a safe pair of hands, not a colourful figure.'

Privately, Albanese characterised the first task for Labor after the 2019 loss as the need to 'de-Bill the message' — a matter of leadership style as well as policy substance. It wasn't all about the leader, though. Labor struggled to understand why it couldn't beat a second-rate government that was onto its third prime minister. It had the right cattle in its paddock — an experienced and smart front bench. The third Labor election loss in a row fuelled the party's natural pessimism. At first Albanese wasn't certain he could win the next election, or even survive the parliamentary term as Labor leader. However, Tony Burke thought 2019 would resemble 2004 — the heart-breaking election loss before success in 2007. 'We need to stay positive,' was his message to the new leader and anyone who would listen.

Chapter 2

Loyalty matters

Being the leader of the Australian Labor Party meant the world to Anthony Albanese, more so than being opposition leader. Shortly after taking over the job he would remind colleagues privately, when they referred to him as the leader of the opposition, 'I'm the Labor leader, whether that's in government or opposition.' As a lifetime member of the left he didn't really believe he'd ever become leader. Albo saw the Labor Party as his family, his friendship circle, his life. Labor is far and away the more tribal of the two major parties and, within that tribalism, Albanese was a party man to his core.

If Albanese could win the next election, he would lead a depth of talent into government. The Rudd government was dominated by a so-called gang of four: the Prime Minister, Deputy Julia Gillard, Treasurer Wayne Swan and Finance Minister Lindsay Tanner. By the time the party had to pick up the pieces in opposition, these experienced members were all gone, but a host of senior ministers stayed on: Chris Bowen,

Penny Wong, Richard Marles, Tanya Plibersek, Bill Shorten, Tony Burke and Mark Butler. In fact, Wong had only stayed on after the 2019 defeat because Albanese convinced her to. 'I wanted Penny to stay,' he told us. 'She's outstanding. I said she was an important part of us being able to win the next election. She needed a bit of convincing but you can't be a conscript either. You've gotta be all in.'

Other ministers during the Rudd–Gillard years who made it to shadow cabinet under Albanese included Catherine King, Don Farrell, Mark Dreyfus, Julie Collins, Brendan O'Connor and Jason Clare. They were joined by two former state or territory leaders, Kristina Keneally and Katy Gallagher. It was the nucleus of a good team — *if* they could win. A new Labor government would bring the prospect of a front bench better than any since the early Hawke years. During the election campaign, Albanese would promote this as 'the most experienced incoming team Labor has ever had'. After years in opposition, though, such talents could either be fired up or jaded. Which would it be?

Many questions were being asked of this new leader's background. What was his ideology? From where, and whom, did he draw his support? And, crucially, was there a 'real Albo' underneath that small-target strategy?

A man of the left

Albanese became the fourth Labor leader since the end of the Second World War to defeat a Coalition government and become prime minister. The others — Whitlam, Hawke and Rudd — took different approaches to leadership and governing. Albanese sought to emulate none of those men, neither in style nor substance. Among these post-war Labor PMs only Bob Hawke served more than three years. Gough Whitlam is a misunderstood figure. While his government looks a model of progressive reform in retrospect, as opposition leader Whitlam had to rein in the left and the organisational wing of his party. Yet, Whitlam and Hawke — less so Rudd — provide the mythology of bringing a strong policy program into government.

Hawke's 1983 victory had a profound effect on a young Albanese. While this win ushered in an era of Labor reform, few of those reforms, particularly the liberalisation of the economy, were foreshadowed during election campaigns. Hawke and Treasurer Paul Keating sought mandates for controversial policies such as tax reform, financial deregulation and privatisation through consultation and summits, only putting them to elections after they had been introduced. It was a different approach to the programmatic Whitlam ascension in 1972, with a different political result — five election wins rather than two. Yet, Albanese's political style in university and Young Labor politics was more akin to Whitlam's 'crash through or crash' style than Hawke's consensus approach. Nonetheless, Albanese channelled Hawke in the lead-up to the 2022 election. 'We must rediscover the spirit of consensus that former Labor Prime Minister Bob Hawke used to bring together governments, trade unions, businesses and civil society around their shared aims of growth and job creation,' he said, seeking the strongest possible contrast with the divisive Morrison. 'He brokered reforms that yielded benefits for all parties — not just better wages for workers, but stronger profits for businesses, along with the introduction of landmark reforms adding to the social dividend, such as Medicare and universal superannuation.'

From the beginning of his time as leader Albanese focused his energies on what it would take to win the election, still years away, rather than winning the daily or weekly media cycle. It was a contrast to Shorten's approach. 'Kicking with the wind in the fourth quarter' was the way he would sell his strategy, using the vernacular of a different sporting code to where his passion lay. Unfortunately, this cautious approach wasn't the best way to avoid being rolled before getting the chance to take Morrison on in an election campaign. While there were moments during his three-year stint as opposition leader when pressure would build, and could very well have overwhelmed him, Albanese hoped that the leadership rules introduced by Kevin Rudd would protect him from the fate of so many opposition leaders before him.

Albanese often jokes about the fact that, as a member of the left, failure is second nature to him. He has been on the wrong side of almost every internal Labor leadership showdown during his political career. The first time he backed a winner was Kevin Rudd against Julia Gillard in 2013 — a last-ditch effort to retain government, but one that failed. Labor's left have historically been perennial losers in New South Wales and at Commonwealth level. A young Albanese imbibed that pessimism but needed to overcome it to succeed as leader. Virtue in defeat was always their solace. Yet, the left faction has now produced two of the last three Labor prime ministers in Gillard and Albanese. While this says something about the declining relevance of raw factional power in the ALP, it also reveals the poverty of potential leaders produced in recent decades by the party's dominant right faction.

Nevertheless, Albanese would be one of the less forceful leaders of the opposition from either party to make the transition to prime minister. Whitlam, Fraser, Hawke, Howard, Rudd and Abbott never hid their ambition for the top job, and Albanese's predecessor had made no secret of his ambitions. Albanese provided useful contrasts to both Shorten as Labor leader and the incumbent prime minister. Albanese and Morrison both promoted alternative images to the veneer of tough political combatant. But where 'ScoMo' is a marketing creation, 'Albo' is an authentic character, warm and affable. Unless, that is, one finds oneself on Albo's bad side, in which case the less cuddly Albanese is just as authentic. And in contrast to Morrison, who always seems like he has a point to make, Albanese just might be a listener if the moment is right.

Unlike Shorten, Albanese was never a creature of the trade union movement, seeking support wherever he could find it. Yet, of course, he is every bit the party-machine man as Shorten. Shorten's self-conscious cultivation of a public profile prior to entering parliament (remember the Beaconsfield mining disaster?) was not Albanese's approach, partly because he didn't have an eye on the prime ministership until he became deputy leader. Shorten created enemies by campaigning to oust Mark Latham after the 2004 election loss. Once in parliament, and as a junior minister, Shorten liked outshining his more senior counterparts. Not all his colleagues enjoyed the experience.

Albanese also comes across as a more natural political talent than Shorten or Morrison, archetypes of the era of spin and stage management. This gave him an edge in responding to the numerous natural disasters of the past few years. He empathises and cares, which comes across on television. His sense of humour helps. Albanese leans into these perceptions. 'What you see is what you get with me,' he likes to say. 'I'm a bit rough at the edges, but I think that Australians don't want someone who just utters talking points.' He utters talking points with the best of them, of course, and he's capable of dissembling and evasion when it suits. It's the contrast with one's opponent in a two-party system that matters.

Labor's factional politics remain mysterious to most Australians. Shorten, perhaps unfairly, never shook off the tag of factional political operator. Albanese has the chance to transcend partisanship in a way that Labor prime ministers can only do when their rise was seen to be above factional politics. Yet, the badge of the left also brings with it the idea that Albanese stands for something. On this front, his leadership was sometimes disappointing to fellow progressives. A small-target strategy might be doubly perplexing when left-wingers the world over were welcoming a more interventionist politics to deal with financial crises, climate change and the pandemic.

Albanese's caution was enough for *The Monthly* to dub him 'the disappearing man'. Yet, this is to misunderstand Albanese's political pedigree. Under Uren's tutelage, principle was tempered by pragmatism, and a careful eye was kept on the party organisation. 'Tom was a believer in coalitions and bringing people with you on the journey of change,' Albanese told us.

We asked Albanese what Uren would have said upon him becoming prime minister. Albo was adamant:

> 'I told you so,' he would have said. In 2013, when I was still not sure I was going to run for the leadership, he rang me and he said, 'You have a responsibility to run. You're the leader that we need.' I didn't come to Canberra to be leader of the Labor Party. He gave me a great deal of confidence to pursue higher office. Tom was always into building those broad relationships, which is one of those things that I, as leader of the Labor Party, have tried to do, to spread the base of support for various policies. Before I went to work with Tom I had no relationships with anyone who wasn't in the Labor Party.

As if to underline the point, during one of our interviews shortly after Albanese's first National Cabinet meeting he received a text from a former prominent Liberal. 'You're smashing it' was the message.

Joining the New South Wales Labor left faction was a move away from the more radical crowd Albanese ran with in university and Young Labor politics. He still portrays the Greens, for example, increasingly competitive in inner-city seats like his own seat of Grayndler in Sydney, courtesy of the gentrification of the inner suburbs of the capital cities, as committed to protest rather than policy. In answer to the allegation that Ben Chifley would not win Labor pre-selection in the contemporary middle-class-dominated Labor Party, Albanese would say that the point of the ALP as a social democratic rather than socialist party is to improve the lot of the working class — not just represent them. He embodies this transformation, and he would talk about his upbringing in public housing at every opportunity on the campaign trail, sometimes at the cost of quiet mockery from colleagues.

Albanese once said, 'I like fighting Tories. That's what I do. That's what I do. And I have lifelong friends who disagree with me on this. It has been very difficult.' 'Fighting Tories' is an odd formulation, since Tory is not a widely used epithet in Australia. The term was designed for internal party consumption, papering over the fact that Albanese has expended plenty of energy on fights within his own party, including within his left faction, taking on those he dislikes inside the caucus and the wider labour movement, such as former Senator Kim Carr, a Victorian left-winger.

Yet Albo has always had the real Tories, the Liberals, in his sights. Albanese first came to notice as an MP with a class-based attack on then-Prime Minister John Howard, reversing the usual battler-made-good formula that Howard revelled in by labelling him a class traitor for his move from the inner west of Sydney across the harbour to find a seat in parliament:

His father owned a service station on the corner of the street where I now live. These were the halcyon days of little Winston's life — when the working classes knew their place and when all migrants were British. Lucky John Winston Howard moved further north, across the harbour; he certainly would not be comfortable living in the inner west of Sydney anymore. A bit too much change for his lifetime.

Kim Beazley said, at his first caucus meeting after the 1996 election loss, that he expected everyone to be constructive. But he separately called Albanese into his office. Albanese shared with us what happened next. 'He said, "That issue about being positive and constructive? Not you!" We were devastated in 1996. You need some people who are prepared to have a crack at the government.' Not a lot of MPs make the transition from hitman to prime minister. Keating is notable, but he always had a reputation for serious policy work alongside the barbs.

'You've gotta be all in'

Albanese gives and receives loyalty in equal measure. 'There are people who are lifelong supporters, who get me, who know me, and that gives me comfort.' These include long-term staffers as well as confidants, and friends outside politics. 'We'd have walked over broken glass for the bloke,' Tim Gartrell, his chief of staff, once said. Gartrell had been Albanese's first campaign director for Grayndler, before rising to prominence in 2007 running the 'Kevin 07' campaign nationally. Before that, Albanese had helped Gartrell become Labor's national secretary, in which position in 2004, he learned what it was like to lose, and how difficult running a campaign could be when working for a volatile leader. Being national secretary with Latham as Labor leader was an experience. Once Albanese was Labor leader, bringing Gartrell back as chief of staff was a natural move — valuing the experience of a man who had run a successful national election campaign.

The first rule of Albo's circle is that you are either a mate or not a mate. He helps mates out and expects them to help him in return. Long-term factional ally Mark Butler is his closest friend in the parliament. Seven years younger than Albanese, Butler joined the national executive in the late 1990s and they worked together to unite the splintered Labor left. With the exception of a group around Victorian stalwart Carr, they were successful. Butler entered parliament from South Australia in 2007. He describes Albanese as a factional opponent within the left who became a friend.

Tony Burke remains a mate. 'Both of us are interested in the parliament,' Albanese said of Burke. Burke is a senior figure in the NSW right, but that didn't prevent him advocating for an Albanese leadership, even when fellow right-winger Bowen had put his hand up. 'We have similar views on a whole range of issues,' Albanese tells us. 'We're both interested in the arts and workers' issues. We became close over a period of time. He's in a neighbouring seat.'

The alliance with Marles as his party deputy started out as transactional. Marles and Shorten were close friends and Victorian factional allies — until they weren't. When that moment came, the mutual benefit of Albo and Marles joining forces for advancement forged their loyalty to one another. Low moments during three years of opposition only brought them closer.

Albanese's other friends within the parliament include Wong, Gallagher, Tim Ayres and Andrew Giles. He added Murray Watt, an eye-catching performer in Senate Estimates, and the senior left-winger in Queensland, to that list. 'People like Penny and Mark, Burkie, people who have been there a long time, people in the wider movement. Sally [McManus] was in my local branch. People who have been with me for forty years.' To be Albo's mate is to receive loyalty over decades.

There is no secret about those high on the list of 'not Albo's mate': Shorten and Carr, certainly, but also Tanya Plibersek. Continuing one of the more enduring feuds in Australian politics, Carr had moved some left faction votes in the 2013 leadership contest to Shorten. Albanese returned the favour when he became opposition leader by mobilising the left to deny Carr a frontbench position and, later, his Senate pre-selection — Carr jumping both times before he was pushed. On becoming prime minister, Albanese decided that parliament would return in July rather than June, enjoying the happenstance that this would deny Carr a final appearance in the Senate before his term expired. In the 2013 contest, Plibersek had to vote for fellow left-winger Albanese but also made it clear that she would be prepared to serve as Shorten's deputy. This annoyed Albanese. Between the two of them, Carr and Plibersek could have been the difference between victory and defeat for him. She, too, felt Albanese's wrath, being denied a substantial role in the campaign and being demoted in the ministry after the election.

How to reconcile this rough treatment of supposed factional allies with the self-described conciliator who had learned consensus politics under Uren? Even political leaders with decades of experience sometimes use their heart instead of their head. There is still enough of the old-fashioned Labor hater in Albanese for him to act on these feuds even when he has other rather important things to do as party leader.

In a similar paradox, Albanese has plenty of mates, but also a reputation as a lone wolf. It is not an uncommon character trait for an only child. It can manifest in a lack of consultation with his staff, such as when he deals directly with journalists, to the despair of his media team. Delegating was a difficult transformation for Albanese. His journey from staffer to candidate to MP, cabinet minister and Labor leader required a continual reassessment of who he allowed in his inner circle, and to what extent he could personally deal with journalists, lobbyists and the other hangers-on who like to surround politicians on the rise.

Becoming leader meant that Albanese nevertheless needed to widen his circle of trusted allies to the parliamentary leadership group. In different ways, the fortunes of Marles and Wong were tied to their leader. Marles would not survive as deputy if there were a change of leader. Albanese and Wong had been senior ministers in the previous Labor government but not part of the gang of four. Albanese promised to bring Wong into his confidence. They became close allies, not just mates.

Chalmers wasn't a mate for much of Albanese's time as opposition leader. He became shadow treasurer almost by default after serving as shadow finance minister, and once Bowen was damaged goods after the 2019 loss, along with his failed and short-lived bid for the leadership. Albanese's office thought Chalmers had been responsible for leaking against his leader. Chalmers believed that pulling out of the leadership contest in 2019 before ever declaring was evidence that he could be trusted and was working for an Albanese prime ministership, but his leader didn't see it that way, nor did Albanese's closest supporters. They believed that Chalmers was positioning himself for a late-term tilt at the job if Albanese faltered, or in the aftermath of an election defeat. Chalmers denies this. Either way the pair ironed out their differences well in advance of the 2022 campaign, by which time Albanese needed his shadow treasurer to counter Coalition claims that Labor couldn't manage money. Whether this improved relationship survives the pressures of government remains to be seen. Bowen, who was stripped of the treasury portfolio after the 2019 loss, isn't close to Albanese, but they do respect one another. The pair developed that mutual respect during the debilitating feuds between Rudd and Gillard.

Team Albo

Winning is a team effort; even a loner like Albanese knows that. Those around him in key positions both in his office and in campaign headquarters were an important ingredient in the victory. Senior members of the leader's office and the national secretariat are more important sources of advice than most shadow ministers on election matters.

Two key figures were press secretary Matthew Franklin and deputy chief of staff Jeff Singleton. Prior to becoming opposition leader, Albanese had worked closely with Franklin, the former chief political correspondent for *The Australian*, for six years. Singleton had worked with Albanese for over twenty years. Singleton started out as a media adviser in Tebbutt's office before becoming Albanese's right-hand man working on policy ideas. Franklin had switched out of journalism to work for Kevin Rudd when he returned as PM in 2013, staying on with Albanese after that. Albanese liked to tell journalists and colleagues alike he had nabbed the former senior *Oz* journalist, convincing him to stay on with him in opposition. The original plan was that Franklin might do so if Albanese had won the leadership showdown against Shorten, but getting to know him better, Franklin decided to work for him as a shadow minister anyway.

Shadow ministers only get one or two extra staffers beyond their electorate entitlement, so it was a small office working together for an extended period of time during what might be termed Albo's 'wilderness years'. Both men stayed on as senior advisers when Albanese was elevated to opposition leader. With his media adviser background, Singleton would interact with senior journalists, but for the most part his role was to engage with shadow ministers and their staffers about the policy ideas Labor might junk or promote. Franklin's task was to float between the Labor tactics committees and the gallery, putting out fires or stoking issues Albanese wanted attention drawn to. He had the connections to do both.

Having Gartrell as chief of staff gave Albanese more confidence in the much younger Paul Erickson when he put his hand up to become national secretary of the Labor Party after the 2019 defeat. Erickson had made a name for himself as the key seats coordinator winning difficult by-elections for the Labor Party under Bill Shorten's leadership. First Batman, then holding all the seats up for grabs at the super Saturday showdown that played a role in Malcolm Turnbull's demise. Albanese had told Erickson he should be the next national secretary back in 2015 at the National Conference, but most thought he was too young at the time. George Wright — who Erickson describes as his mentor — handed the reins over to Noah Carroll instead. When Erickson was seeking support to take over in 2019, Shorten threw what clout he had left behind Erickson. The former leader regarded him as a 'straight shooter'.

Four communications professionals joined Albanese's media team in 2020: Alex Cramb, Alex Beech, Liz Fitch and Katie Connolly. Cramb, the oldest of the bunch, had worked as the communications director in campaign headquarters (CHQ) at the 2007 election with Gartrell before becoming chief of staff to NSW Home Affairs Minister Bob Debus in government. He had also spent some time in the private sector doing government relations and strategic comms. Returning to life as a political staffer was a temporary change to help a leader he had known for decades.

Beech had been Sabra Lane's producer on the ABC before switching over to political staffing. Prior to the campaign, her involvement was focused on radio. On the campaign trail, she was tasked with wrangling the travelling press pack. Liz Fitch came to Albanese by way of Chris Bowen, starting out as a senior media adviser, like Franklin and Cramb, but roughly a year out from the election was promoted to director of communications in the Leader of the Opposition's media unit.

Katie Connolly was the Opposition Leader's director of strategic communications, responsible for speech writing, political messaging, framing and management of the digital team. She came back from the US to help Albanese out, having spent over ten years working for the Democrats — first for the

Obama administration, then the campaign for presidential candidate Pete Buttigeig.

James Jeffrey had joined Albanese's staff as speechwriter not long after he became opposition leader. Jeffrey had, for years, written the 'Strewth' political satire column at *The Australian*. He worked with Connolly, prepping jokes and clever turns of phrase, and had licence to jazz up Albanese's speeches.

With his experienced and capable team assembled and his small-target strategy conceived, Albanese should have been full of confidence, but he was not. Not yet. It was after his first holiday upon assuming the leadership that Albanese set a tone of despair rather than hope. Taking some time off in August 2019, he told Paul Erickson, 'Well, my portrait is on the wall, they can never take it off me,' referring to his photo as leader in the opposition party room. Erickson took that as a worrying sign Albo lacked confidence that he could get through to the election. Other parliamentary colleagues too, noticing that Albo seemed to see assuming the Labor leadership as the pinnacle, also wondered: did he have what it would take to defeat Morrison?

Albanese's strategy prior to the pandemic was for Labor to be noticed as little as possible while it debated a new direction internally. The debate about the extent of 'convergence' between the two major parties is an old one, going back to the 1980s when Labor, under Hawke and Keating, did the heavy lifting on liberal economic reform. There have been important differences between the parties since then, although the public tends not to pay much attention. Albanese was keen to make this point. Indeed, it was difficult to think of policy areas where there wasn't some distance between government and opposition. When the government sought to legislate its tax-cut proposals right after the 2019 election, the stage was set for Labor to think seriously about the extent of those differences.

Labor had attempted to amend the legislation so that the third stage of the cuts, the stage most generous to high-income earners, would not be enacted. Having been unsuccessful at this, the opposition needed to decide whether to go to another election promising tax rises, and in any event would struggle to pass such legislation even if they won. Working on the principle of 'no one left behind, no one held back', Albanese was reluctant to insist on further changes. Shadow cabinet backed the leader, although there were dissenters. Kristina Keneally was particularly vocal, labelling the new tax rates as too flat for Labor to support. The tax cuts were aimed at saving marginal seats, rather than a calculated fiscal strategy, in what was supposed to be an unwinnable election. Another wedge. Supporting the tax cuts after the election loss made Labor competitive with voters with household incomes over $150,000, according to Newspoll, which they hadn't been under Shorten. Albanese didn't want his leadership defined by the re-elected Coalition government as obstructionist and negative.

Nevertheless, such debates could have been more embarrassing for Labor were it not for events not anticipated at the 2019 election. While he was surrounded by a strong team, Albanese had yet to show the country that Labor was ready for government.

Chapter 3

We can do this!

Fire, plague and a small target

Winston Churchill, in a phrase misattributed to one of his successor prime ministers, Harold Macmillan, described the greatest threat to a sitting government as 'the opposition of events'. Until events conspired to test the Morrison government, the actions of the opposition were of limited interest. The first of these events was the bushfires of 2019 and 2020. While Australia burned, Morrison secretly took his family on a holiday to Hawaii. When it was revealed that the nation's leader was missing in action, Morrison was widely criticised. Albanese was in the Hawkesbury near Sydney and then the Blue Mountains when Morrison made his notorious statement on Sydney radio 2GB, calling in from Hawaii. 'I don't hold a hose, mate,' he said in response to criticism of his role.

Albanese thought it was extraordinary. 'I was amazed he'd done the interview from Hawaii. The thing that struck me about the interview, he had told me he was going on holidays.

I had kept his confidence.' Much to the Opposition Leader's annoyance, Morrison subsequently tried to use Albanese's knowledge of the trip as a shield.

Albanese had no respect for Morrison, which only added to his ultimate desire to beat him. Some political leaders have respect for their opponents even if they dislike them personally. Albanese hated Scott Morrison. 'I had a meeting with him on the first day of parliament here when I became opposition leader,' he said, referring to the prime minister's suite where we interviewed him, 'and I don't think I entered this office afterwards other than at Christmas to put gifts under the tree. That's extraordinary, given I was opposition leader.'

Albanese had written to Morrison in November 2019 before the Prime Minister jetted off to Hawaii, suggesting rewarding volunteer firefighters for the work they were doing and subsidising leave during their service. Morrison was dismissive, citing federalism and the perennial conservative excuse — 'Now isn't the time.' Weeks later, Morrison took up the Opposition Leader's suggestion, along with similar advice on expanding aerial firefighting capacity, assessing the damage to flora and fauna, deploying the military to assist firefighting efforts, providing mental health support to victims, and establishing a national agency to coordinate emergency responses. No credit for the appropriation was given.

It wasn't just Morrison's conservatism that bothered Albanese. He recalls an occasion when he received a call from Morrison about his decision to change the national anthem from 'young and free' to 'one and free'. In Albanese's mind, Morrison not only called to tell the Opposition Leader very late in the piece, also explaining that he was ringing around former prime ministers to word them up on the change as well, the then PM was also aggrandising a change Albanese thought was the very least that government should do to support Indigenous Australians to feel respected and included in the national story. 'There was no relationship and there were times when he lied, or told an untruth, I don't know whether he even believed it, which was so unnecessary.' Albanese relates an incident where Question Time had started late and Morrison asked the Opposition Leader if he wanted to finish on time. Having agreed to extend the session, Morrison went back on his word. 'There were a few occasions where he would just say "black is white". That was what a range of his colleagues would say publicly and privately as well. It was difficult to have a relationship with someone who does that.'

Albanese felt that Morrison's constant references to his family throughout 2019 were designed to undermine the recently separated opposition leader; to undermine his character and standing as a family man. It made it easier for Albo to ruthlessly exploit the character failures of Morrison in due course. Whether or not that was the PM's intent, it also played with Albanese's confidence. The marriage breakdown was still very raw. He was struggling in his new role and had yet to meet future partner, Jodie Haydon. Such behaviour by Morrison was all par for the course, in Albo's eyes.

Yet, even when the bushfire emergency exposed Morrison's weakness as a leader, it was far from inevitable that Albanese would benefit. It can be state premiers or the media who instead put the most pressure on a prime minister. The fire disaster was a charged and dynamic environment, cutting across state and Commonwealth responsibilities, and carrying the danger of the opposition being seen to politicise human tragedy.

The Auditor-General had a late Christmas gift for the opposition — a report into the Community Sports Infrastructure Program, which quickly earned the moniker 'sports rorts'. Sports Australia had dutifully ranked applications for the program's grants based on strict criteria. Meanwhile, in the Minister for Sport's office, the rankings were based on political need. The politics was ugly enough for Morrison to stand down his minister. Such programs also became a byword for wasted expenditure, allowing Labor to nominate some of them for the axe when the subject of spending cuts inevitably arose.

While the bushfires and sports rorts scandal gave the opposition a higher profile, Albanese was determined to stick to developing a small-target strategy. After an indifferent start to the leadership, he had a good run. In January, Labor briefly took the lead in Newspoll's two-party preferred measure for the first time since the election. Morrison's 'I don't hold a hose' phrase had caught people's attention, Albanese's in particular. He jumped all over it, believing it defined deficiencies more broadly in Morrison's character as a person who doesn't take responsibility.

Fire gave Albanese a sniff of victory. Plague took it away. Looking back after his 2022 victory it is easy to forget just how precarious Albanese's position was throughout 2020. The betting markets had him well beyond three dollars to even make it to the next election as leader, much less win it. 'You should be sure and include that,' Albo told us with a smile from the comfort of his prime ministerial office. Morrison's approval ratings were high in 2020, Albanese languishing well behind the incumbent as preferred prime minister. Without a good working relationship with his shadow treasurer, whom Albanese remained convinced wanted his job more than he wanted to become treasurer, the pressure was on.

National cabinet, featuring the prime minister and the premiers, provided plenty of opposition for Morrison. The media didn't need an invisible federal opposition to find conflict about pandemic policy. The battle between the Commonwealth and Victoria provided plenty of drama. National cabinet gave the media contrasting views on lots of COVID-related issues through the differing approaches of each state, and on Commonwealth–state conflict on responsibility for aged care, quarantine and the vaccine rollout. Combined with the lack of parliamentary sittings, the media's focus on state and Commonwealth governments at the expense of their respective oppositions was simultaneously a blessing and a curse for Albanese. It allowed him to fly under the radar in the years before the election campaign began early in 2022 — useful for a party debating a change of electoral strategy. The problem was, voters seemed very patient with their governments dealing with extraordinary circumstances. The personal approval ratings of all incumbents, state and federal, shot up. And there was little sense of when things would return to normal, or what the new normal would look like.

There was less room in the first stage of the pandemic for criticism of the government's failures than there had been during the bushfires, when Morrison's lack of leadership was the key issue. Chalmers was effective during the missteps involving JobKeeper, when the government massively overestimated the cost of the scheme. This only elevated Albanese's distrust towards his shadow treasurer, keeping Chalmers outside his inner circle and limiting their cooperation on economic policy development. The JobKeeper scheme, intended to encourage employers to retain staff, ended up showering billions of dollars on companies that actually increased their revenue over the qualification period. Had a Labor government made such errors, the pillorying from the media would have been relentless. While we will never know what might have happened to the economy without this quick and dirty stimulus, the scale of waste remains eye-watering.

Yet JobKeeper also provided an example of why the public perceives Labor as the bigger spender. The Morrison government ended JobKeeper in early 2021. Chalmers' response was that cutting the program would have 'diabolical consequences for workers and small businesses, and the jobs that people rely on to feed their loved ones'. Labor could either criticise expenditure priorities while lamenting waste along the way, or cast itself as the safer economic manager by embracing fiscal conservatism.

Chalmers' rhetoric that the Coalition should be judged on the unemployment rate would come back to bite him during the campaign when it reached a record low. Albanese got his lines in about border control failures such as the farce of the COVID-stricken *Ruby Princess* cruise ship in Sydney. More constructive policy suggestions, though, were harder to handle. The Commonwealth was bickering with states about issues such as aged care and hotel quarantine. Events were moving too quickly for the opposition to be an effective affirmative voice.

It was a feat of leadership on Albanese's part to keep his party united behind the small-target strategy while substantial policy work was under way. Being of the left made it a little easier for him. In a few areas, such as environmental protection, Labor held the line in the Senate along with the minor parties. Some time later, in early 2022, Labor caved on a pointless change to the migration bill to provide specific guidance to ministerial discretion for deporting or refusing entry to convicted criminals. Given the government tactics were primarily about keeping the issue on the agenda, Labor's response couldn't always be based on policy merits but had to be calibrated against government spin.

The biggest test

For leadership rumours to transcend mere scuttlebutt something obvious would have to go wrong for Albanese. On 30 April 2020, the Member for Eden-Monaro, Mike Kelly, announced that he was retiring from politics, forcing a by-election in the key marginal seat Labor had narrowly retained in 2019 and providing that leadership test. And this was at the height of COVID, when the Prime Minister was ascendant. What would defeat have meant? 'It would have been disruptive, and it would have been difficult, but I was always very confident, from the time that I was leader, that my cross-section of loyalists was very strong across the factions, across the states.'

'I never felt vulnerable,' Albanese told us, 'not because of the [revised caucus leadership] rules, because rules can always be changed, but because there wasn't a clear alternative.'

Others weren't so sure. For months between Kelly's retirement announcement and the by-election on 4 July, the speculation was that losing the seat could bring about Albanese's end. One of his senior staffers told us it was a 'piss or get off the pot' moment, the pot being the Labor leadership. Even without an obvious alternative candidate for leader, factional heavies were circling. Sections of the right briefly toyed with offering up Plibersek, certain that the next election would be lost and then the leadership would return to its rightful place back in their orbit.

Albanese picked Kristy McBain as the candidate, staring down the factions, knowing his future in some form would be tied to her success. McBain had shone as a local mayor during the bushfires. A woman, not a Labor careerist, and a local. Almost nobody outside the electorate was paying attention. At this point in the pandemic, the media was all COVID, all the time.

The poll would be an equally important test for Erickson. Labor's federal president, Wayne Swan, had told Erickson the party needed a better advertising team, and recommended Dee Madigan, of *Gruen Transfer* fame, whom Swan had worked with in Queensland. Her company, Campaign Edge, had run successful advertising campaigns for Labor for a decade. The Eden-Monaro campaign was a chance for her to build a relationship with Erickson and win the contract for the national campaign.

Albanese campaigned hard for McBain, driving all over the electorate every day that he could spare. The swing against Labor was less than half a per cent. The result wasn't known on the night, which gave Albanese's detractors a chance to plot, but the leader was confident the numbers would see McBain get over the line and win her way into parliament. At the after-party, standing with journalists and supporters, with his candidate next to him, and with beer in hand, Albanese casually declared victory: 'We've won, don't worry about that.'

NSW Deputy Premier and Nationals leader John Barilaro saved Albanese's bacon. He was advocating a preference flow Labor's way for anyone voting National in the three-cornered contest. Barilaro was no fan of the Liberal candidate. Barilaro's words carried extra weight because his state seat was within the federal electorate. To have the state Nationals leader and local state MP advocating preferencing Labor ahead of the Liberals was enough to deliver the seat to McBain. If Nationals preference flows from the general election in 2019 had been replicated at the by-election, Labor would have lost, and who knows what might have followed for Albanese's leadership?

'I'd outlined both publicly and privately the fourth-quarter strategy,' Albanese told us. 'If you're worried about the leadership, then you're making decisions that have an impact in a week or a month and that is one of the things that can affect your ability to win an election. I made a decision very early on that I wouldn't be worried about any of that.'

The Eden-Monaro campaign was a template for how Albanese planned to fight the general election. It was a chance to road-test his strategy: condemning Morrison as a blame shifter and using community events to build support. The real Labor campaign for government only started after this win. It was all happening in the shadow of a dominant Morrison and of COVID. In that shadow Albanese started to transform his relationships with colleagues to build better unity, and his sense of identity as leader became stronger. 'He became an alternative PM not just a Labor leader,' one colleague reflects. McBain became an Albo mate and two years later she was fast-tracked to the outer ministry. 'The result built confidence across the party and the movement that rebuilding our campaigning machinery was well underway,' Erickson told us.

The economic management issue

There is no justice in politics. The idea that the Coalition are superior economic managers to Labor seems unrelated to evidence and instead leans on public stereotypes about the major parties. But published polls consistently confirm the misapprehension. Journalists could do more to challenge these stereotypes, but Labor often fails to provide ammunition for them — walking away from the Hawke and Keating legacy of economic reform at times in opposition; or failing to point out the high-taxing records of both the Howard government and its Coalition successors. Chalmers' biggest contribution to the election of the Albanese government was to relentlessly challenge this stereotype, doing so with increased vigour as the term of government closed and the election drew nearer, and the more the Coalition racked up debt. A big-spending conservative government — and there have been many since Menzies —

presents a dilemma for the Labor opposition. Chalmers would become increasingly confident in critiquing government fiscal policy, but his leader would have a long list of things he thought a Labor government should be spending more money on. Shadow Expenditure Review Committee battles were robust.

Labor needed to neutralise the economic management issue to win public confidence and fit their arguments on health and welfare into an overall narrative. Otherwise, only obvious Coalition failures would set the stage for a change of government. Breaking economic issues down showed where Labor could win an advantage, and where the issue agenda in 2022 would favour them. An Australia Institute poll at the time of the 2019 election found the Coalition had a decisive lead on the general question of economic management but found variation in age and gender — older voters and men favouring the conservatives — and in the results on a wide range of individual economic issues. Labor had the edge on job creation, inflation, wages and spending on government services but trailed on economic growth and business investment.

Pollster Essential had another way of breaking down the economic management question, asking voters which party would 'ensure the economy works in the interests of everyday Australians', and providing a decisive result for Labor. This is an issue where opinion may seem static but its salience is highly dependent on framing or 'agenda priming', as political scientists call it. Inflation (or is it 'cost of living'?) making its way back onto the domestic political agenda is a good example.

An alternative way of looking at the economy is that, regardless of which party is in government, a strong economy will favour the incumbent. However, a stable economy can also reduce the salience of economic management as a vote winner, as Howard found in 2007. Or, as Keating found after the 1990 recession, the opposition might make a spectacle of themselves with a large policy program when they should be focusing on government failures. Albanese had a range of models to choose from when positioning Labor on economic issues. Kevin Rudd addressed this question with a YouTube appearance claiming that he had been called a fiscal conservative. His advisers scrambled to find an actual example of the label. Shorten tried to change the subject in 2019, succumbing to Morrison's relentless attacks.

The second half of 2020 was a chance for the Shadow Treasurer to find his voice and provide a strong economic dimension to one of Labor's main indictments of Morrison: that he and his government over-promised and under-delivered. The government tried to press an advantage on economic management. Ignoring Albanese's time in the infrastructure portfolio during the Rudd government, Morrison continually claimed Albanese had 'never held a financial portfolio, never done a budget, never held a national security portfolio'.

Albanese, though trained in economics, doesn't appear invested in economic policy. He would use Howard to compare that prime minister's approach to economic reform with that of the successor Coalition government: 'A former Liberal prime minister once said that, in the race for economic reform, you would never reach the finish line because it was always advancing and there would always be something else to do to make our economy stronger and more productive.'

These really just sound like empty words from Albanese, though. He talks about economic reform but doesn't revel in it. For all his talk about the Hawke government's conciliatory style, he seems neither enamoured with nor ashamed of the record of economic liberalisation that is most notable about that period. 'The great thing about the Hawke government,' he explained to us, 'was that it entrenched reforms.'

> It had economic reforms based upon a social dividend. It was about inclusive growth, so you had some radical changes in opening up Australia to the global economy that were necessary but at the same time you had the creation of Medicare, universal superannuation, improvements in the social wage. Really significant environmental reforms as well. You had increases in productivity growth but sharing of that growth through enterprise bargaining. I was never a fan of privatisation. I'm still not an ideological fan of privatisation for its own sake. We have to rebuild the public service.

Labor's left has long emphasised the internationalist elements of economic reform to make it palatable. Having grown up among light manufacturing plants in Marrickville in Sydney's inner west, Albanese romanticises domestic industry but doesn't challenge the basic principle of open trade. On matters of inequality, though, we can expect Albanese's fundamental values to come to the fore. 'A fair society has to be the objective of Labor governments,' the new prime minister told us. 'It's what we do. I want to create wealth but I'm also concerned about the distribution of wealth and opportunity.'

Albanese's 2020 and 2021 budget reply speeches centred on differentiating broader policy priorities — on health and energy, for example — more so than fiscal policy. The fact that women largely missed out on assistance from the government was a gift for Labor. Albanese's lines on more affordable childcare would become particularly apt as the election approached. They did nothing to convince the electorate, though, that the government's fiscal policy had erred.

It's one thing for an election review to criticise a cluttered agenda. It's another for an opposition party to decide which signature areas to prioritise and which would have to wait. Childcare had long provided a model for political and policy needs converging on greater spending. Labor promised a further step: lifting the maximum subsidy to 90 per cent for the first child. This was a clear choice on Labor's part on how to prioritise any increased expenditure. However, it is also another area where supply-side reform and not just additional spending might be expected. Given Labor's conservative fiscal approach overall, such a choice made additional spending in other areas hard to come by. Since the departure from providing school funding according to the Gonski formula, as introduced by the Gillard government, we might have expected schools to become a higher profile election issue. However, both sides emphasised skills training rather than schools and universities, for which Labor promised spending on specific programs rather than a return to previous policies or spending levels. Adopting the demand-driven system of allocating university places, which Shorten had promised in 2019, would be both expensive and not necessarily the optimum policy choice.

The most important internal policy debates within the party dealt with the issues perceived to have cost Labor government in 2019 — climate change and taxation. Climate change was a particularly messy debate, with Joel Fitzgibbon quitting the front bench and calling for Mark Butler to be moved from the climate portfolio. 'Joel was always a supporter of mine. Joel had a view that he had been too quiet in the lead-up to the 2019 election and he was correcting the other way,' Albanese told us. 'It was never aimed at me personally or my leadership. It was a genuinely different view. We had very frank conversations.'

Husic and Fitzgibbon made a deal within the NSW right at the beginning of the term so that Fitzgibbon would eventually step aside for his factional ally Husic to move up, because Husic had made way for Keneally to take a front-bench role after entering the Senate. It was a selfless act designed to avoid the odium of a former premier — a woman at that — languishing on the back bench because the factional boys' club wouldn't accommodate her. Besides, Kenneally was Husic's mate. While Husic wasn't close to Albanese, Kenneally was, and the leader appreciated Husic's gesture (not that he told him that). Fitzgibbon, of course, hoped that he could manoeuvre his way back into a front-bench spot. He was Albo's mate, after all, having helped him get the numbers together to take the leadership unopposed.

It wasn't to be, and the pair's friendship fractured publicly as Fitzgibbon refused to go quietly. The Otis Group — a collection of largely right-factional MPs and senators who wanted closer cooperation with the mining sector — kept meeting, despite bringing Labor bad publicity. The name came from the restaurant where the first meeting occurred: Otis Dining Hall in the Canberra suburb of Kingston. Albanese tried to brush off the get-togethers in early 2020 when they came to public attention, courtesy of a group email accidentally sent to a Liberal staffer with the same name as one of the attendees. The government revelled in the spectacle of Labor MPs, including a small number of frontbenchers, meeting to discuss what was wrong with opposition policies. Fitzgibbon issued more parting shots at Albanese, and especially his close ally Butler. The pair had been quietly at war for years. It was Fitzgibbon's belief that his personal vote was all that stood between Labor and a loss of seats in the Hunter region, with the margin in the seat of Paterson tight, and Shortland occupied by Pat Conroy, a member of the left and a strong climate change activist.

Butler was keen to move from the climate portfolio but Albanese didn't want to look as though he was giving in to Fitzgibbon's wishes. 'I think we made absolutely the right calls and did more change than I would have, had the accident not happened,' Albanese told us, referring to the car accident he'd had in 2021, which had given him pause for thought. 'We had no one in a domestic portfolio in the leadership group so we gave Keneally government accountability and moved Marles into employment and skills. We moved Chris [Bowen] to climate and did a straight swap with Mark [Butler, to health], which is where both of them wanted to be.'

Shaping up

Senate leader Penny Wong, her deputy Kristina Keneally and Albanese's good friend Tony Burke individually sought out the Opposition Leader about things he needed to work on. While COVID had made life difficult for opposition parties everywhere, his colleagues were not impressed with Albanese's sluggish performance in parliament. 'Shape up or ship out,' was the message. 'You look like a loser' was a tougher appraisal from one MP. He needed to work harder, some colleagues thought, discussing this among themselves. While there was no collective intervention, senior frontbenchers one by one took their concerns to the boss.

Lethargic performances in parliament weren't the only concern of colleagues. Keneally emailed Albanese after a performance on ABC's *Q+A*, taking him blow by blow through what had worked and what hadn't, and why he needed to start preparing properly for such opportunities. 'An hour on national television doesn't come along all that often,' she wrote. She believed that he was better at taking advice when it was delivered in writing, giving him time to privately absorb it rather than bristle at a verbal exchange. Other colleagues employed the same strategy.

Towards the end of 2020, Labor MP Michelle Rowland talked to Albanese about him needing to lose weight. 'If I can do it so can you,' she said, vowing not to share their meeting with anyone else. In the end Albanese would talk regularly to colleagues about how he was 'on the Michelle Rowland diet', which was essentially the low-carbohydrate keto diet with a few extra rules. Rowland had a hamper delivered to him with all the ingredients he could consume. But it was only after his January car accident that he took the diet seriously, and the weight started to fall off. A recently purchased treadmill in the Parliament House office finally got some use. Albanese had started the turnaround that would see his girth become a smaller target, a match for his small-target policy strategy.

Some thought Albo was drinking too much of an evening during the few sitting weeks in 2020, though not to the point of intoxication. As opposition leader they wanted him to 'bring his A-game', one colleague told us. By 2021, he was all but off the booze, as part of his diet. It is not that his consumption of alcohol was a problem, but for someone tasked with unseating Morrison it needed to be brought under better control. Leader of the House Christian Porter noticed it on Albanese's breath at times when the pair discussed procedural issues late in the evenings behind the Speaker's chair. When Albanese did become more disciplined, these earlier moments contributed to the government underestimating him.

In early January 2021, Albanese's car collided head-on with a Range Rover near his home in Sydney. A teenage P-plater was driving in the wrong lane of a two-lane street when he came around a bend, giving Albanese little time to react. 'All of a sudden, he was right in front of me and headed straight for me,' he later said. Time stood still for a split-second. 'It wasn't so much a scary event as a matter-of-fact event,' he told us. 'This is how it ends. The noise was something I will never forget. I was sitting in the car thinking "Is there going to be a bit of me somewhere else?" You think immediately, "Can you move your limbs?"'

His Camry was totalled. The collision was heard two blocks away. 'I had a guardian angel up there looking after me,' Albanese recalled. It was the third car accident to land him in hospital, the first two back in the 1980s. After being treated for shock and mild injuries overnight at Royal Prince Alfred Hospital, he praised hospital staff and took the opportunity to make a policy point: that both Kerry Packer and his own mother had been treated there. 'Whether you're the richest Australian or a pensioner you get the same level of care,' he said. He empathised with the driver, who had apologised at the scene of the accident. 'I hope that this experience leads this young man to commit to becoming one of the safest drivers that Australia has ever seen.'

Was this a life-changing moment? 'I was always very confident that I could deal with any of the challenges that 2021 threw up. After yesterday I'm not just confident, I'm absolutely certain of that.' He took a while to recover:

I was getting dizzy spells. I had concussion. When I stood up in the caucus room to announce the shadow cabinet I had to stop the conference for a while because I was dizzy. For the politics, I had to be strong and forward but it was a difficult period and some people were aware of that — Penny [Wong] and Richard [Marles] were aware. I had a neurologist and a cardiologist and a haematologist and had all these tests. I was reasonably healthy for my age but I was also determined to get healthier and that made a difference in my capacity to work and my energy but also the public perception, showing that discipline was there.

He was mindful of what Uren had impressed upon him. 'It was a real reminder of the need to not waste a day, and that really hit home. To be less tentative, to lead more, to be more decisive.' He told us, 'We'd been through a tough 2020. We were thinking about the reshuffle that was imminent. It had an impact on my decision-making in that it was more of a "go for it" approach after that.'

All the COVID-policy activity provided Albanese the cover to ditch the least popular of Shorten's policies in early 2021: the less generous treatment of franking credits for retirees, capital gains and investment properties. 'Whitlam, Hawke and Rudd had in common,' he told us, 'not going to an election from opposition advocating new taxes. You needed to learn from history rather than repeat it.' Yet given that each tax policy was sensible in its own right, it was a humiliating performance. Echoing Whitlam's observation that 'the impotent are pure', Albanese greeted the derision this decision generated from many in Labor with this rebuttal: 'One of my Labor principles is for Labor to win elections.' It was an example of wanting to kick with the wind in the fourth quarter.

As we saw in 2019, fear can be a more reliable driver of votes than hope. It is one of the reasons Albanese's inner circle referred to their small-target strategy as a 'smart-target strategy': denying the Coalition a scare campaign. However, this is a more complex question than the advice to 'leave tax reform for government' would suggest, given that Rudd tried and failed at that gambit. And while Shorten conceded that his policy platform was 'cluttered', he warned his party, 'the polar opposite of [embracing] a tiny agenda is not the right way either. We must be an opposition that stands for something.' Better, though, to be a government that stands for something.

It wasn't until March 2021 that the Opposition Leader was finally secure enough in the job that he could be certain he would contest the next election. He had seen off the Otis Group agitators, politely walked Fitzgibbon to stage right, won the crucial by-election in Eden-Monaro and stared down leadership rivals. Albanese quietly went about capturing his approach to leadership in a series of 'vision statements' — mostly a collection of speeches and statements on key topics. Albanese preferred to describe himself as a 'values politician' in his first statement as leader, which became the first values statement. An economist who places the economy in its social context. A consensus-seeker. Mindful of his public image as parliamentary enforcer, he laboured the point. 'People want solutions, not arguments,' he said in comments directed at the Prime Minister. 'They have conflict fatigue. Some reforms require bipartisan support.' He referred to his work on Infrastructure Australia as an example of government, business and unions working together. Later, during the campaign, he would note that his approach to opposition — and his hopes for government — were all contained in that speech.

The context of the speech was also important to the small-target versus big-target approach. Morrison had won his miracle election off the back of attacks on Labor's proposed tax changes. Nobody could have predicted the crises to follow, and their effect on politics. With hindsight, a stronger platform could have shifted votes more decisively Labor's way. However, any electoral strategy had to take into account a range of scenarios. Erickson was concerned about 'change fatigue' among voters.

More promising from Labor's point of view was the way the economic debate was evolving. Big government was back in fashion. It never really went away where fiscal policy was concerned, but expansionary budgets during the pandemic were accompanied by growing scepticism of the reliability of global supply chains in times of crisis. While the strategy of the government to make a virtue of higher levels of government intervention had its merits, the longer-term effect has been to promote spending and social priorities in Labor's wheelhouse. The focus on aged care during the pandemic underlined the weakness of the Coalition's position.

The government made a range of announcements to buttress sovereign manufacturing policy in the year before and during the campaign. Moves towards more manufacturing capacity in pharmaceuticals paved the way for a more extensive industry policy debate. This had long been an area of interest for Albanese. 'Australia must be a country that makes things,' was the refrain. Apart from leveraging government spending on defence, transport and infrastructure to boost training and domestic capacity, the policy proposals were fairly thin. Romanticising the heavily subsidised car manufacturers of days past, plans were put in place for a $15 billion National Reconstruction Fund modelled on the Clean Energy Finance Corporation established by the Gillard government. This model keeps the funding decisions independent of ministers and is funded off-budget. Labor nominated tasks as diverse as commercialisation of medical research and processing of rare earth minerals as potential recipients, and cited research from the OECD showing that Australia lagged other developed nations in manufacturing. Yet, with Albanese only promising modest steps in this direction, the issue didn't provide the sort of advantage for Labor that he would have hoped when he became leader.

With policy deliberations mostly locked up between the factions, the 2021 ALP National Conference was more significant for what happened behind the scenes rather than on the floor. There was more consensus than usual over an interventionist economic policy and some agitation for friendly language about gas production from the resource-rich states. The combination of a small gathering in Sydney supplemented by online attendance made the grandstanding from left-wing unions less dramatic. The hard work on policy had already been done. The conference was the backdrop for the announcement of the National Reconstruction Fund and a coronation for Albanese, who was introduced by Shorten in a delicious moment. The theme of Albanese's speech was 'we are on your side.' While that line didn't last long, the concentration on the failings of the Morrison government would become very familiar.

Behind the scenes, Albanese got to know and like Dee Madigan. After the successful campaign in Eden-Monaro, Erickson decided to hire her company to produce video and branding for the conference. Once Albanese and Madigan were comfortable with each other, and the conference was a success, Madigan accepted the role in charge of television advertising for the upcoming election. With Madigan sitting in on focus groups from July, she and Erickson discussed messaging almost daily. Madigan felt that the relationship between the creative director and the campaign director was more important than that between the creative director and the leader but she wanted to know that Albanese would listen to her. Filming for video overlay, which could later be inserted into topical campaign advertising, began in March 2021, with more sessions in July. Madigan's young daughter was at an early shoot and got a photo with Albanese. Madigan noticed that this produced a more natural smile than he usually produced on demand.

The year 2021 also provided more opportunities for Labor to attack the government over the botched vaccine rollout and endless changes to the planning for an end to lockdowns. Morrison played down the effects of Health Minister Greg Hunt's failure to purchase sufficient vaccine supplies. At every step of the pandemic after the initial response, Morrison seemed to hope things would get better, only to be mugged by reality. Labor released its own plans in response, but they amounted to doing things more competently rather than differently. The point of such appearances was to look constructive rather than to have a material effect on events in the way Albanese had been able to do during the bushfires.

The onset of the Omicron COVID variant late in 2021 gave the government another chance to show its determination to learn nothing. Erickson thought this period decisive. The public's willingness to support difficult government decisions was compromised, he said, by 'two impulses that the Liberals seemed incapable of controlling: hubris and mindless partisan tribalism'. Joined by New South Wales, and later Victoria, in pursuing a 'living with COVID' strategy despite the more contagious new strain, Morrison again showed a slapdash policy approach. In September, NSW Premier Gladys Berejiklian, with whom Morrison had clashed over pandemic strategy, resigned due to an investigation by the Independent Commission Against Corruption. The new premier, Dominic Perrottet, was more in sync with Morrison's hit-and-hope approach, but Perrottet couldn't stand Morrison, their factional fighting predating any policy disagreements.

Having shifted rhetoric to emphasise freedom and personal responsibility, Morrison invited Albanese's allegation of a 'let it rip' approach, even though it was far from that. Morrison in turn accused the opposition of wanting a return to lockdowns. Not an especially enlightening debate. There was little sense of a considered plan for reopening. The Commonwealth had to scramble to order rapid antigen tests to allow for self-testing, although the states also dropped the ball on what became a vital component of the changing approach to the pandemic. However, Albanese's idea for a cash incentive for immunisation and for free rapid antigen tests didn't go down well. He was forced to clarify Labor's position on making RATs free. Why any policy was necessary on such an ephemeral issue wasn't clear to most voters. When daily cases in New South Wales topped 40,000, many Sydneysiders chose to stay home rather than exercise their newfound freedoms. Death rates that would have been scandalous early in the pandemic barely registered in the public consciousness. Around the world, citizens were impatient with lingering restrictions. The consensus behind a restrictive approach to the pandemic was breaking down.

The difficulty of finding clear air to put a policy position in such a fast-moving environment caused Labor its share of problems. Raging at the government's incompetence was fair enough. Yet, Labor's mantra that the economy wouldn't recover unless health was prioritised looked less viable as an electoral strategy as the pandemic entered a third year. The combination of public loyalty to incumbents during the pandemic and a recovering economy should have seen Morrison in the box seat. However, it wasn't just vaccines that caused the prime minister headaches throughout 2021. He also had a woman problem.

A PM past his prime

Morrison's approach to women belied common sense, especially for an essentially pragmatic leader. On the one hand, much of his 'daggy dad' persona was aimed at shoring up the women's vote, in which the Coalition often had an advantage over Labor until the Gillard–Abbott clashes early in the last decade. He had made noises behind the scenes prior to the 2019 election to consider gender quotas for pre-selections. Yet the issues where the Coalition usually outpointed Labor — the economy and defence — provided an advantage among men. Improving the workplace culture in Parliament House should have been both a moral and political winner for the PM. Not only did he not take advantage of this but the issue would also consume him like no other for more than a year.

In late 2020, two incidents foreshadowed what was to come and Morrison's failure to adopt a more sensitive approach. They followed the notorious 'blokes' budget' and the lack of attention to women in the COVID support measures. In October, a Senate committee heard that Australia Post chief executive Christine Holgate authorised a $19,000 purchase of Cartier watches as executive bonuses for securing a deal worth hundreds of millions. The Prime Minister thundered about this in the House, as though the 'pub test' set standards of corporate behaviour. 'She can go,' he said. He looked unhinged. A government that detested accountability wanted the scalp of a high-achieving female CEO. He refused to apologise for the procedural unfairness after Holgate resigned.

In November, the ABC's *Four Corners* program interviewed Rachelle Miller, a former staffer of Education Minister Alan Tudge, about the toxic culture in parliament. The family-values politician had a consensual affair with Miller in 2017. The program made various allegations about Attorney-General Christian Porter, but worse was to come for him. Morrison dismissed the idea that ministerial standards had been breached — Malcolm Turnbull's notorious 'bonk ban' having been introduced separately to the Tudge affair. The PM's response ignored the most important part of Miller's story: that she had been pressured to keep the affair a secret as part of the culture of misogyny. Frustrated by the ongoing government failures throughout 2021, Miller made further allegations against Tudge, which prompted him to stand aside from the ministry pending an investigation into whether he had breached ministerial standards.

To kick off 2021, Grace Tame, an advocate for survivors of sexual assault, was announced as Australian of the Year. This would prove to be one of the award's more interesting choices. Albanese developed a good rapport with Tame. A soft interview with Tame in *InStyle* magazine dropped just in time for the election.

Morrison refused to stand down Porter when Porter revealed he was the minister facing rape allegations dating back to 1988. The woman concerned had taken her own life in 2020 and NSW Police had chosen to end their investigation. A letter detailing the allegations, including supposedly contemporaneous diary entries, was sent to the Prime Minister's office, the opposition and journalists by friends of the complainant. Given the woman's detailed account, there were widespread calls for an independent inquiry. Porter publicly denied the allegations. Morrison ultimately did Porter no favours by not standing him down, particularly after Porter launched defamation action against the ABC, and given that a ministerial reshuffle was in the works, in which Porter was moved sideways. Having settled the defamation action, Porter eventually resigned from cabinet rather than reveal details of the funding of his legal costs through a blind trust.

Morrison did manage to strike the right note occasionally. However, his change of tone seemed to be a response to the snowballing of issues after the allegations against Porter, and a staffer being sacked for sharing images of another staffer engaged in a sex act on a female MP's desk. A snowballing response to the PM's inaction was also well underway, culminating in a large protest in Canberra, which Morrison declined to visit. By contrast, Albanese nominated to us his speech to the rally as one of the key points of the parliamentary term for him.

The Prime Minister was on the back foot politically, and behind the times socially. Morrison's attitude to all of this fuelled a movement of independent candidates who would take their revenge on the government at the election — almost all the 'teal' independents would be women. Having resisted quotas to pre-select more women into his own party, by governing so badly Morrison helped increase the number of women in the parliament, but they were teal rather than blue.

Victory in sight

Labor's clear position favouring an anti-corruption commission looked better and better as the government floundered. Member for Bass Bridget Archer crossed the floor in November 2021 to bring on debate over Helen Haines' private member's bill to establish an integrity commission. Archer and Morrison gave different accounts of a subsequent meeting, which Archer had not wanted to attend and which she characterised as a 'frank' exchange of views. Morrison described Archer as a close friend whom he wanted to make sure was being supported.

In January 2022, Morrison proposed to cabinet to introduce strengthened legislation for an integrity body, incorporating some features of the Haines bill in exchange for moderate MPs passing the Religious Discrimination Bill. Communications Minister Paul Fletcher and other moderates objected. There were also the usual concerns about retrospectivity. Others were concerned that the politics would again leave Morrison looking tricky. Morrison was taken aback when he was rolled and his cabinet humiliation was in turn leaked to the media, a sure sign of trouble at the top. Labor, of course, was happy for the government to make headlines for all the wrong reasons. During the pandemic, Morrison had become used to executive decision-making at Commonwealth level, then twisting the arms of premiers at national cabinet. It was a remarkable misjudgement of both the moral and political pressures facing his backbenchers. Morrison simply couldn't comprehend the fact that some politicians would not horse-trade over these issues for the sake of legislative neatness leading up to an election. Archer wasn't having any of it. 'That's the way Morrison thinks, not me,' she told us. All eyes would be on Archer and Morrison when they campaigned together in Bass.

Labor was finally set to unveil its climate change policy in early December after parliament rose for the year. 'We went through proper processes of shadow cabinet then caucus,' Albanese told us. '[The government] had their pamphlet rather than a policy. They had come out with net zero by 2050 but there was nothing beneath it except the slogan.' A higher 2030 emissions target of 43 per cent was Labor's centrepiece, with additional investment in renewable energy and a promised cut in power prices. There was also a plan to transition the Commonwealth vehicle fleet to electric. The sleeper issue was Labor's plan to tighten the existing Safeguard Mechanism, requiring the highest carbon emitters to keep their net emissions below a certain limit. This would later trip the opposition up during the campaign but Albanese was happy that the internal debate about climate policy was out of the way.

A few days after the release of Labor's climate change policy, Morrison was in Bathurst, taking a lap of the famous racing circuit at Mount Panorama with Supercar driver Mark Skaife. He looked a little nervous as Skaife clocked 230 kilometres per hour. The Bathurst 1000 wasn't the right forum to repeat his line about the vaccination rollout not being a race. By then, Australia's rate was indeed globally competitive. 'It's just showing where we're heading,' he said. 'Looking out of the front windscreen, not in the rear view mirror.'

Albanese was unimpressed. 'It was just another photo-op,' he told us. 'Morrison should have gone to an election last year [2021] with the same playbook as he did in 2019. It was never going to get better for him. People were on to him by then. We had a few themes running through — "all about the photo-op, not the follow-up", "always about the promise, not the delivery" — all of those things he kept reinforcing by his own actions.'

An election campaign based on the public's lack of trust in the Prime Minister was coming into focus for Labor. How, though, to package the idea of a government led by Anthony Albanese? Erickson was concerned that the electorate would be risk averse. 'It was a widespread and deep sense of fatigue, anxiety, and aversion to risk after some of the most difficult years we've endured,' he told the National Press Club after the election. 'Normally, these sentiments would drive fence-sitters decisively back to the government of the day and weigh heavily against an effort to build a majority for change.' This concern, and the sustained period of intense policy debate during the pandemic provided a post-hoc justification for a small-target approach. Would voters be weary of policy change in a way that justified Labor's approach, leading to the adoption of the Tony Blair-like rhetoric of 'safe change'? Yet, precisely because so little of consequence had been achieved on the policy front over the last nine years, the next parliament would have to embrace serious reform: the federation, the tax system, a coordinated response to climate change, and difficult decisions on pensions and superannuation to ensure fiscal sustainability.

'So, when voters go into the ballot box, they ask themselves: Do I really want another three years of this shit? No thanks,' Erickson told *The Monthly*. Albanese just needed to be plausible. 'Some voters used to worry he's a nice bloke, but they couldn't see him representing us on the world stage,' Erickson said. 'We stopped hearing that in focus groups.'

Howard faced the same questions prior to the 1996 election, and Abbott prior to 2013. At some point, voters start to have more questions about the prime minister than about their opponents. Morrison's everyman persona was effective in the absence of a record. Ordinariness is a two-edged sword, though, when it is the government's performance in the following parliamentary term that could only charitably be described as ordinary. Morrison was the first prime minister since Howard to take their record of a full parliamentary term to the electorate. As Albanese put it, 'people are far more cynical about our opponents this time around'.

Where to win?

Any confidence on Labor's part was tempered by a hard-headed look at the electoral map for the House of Representatives. A solid lead in the two-party preferred polling would not necessarily translate into a majority. This was a point Chalmers, a political scientist by training, would often make. Labor could elevate its two-party vote beyond 52 per cent nationally, but if it didn't do better than that in marginal seats it could come up short. Redistributions since the 2019 election had abolished a Liberal-held seat in Western Australia (Stirling) and created a Labor-held seat in Victoria (Hawke), changing the notional House of Representatives balance to seventy-six Coalition — bang on the majority needed to govern — and sixty-nine Labor. If Labor held all of its seats it would need to pick up seven Coalition seats to form majority government. Erickson believed Labor would lose one or two seats at the election. 'It was a case of knowing which ones,' he told us. 'Every opposition has lost at least one seat since 1998. We therefore assumed so would we.'

Labor strategists identified twelve seats they hoped to win, which would deliver a majority even if they lost a few seats of their own. The hit list included Bass in Tasmania; Flynn and Brisbane in Queensland; Reid, Robertson and Bennelong in New South Wales; Chisholm and Higgins in Victoria; Boothby in South Australia; and Swan, Pearce and Hasluck in Western Australia.

Five of the seats were occupied by retiring government MPs (Boothby, Swan, Pearce, Bennelong and Flynn), which robbed the Coalition of name recognition, also creating some friction in the local campaign for the conservatives over things like voter databases and volunteers. Erickson was alive to this.

Western Australia looked strongest for Labor. Swan, at 3.2 per cent, was the most marginal WA seat and, coupled with the retirement of Steve Irons, looked as likely a loss for the Liberals as any seat around the country. Pearce, on 5.2 per cent, would be difficult to hold for the Liberals because of the controversies surrounding the outgoing member and former attorney-general, Christian Porter. Indigenous Affairs Minister Ken Wyatt held Hasluck with a 5.9 per cent margin, but Labor was confident with the halo effect of the popular Labor Premier Mark McGowan Hasluck would be won. Labor had expected to win seats in the west before and fallen short, which perhaps explains why it ignored the state party's confident assertions that the seats of Tangney and Moore should also be considered for key seat status. Perennial swinging seat Bass in Tasmania had the tightest margin for the government at 0.4 per cent, but Erickson was never confident of winning it. The Liberals' Bridget Archer was trying to become the first MP for Bass re-elected since 2001. Chisholm in suburban Melbourne was on just 0.5 per cent, and Boothby in Adelaide 1.4. It was a miracle the Liberals held Chisholm in 2019. Their track polling suggested it was gone. If Labor didn't win there, they had zero chance of winning the election. Each party runs a five or six-day rolling tracking poll of key marginal seats. It has a small sample size in each seat, and therefore bounces around day to day, but measuring 25–30 seats can be more accurate than published polls in picking up changes of sentiment, and in breaking those numbers down by demographics such as gender and age.

Boothby Liberal MP Nicolle Flint was retiring. She had faced a vicious campaign in 2019 and cited the sexism in that contest and in parliament more generally when announcing her retirement. The seat had been held by the Liberals since their inaugural national election win in 1949, so Labor was concerned that they had already done as well there as was possible, given the demographics. It was on their target list, but an outlier.

The inner-city Melbourne seat of Higgins was on 3.7 per cent. Incumbent Liberal Katie Allen was keen to brandish her moderate credentials, tweeting photos of herself with her electric car, which, for those who like metaphors, would go on to be smashed by a truck during the campaign. While Higgins was not regarded as a likely gain in wider Labor circles, Erickson was confident they could win the traditional Liberal electorate. And he wasn't quietly confident; he'd told guests at a fundraiser in February 2022 that Higgins looked like a good bet for Labor. He waited for Albanese to leave the room on a phone call before making the bold prediction. 'I don't bet, that would be unethical as national secretary, but there is money to be made there for anyone who does,' he told the room.

The two Queensland seats on Labor's list were Flynn and Brisbane, with margins of 8.7 per cent and 4.9 per cent respectively. Flynn, while held by the government with a strong margin, had a retiring MP, and Labor's candidate was strong. Albanese hoped it could swing his way; Erickson was less confident. The lax government response to the March 2022 floods put Morrison on the nose in Brisbane. Right until the end, Labor didn't believe the Greens would come through the middle to steal the seat. Longman at 3.3 per cent had been snatched from Labor in 2019 by Terry Young, and its margin made it appear more vulnerable than Flynn or Brisbane, but its demographics suited Morrison, which is why it wasn't on the dozen key seats list.

In New South Wales, Reid is a traditional Labor seat, first won by the Liberals in 2013 when Craig Laundy entered parliament. Fiona Martin held on by 3.2 per cent in 2019 when Laundy retired, but the outgoing member worked tirelessly for the incoming candidate. Labor expected to pick it up in 2022 and Liberal strategists were anything but confident they could hold it. Robertson, on the New South Wales Central Coast, is a swing seat. As Labor had held the nearby seat of Dobell from the previous election, Erickson was hopeful of making it a double. In Sydney, Bennelong, John Howard's old seat, rounded out the targeted dozen. But with a margin of 6.9 per cent it was one of the long shots in the eyes of Erickson, despite the retirement of the Liberal MP John Alexander.

'We entered 2022 feeling pretty good about our prospects,' Erickson told us. 'Anthony was getting the best reception he'd received during his leadership, and Morrison had once again stuffed up when Omicron arrived by not ordering enough RATs. We weren't complacent but the mood was shifting in our favour.'

The Opposition Leader was also confident. 'The big calls I made were right,' he said. The climate change policy, the Religious Discrimination Bill. People close to him had faith in his judgement. It gave Albanese the confidence he could win. 'We were totally in play to win,' he told us. 'I said to people, "We can do this!"'

Chapter 4

The phoney campaign

It was 1 February 2022. Anthony Albanese and his senior staff were doing something unusual: watching their opponent speak at the National Press Club. They were aware of how important the event was to both leaders. Having undergone a transformation of his own, Albanese had held court at the Press Club a week earlier, performing credibly but not making a big impact. Prime ministers often use the Press Club to set the political agenda for the year ahead. Incumbency gives them the clout if they can get it right. In an election year with the government well behind in the opinion polls, Scott Morrison hoped to use his speech to reset his government's fading political fortunes. Parliament was returning for the new year the following week and the budget would be handed down soon thereafter — early again, as a momentum-builder for the election, just like 2019.

'I watched it and I just thought the speech had no substance, and that he wasn't capable of resetting because he wasn't capable of admitting any mistakes,' Albanese told us. 'Even in that speech, he sought to blame others for all of the problems that there were. To me, it just didn't work at all.' Morrison's come-from-behind win in 2019 left Labor strategists and supporters paranoid about what he had up his sleeve in 2022, notwithstanding the poor start to the election year.

Morrison can be an effective speaker. At least, he would be if his every utterance wasn't marred by years of undermining his own credibility with evasions, hypocrisy, spurious comparisons and outright lies. Exactly one year earlier at the Press Club, he was riding high, enjoying the glow shared by leaders in most of the world battling a global pandemic. This 'rally round the flag effect' has been well documented. The Queensland government was returned easily in October 2020 and Western Australian Premier Mark McGowan won an astonishing victory in March 2021. McGowan's triumph got Anthony Albanese thinking about opportunities for federal Labor in the west. Victorian Premier Dan Andrews had barely lost any paint in the face of a brutal attack from the *Herald Sun* over some poor decisions by his government regarding quarantine and aged care. However, this boost to incumbents was temporary as 'pandemic fatigue' set in, just as it had in the 1919 influenza pandemic. The further into the pandemic we went, the less consensus there was about how to proceed both in terms of public health measures and fiscal policy. And, as Morrison was to say in his speech, we were exhausted. Unlike the 2019 campaign, the Prime Minister no longer enjoyed the benefit of the doubt from journalists or voters. His public events would be interpreted with understandable cynicism.

During the speech, Morrison tried to show empathy for those affected during 'the past three years ... some of the most extraordinary that our nation has ever experienced'. 'For so many Australians,' he continued, 'it has been exhausting — financially, physically, emotionally.' He conceded some mistakes. He canvassed changes to domestic manufacturing capacity considering the pandemic and outlined his efforts on national security and federalism. He commented on the resilience of the economy but gave cost of living pressures short shrift by highlighting falling electricity prices. His 'announceable' was a temporary boost in wages for aged care workers. There was only an oblique reference to Labor and its leader: 'we cannot take this for granted; now is not the time to turn back.'

Morrison's speechwriter, Paul Ritchie, would not have been surprised that his painstaking efforts prompted not one question from a journalist on the substance of the speech. Chair Laura Tingle met Morrison's concession of mistakes by helpfully providing an impressive list of them and asking for an apology on behalf of the nation. Morrison played for time by thanking Tingle for the question and pausing for the laugh from the audience, ably provided by the many ministers, MPs and staffers in the room, including Morrison lieutenants Ben Morton and Alex Hawke. A few of the journalists joined in. His brain was ticking over.

He was sorry. Sorry that shit happens rather than for anything he may have done. Oh, he was sorry for being 'too optimistic' about the pandemic as Omicron loomed over Australia's summer. He regretted not militarising the vaccine rollout earlier. Now it's possible that Lieutenant-General John Frewen would have done a better job than Health Minister Greg Hunt in negotiating with the multinational drug companies to get more doses of the vaccine to Australia earlier, but it was just more sleight of hand from Morrison, pretending that the vaccine 'strollout' was about logistics rather than complacency. Albanese had observed this tendency towards hope over experience during the pandemic. 'He had been too optimistic at a range of times,' he reflected to us. 'Congratulating Gladys [Berejiklian] for not having [taken] action when the debacle that led to the shutting down of News South Wales, Victoria and New Zealand occurred.'

Nine's Chris Uhlmann provided the cost-of-living numbers Morrison had left out and invited the PM to repeat John Howard's manoeuvre in 2001, when he cut fuel excise as GST-influenced inflation rose. Morrison had clearly not given this topic enough thought. The cost of living rated nary a mention in Treasurer Josh Frydenberg's 2021 budget speech. Uhlmann made the mistake of referring to what the PM had said about house prices, providing Morrison the fig leaf to ramble on about anything but inflation. The third question was about something studiously avoided in the speech: the culture in parliament. Then sluggish wage growth and the price of a loaf of bread. The tactic in dealing with such questions is to avoid providing anything quotable to help put the focus on the positives. It wasn't to be.

Tingle called upon author van Onselen in his capacity as Network Ten political editor. Van Onselen read from an SMS exchange between a current Liberal cabinet minister and Berejiklian during the 2019–20 bushfires. The senior minister had referred to the PM as a 'fraud' and a 'complete psycho'. The anonymous senior minister was the source of the text, giving van Onselen permission to quote from the exchange. The former premier, whom Morrison described as a close friend, had texted that he is 'a horrible, horrible person' more concerned with politics than people. Morrison visibly winced when van Onselen read from the texts. His eyelids flickered uncontrollably as he processed the question before starting his answer. The PM had tried to persuade the former premier to contest Warringah at the federal election. It's harder to ignore questions in the formal Press Club format compared to a press conference or doorstop. The smirk turned upside down. He could muster only a couple of sentences in response.

'It just reinforced what people thought of him,' Albanese told us. 'There were enough people who were close to him in the government and at other levels of government who would make similar comments to you. It was always the case that the reality of the failure to have proper relations with people would catch up with you.' Albanese's phone started to vibrate from the messages coming in about Morrison being skewered by his own colleagues. For years the Opposition Leader had been slowly and steadily putting out his take on the Prime Minister; now he saw his views reflected in the judgements of Morrison's closest colleagues. It was a devastating blow.

Paul Erickson was watching the speech from his office at Labor headquarters in Canberra just down the road from the Press Club. '[Morrison] looked quite flustered. He definitely didn't get the reboot he wanted,' he told us.

Recognising that 'suddenly his own side were going after him,' a Labor staffer at HQ popped his head into Erickson's office: 'Did you see that?'

'We shouldn't buy into it,' Erickson responded. 'They are better at a campaign to destabilise Scott Morrison than we are!' What transpired confirmed the worth of Labor's subtle campaign for Erickson. 'We had to bring down his popularity so we could compete. Suddenly we looked up from our work and everybody agreed with us.'

Erickson texted Dee Madigan asking her to put together some advertising options including the text message quotes so they could be tested on focus groups. 'In the end we had so much material I don't think we used them,' Madigan recalls. Focus groups told Labor that the electorate had well and truly heard what Morrison's colleagues had said about him. They were still thinking there was a chance Morrison would call the election early, for 5 March. The way Morrison's reset just landed, however, put an end to that idea, Erickson thought.

The following days were dominated by the 'psycho' story. Coffee mugs were produced with Morrison's image and the words 'complete psycho' underneath. A text emerged from Barnaby Joyce from prior to his return to the Nationals leadership referring to Morrison as 'a hypocrite and a liar'. Joyce's leaked text went on, 'I have never trusted him, and I dislike how earnestly [he] rearranges the truth to a lie' — as penetrating an appraisal of Morrison's rhetorical technique as could be offered. Speculating on the identity of the anonymous minister texting with Berejiklian became a national pastime. Fellow MPs were in no doubt, though, as to motive: this was a calculated attempt to sabotage a sitting prime minister just months away from calling an election. There Morrison stood, looking less like Shelley's Ozymandias than one of Elon Musk's rockets bursting into flames on its launch pad. Reset over.

Cautious optimism

Roy Morgan Research found that levels of trust in government fell during late 2021 and early 2022. Any goodwill towards the government due to the pandemic was receding. The sweet spot for holding elections in Australia is late February or March. Christmas and New Year provide a natural break from politicking, leaving little time before a formal campaign period gets under way. An election in May leaves the early part of the year as one long phoney election campaign. Especially when parliament is due to sit in February and every action is directed towards the campaign.

For Albanese, election year had started with a long road trip through Queensland in January in case Morrison called an early election. Chalmers was with him much of the time, an important period in their improving relationship. Accompanying them were Senator Anthony Chisholm, a friend of Chalmers, and Senator Murray Watt, a friend of Albanese. 'We did twenty towns in ten days and I really like doing that stuff,' Albanese told us. 'I get energised by being out there on the trail and it's something that I'll do as PM as well. That trip was really successful. Jim and I got on really well.'

Madigan joined the Queensland roadshow, having realised just how different Albanese looked after losing 18 kilos. She had long since shot video overlay for the campaign. They were now unusable. 'We need new overlay,' she told Erickson, 'he's lost too much weight.' She jumped on a plane to Cairns.

A run of newspaper and magazine profiles of the slimmed-down Labor leader were timed as a reintroduction of Albanese in the new year. A *Women's Weekly* cover story with partner Jodie Haydon emphasised the new look — more fashionable glasses and suits to cut a more contemporary figure. Albo chose his own glasses, everyone was at pains to tell us. As 2022 commenced and Albanese needed to start travelling around the country to campaign, Haydon started to play a more visible role. The *Women's Weekly* feature was her first major interview and an attempt to softly sell them as a couple prior to the campaign. Albanese was very protective of their bourgeoning relationship, not wanting to thrust Jodie into the spotlight, but also not wanting to be accused of hiding Haydon from view. Journalists asked to do profiles and sit-down interviews with the couple, but Albanese largely resisted. He was also wary of how Morrison might frame the contrast to his own family life. Albanese didn't put it past the win-at-all-costs Morrison going below the belt, even though he had nothing to hide.

There was also the obligatory pre-election *Four Corners* episode and a sympathetic profile on *Sixty Minutes*, which outrated a prior segment featuring the PM. Albo yukked it up with Karl Stefanovic at a keto-unfriendly Italian restaurant. 'I'm hungry,' Albanese joked about his diet. This lengthy appearance on prime-time commercial television provided the Albanese biography to hundreds of thousands of voters who barely knew him, relating the story of his search for his Italian father and showing him laughing with friends from outside politics. There wasn't much policy talk, Albanese solemnly telling Stefanovic that after the near-death experience of the car crash he was 'determined to make a contribution'.

Morrison's tin-eared start to the year continued when he told *Sky After Dark*'s Paul Murray there was something amiss with Albanese's new appearance. 'I'm not pretending to be anyone else,' he said. 'I'm still wearing the same sunglasses. Sadly, the same suits. I weigh about the same size and I don't mind a bit of Italian cuisine ... You've got to know who you are because if you don't know who you are, then how are other people going to know?' This was widely interpreted as too personal an attack. Morrison's taunts aside, Albanese still had work to do to introduce himself to voters. He looked confident, though, without coming across as arrogant. He had the Labor Party's entire history to keep his confidence in check. 'We're the party of big ideas,' he told Stefanovic. 'And we can sometimes be impatient about changing the world quickly.' Referring to the experience of the Rudd government, he commented, 'I've seen the mistakes that were made.'

Parliament resumed the week after the views of some of Morrison's colleagues about him were revealed at the National Press Club. The government used Question Time to rehearse its attacks on Albanese.

Without much scary policy to target, and with its own tax and spending record hard to defend, Morrison sought to portray Labor as a risk. This was reminiscent of the 2004 Coalition victory. John Howard warned that Mark Latham was inexperienced and not competent to manage the economy. That fear campaign worked. A similar campaign against Labor and Albanese had less purchase. Morrison's portrayal of Labor as being the Chinese Communist Party's preferred candidate at the election looked desperate.

The government did a poor job of managing the policy agenda early in the election year. Business that should have been dealt with earlier in the parliament, such as religious discrimination and anti-corruption, lingered in the new year. Albanese was treading carefully on the Religious Discrimination Bill, backing the principle but describing the proposed legislation as flawed, and accusing the Prime Minister of 'dividing the nation'. In the end, Morrison wedged himself, losing backbenchers over his decision to send the question of discrimination against transgender students to the Law Reform Commission. When the bill passed the House, five Liberal MPs crossed the floor in favour of a crossbench amendment to extend protection to transgender children. For Trent Zimmerman, Dave Sharma, Fiona Martin, Bridget Archer and Katie Allen, it was an emotional combination of principle and electoral necessity. Rather than face defeat in the Senate, Morrison pulled the bill. He hadn't expected Martin to cross the floor. Her diverse multi-cultural electorate was religiously conservative; Liberal strategists believed it would penalise her for the stance she took. (After Martin's defeat in Reid at the election, Morrison conspicuously refused to call with his commiserations.) Martin copped the brunt of the internal criticism because of her close factional and personal friendship with moderate Liberal Senator Andrew Bragg. The Prime Minister's team was convinced that Bragg was responsible for leaking internal polling during the campaign showing the Coalition behind Labor.

Another distraction for the government was the factional fighting in New South Wales over pre-selection. Amid court challenges, a three-person committee appointed by the federal executive briefly took over the branch and guaranteed the selection of Morrison's proxy, Alex Hawke, key moderate Zimmerman and Environment Minister Sussan Ley. Factional critics argued that it was Hawke who had done the most to delay the pre-selections. Days before the election was called, the federal executive intervened once again in New South Wales to finalise the bitterly contested remaining pre-selection contests, including seats such as Parramatta, Eden-Monaro and Hughes, and the independent-held Warringah. These rushed decisions would have greater consequences than anyone knew at the time.

The National Party's price for acquiescing to a net-zero climate policy soon became clear. Joyce announced funding for a dam servicing the Queensland Coalition electorates of Flynn, Capricornia and Dawson. Morrison visited Townsville to publicise funding for another dam, which had already been announced. Neither project had been vetted by the National Water Grid Advisory Body, established just two years earlier to provide advice on major water infrastructure projects. Showing that the government was incapable of embarrassment, Joyce dissolved the body, saying its work was complete.

Morrison wanted foreign policy and defence to play a role in the campaign. He got his wish when the Solomon Islands' security agreement with China was made public in April, although that wasn't what he had in mind. Morrison had already copped a serve from former security chief Dennis Richardson for politicising policy on China, Morrison having labelled Marles a 'Manchurian candidate'. Just who this kind of rhetoric was aimed at months prior to any election was not clear. Certainly not the voters of ultra-marginal Chisholm, which consisted of nearly 20 per cent Mandarin- or Cantonese-speakers, with Bennelong not far behind. Reid, Kooyong, Goldstein, Swan, Parramatta and North Sydney also had ethnic Chinese voters in numbers that should have given the Liberal Party pause. While Australia's Chinese community is diverse in the way it perceives China, many were wary at the danger of anti-China rhetoric engendering sentiment against Australia's ethnic Chinese. Others with pro-business views did not want to risk commercial relationships with China. The teal independents gave these voters a pro-business alternative to both Liberal and Labor.

After Russia's invasion of Ukraine in February 2022, in a speech to the Lowy Institute, Morrison introduced the short-lived idea of an 'arc of autocracy'. 'A new arc of autocracy is instinctively aligning to challenge and reset the world order in their own image,' he said. Yet, Russia's invasion produced no benefit for the PM, Essential polling finding no clear preference between the parties on which would better deal with the crisis, with a plurality insisting it made no difference, underlining a public preference for bipartisanship on foreign policy which Morrison regularly flouted.

Defence Minister Peter Dutton joined the global rush to foreshadow increased spending on defence in response to Russia's belligerence. He made an absurd announcement about defence force numbers projected to 2040, and leaked options for the location of a nuclear submarine base on the eastern seaboard. None of this was backed with evidence of budget projections. Albanese underlined the government's tendency to make grand announcements about future projects, foreshadowed by a drop to favoured news outlets. 'You can't actually defend the country with a media release,' he said. He resisted the temptation to mock Dutton's re-announcement of Australia's own Space Command.

Labor was rock-solid on national security. Albanese floated ideas to address the capability gap, given the change of submarine platforms, and flagged climate change as a national security issue. Chalmers castigated the $5 billion wasted on an abandoned submarine program. Albanese put this in a larger context of the government crowing about defence spending while extracting very little value from contractors when it came to capital building projects. For the first time since their contrasting approaches to the bushfires, Albanese drew level with Morrison as preferred prime minister, according to Newspoll in mid-March. They were in the fourth quarter.

Floods in Queensland and New South Wales in February–March were met with a slow response from the Commonwealth. Had they learned nothing from the bushfires? A national disaster declaration was delayed and there was blame-shifting to states, Morrison again tangling with Perrottet, who was much quicker to admit failures and apologise. A prime ministerial visit to Lismore, where Morrison met flood victims behind closed doors, showed that he no longer received the benefit of the doubt about his intentions. The media drew comparisons with Morrison's botched visit to Cobargo during the bushfires. It is arguable that the government's response was about what should have been expected, given the scale of the disaster. Yet, even twenty-four hours is an eternity in the social media age for the nation to watch live as entire towns struggle. At first Morrison met any criticism as just a 'Labor narrative'. He and Dutton claimed falsely that criticism was directed at the Australian Defence Force. Contrition was eventually forthcoming in the ungenerous Morrison style. The government also came under fire for providing financial support to citizens in some local government areas but not others, prompting New South Wales upper house Liberal Catherine Cusack to resign. She went on to support the Greens candidate in the flood-affected seat of Richmond.

The same group of emergency services experts who accused the Morrison government of ignoring their warning prior to the deadly 2019 fire season pointed to the floods as evidence of escalating natural disasters. They pointed out that many recommendations of the Bushfires Royal Commission were yet to be implemented. Most of those require joint Commonwealth and state action, but it was nevertheless a sign of a lack of urgency when comparatively trivial issues are relentlessly pursued.

A war on two fronts: The teals

The highest profile independent candidates became known as the 'teals' — teal being a mix of blue (Liberal Party) and green — although some used other colours in their campaigns. Inspired by Cathy McGowan and Helen Haines's success in Indi, they were loosely organised under the 'Voices of' banner — local political community groups — which first endorsed McGowan in 2013. Haines' win in 2019 was the first time that an independent candidate had succeeded an independent sitting member, underlining the fact that this was a real movement. Zali Steggall's successful campaign against Tony Abbott proved the model could work in the big cities, not just in the regional areas, which are often fertile ground for independents. There was also inspiration from Rebekha Sharkie — who represented the Centre Alliance — in Mayo in South Australia in showing that blue-ribbon Liberal seats are indeed vulnerable.

The teals were mostly running against male incumbents, underlining the failure of the Liberal Party to come anywhere near parity of gender representation despite a 50 per cent target for 2025. Twenty of the twenty-two candidates supported by tech investor Simon Holmes à Court's Climate 200 group, which had supported candidates in 2019, were women. As an example of the networks involved, Steggall's chief fundraiser in 2019 became a director of Climate 200.

Apart from their gender, the most noticeable thing about the teals was their list of accomplishments outside politics. A public profile is often vital for an independent to be noticed by the media, particularly given all the competing noise at a general election. The most successful independents had the financial security to campaign full time. McGowan gave a deceptively simple summary of the formula: 'Community engagement, quality candidates and effective campaigns.' Community engagement seems to be the most important factor. Egotists need not apply.

Their policies were consistent but not monolithic. Climate 200 raised over $7 million for a select group of House and Senate candidates for 2022. To receive Climate 200 backing, a trifecta of strong climate action, support for a robust integrity body, and commitment to gender equality was essential. The first two requirements were in place in 2019, the third added subsequently. This program was important so that the teals were not perceived as a protest or single-issue movement. Nothing in this platform was inconsistent with the principles the Liberal Party claims to uphold, but they were all weaknesses of the Morrison government. The targeted Liberal MPs conceded as much by pointing to their own record on these issues. However, it was the record of their government that was most clear in voters' minds. On the three key issues, they were either ideologically aligned with Morrison or ineffective. It did no harm for the teals to have different views on other issues, throwing ideas into the campaign. For example, Zoe Daniel, an award-winning former three-time foreign correspondent for the national broadcaster, was asked by Voices of Goldstein to stand against Liberal MP Tim Wilson. Her policy platform was broader than most of the teals, canvassing a switch from stamp duty to land tax, something that Wilson picked up as a scare campaign but which, outside the adversarial contest between Labor and Liberal, simply seemed like a sensible idea.

Josh Frydenberg's challenger in Kooyong, Monique Ryan, was the head of neurology at the Royal Children's Hospital Melbourne. She was backed by two local groups: Voices of Kooyong and Kooyong Independents. The Liberals would make much of the fact that Ryan had been a member of the Labor Party between 2007 and 2010. She had been fired up by climate change but quit her Labor membership when Rudd retreated on the CPRS. She added health to the policy priorities identified by Climate 200. Kooyong was of particular interest to Holmes à Court, having once been part of Frydenberg's donor group, Kooyong 200, until he criticised Coalition energy policy. He received the boot from Kooyong 200 and gave Climate 200 an echo of that name. His history as a donor to the Liberal Party made their claims that he was trying to buy votes by backing the teal independents particularly laughable. Frydenberg had Holmes à Court expelled from a meet-the-candidate event prior to the 2019 election and was critical of the Holmes à Court family living outside Melbourne during a COVID lockdown. Holmes à Court became something of a lightning rod for conservative criticism during the election year in a bid to undermine the teal candidates.

The Victorian Liberal Party believed that its tough stance against lockdowns in Melbourne would be an asset come election time in Goldstein and Kooyong. Frydenberg had been particularly strident. However, it was far from clear that they had prevailed in that argument with the Andrews Government. More importantly, except in Western Australia, the public was largely moving on from COVID-related issues. The very fact that the teals were part of a movement beyond a single seat was a feature, not a bug. They could afford more sophisticated research than independents of the past. They found, for example, that Kooyong had the highest proportion of young voters of any Victorian seat, and that there were plenty of pockets of low- and middle-income earners to reach out to.

Wentworth's Allegra Spender had been a management consultant at McKinsey and Company and had an Economics degree from Cambridge, and was the managing director of her mother, Carla Zampatti's, fashion empire for a decade before becoming the CEO of a not-for-profit. She had a strong Liberal pedigree: her father, John, and grandfather Percy were both Liberal MPs. Showing how suited she was to wealthy Wentworth, Spender was in favour of increasing the GST rather than meddling with income tax cuts.

The North Sydney independent candidate, Kylea Tink, had been the CEO of the McGrath Foundation and Camp Quality. The danger for Tink was that Labor's candidate, law professor Catherine Renshaw, would poll well. In the end Tink was only a few points clear of Renshaw. Tink's was a familiar story among the teals: someone who was too busy with her own career to think about becoming involved in politics. She was approached by the community group North Sydney's Independent, aligned with Voices of, and agreed to run. The group was started by former Coalition staffer Kristen Lock. Tink, who had voted for Zimmerman in 2019 and preferred 'Tink pink' over teal as her campaign colour, received funding from Climate 200 and added skilled migration to the familiar trifecta of policies.

Mackellar independent Sophie Scamps was a former high-performance athlete and Oxford-educated GP, having worked in both general practice and emergency medicine on Sydney's Northern Beaches. She added health to the Climate 200 priorities in her platform. She had helped found a local climate action group where she was introduced to Zali Steggall. During the bushfires she was unimpressed with sitting member

Jason Falinski's performance as a supposed moderate on the question of whether the fires were linked to climate change. Scamps' story is notable for the number of women involved at all points in this grass roots movement. They formed Voices of Mackellar in 2020, but that group decided not to support a candidate, so Scamps and a friend started Mackellar Rising with the purpose of supporting an independent challenge to Falinski. She stepped aside from her practice to become that person. Falinski complained about Holmes à Court's influence. 'He is attempting to take over the Parliament with money,' he whined.

In the WA seat of Curtin, Kate Chaney, a business consultant with successful careers in the private and community sectors, emphasised the future of the economy in light of the need for renewable energy. Unusually for a Western Australian, she was willing to consider a mining tax as part of broader tax reform. As economically 'sensible' and socially progressive, she felt the Liberal Party was no longer her natural home. 'I think there's a strong sense in Curtin that the Liberal Party has moved away from its traditional base of small "l" Liberals and moved to the conservative right,' she told *AFR Weekend*. Her uncle, Fred Chaney, a former deputy Liberal leader, was a long-time critic of the Liberal Party lurching too far to the right. A group called Curtin Independent, formed after seeing the effectiveness of Voices of, endorsed Kate Chaney, who had been a Labor member as recently as 2021. She would take on a well-respected incumbent, former University of Notre Dame Vice-Chancellor Celia Hammond. However, Hammond lacked one important source of support: long-serving Curtin MP Julie Bishop, who had supported another candidate for pre-selection back in 2019. Hammond was the type of candidate the Liberals need for cabinet, not just parliamentary representation, but her social conservatism cost her local support.

The campaigning skills of the incumbents would be sorely tested. Seats like Goldstein and Kooyong were for future cabinet ministers, not retail politicians. Not all the independent candidates saw their campaigns catch fire. High-flying businessman but low-flying Liberal politician Paul Fletcher was challenged by environmentally responsible investment advocate Nicolette Boele in Bradfield, but Fletcher's primary vote had a long way to fall. Candidates in Casey, Hume and Hughes also had less success. Hume, in New South Wales near the ACT border, increasingly takes in peri-urban developments where the residents commute to Canberra, resulting in a diverse mix of constituents. Angus Taylor had been targeted in Hume because of his climate scepticism in the Energy portfolio. Former teacher Penny Ackery ran a grassroots campaign in the electorate with the support of the local Voices of group. However, she rejected Climate 200 funding, which had proved vital in more successful campaigns in getting communication and fundraising operations in place. In South Australia, Boothby independent Jo Dyer made it clear she was more aligned with Labor and didn't end up having much impact on the seat.

One sign that an election isn't far away is the sound of a Labor leader denying that they would do a deal with the Greens under whatever scenario an enterprising journalist had dreamed up. This time around, with the profile of the teal independents increasing, the questions would flow for both major parties. Steggall's comments about being prepared to support a minority Coalition government (with certain conditions) in the event of a hung parliament showed the tightrope these candidates had to walk. In safe Liberal seats they needed to finish in front of Labor, hopefully by attracting some Labor and Greens supporters to vote tactically in the hope of defeating the sitting Liberal. Any reminder that the independents are in many respects disaffected Liberals didn't help sell that message. Reflecting on the teals' impact on the Liberals, Erickson told us, 'It didn't impact our strategy but it clearly made it harder for [the Liberal Party] to respond to us. Their central campaign wasn't as well resourced as it normally was because they had to invest resources fighting the Climate 200 independents.' Hirst, the Liberals' federal director, has acknowledged this.

Friendly fire

March also brought an ugly debate following the sudden death of Labor Senator Kimberley Kitching. News.com.au political editor, Samantha Maiden, reported that Kitching had complained to Marles about poor treatment from Labor's Senate leadership. Colleagues were filling in the gaps, naming Senators Penny Wong, Kristina Keneally and Katy Gallagher, whom it was alleged had accused Kitching of disloyalty. Kitching had been removed from the tactics committee after she seemed to warn the government about parliamentary questions. The leadership team just didn't trust her. That didn't stop the trio being labelled 'mean girls' by Kitching.

Gallagher felt this barb the most, being as far from a mean girl as one could imagine. Keneally wanted to fight back but had to hold her tongue. Wong had privately apologised to Kitching for her 2019 comment that 'if you had children, you might understand why there is a climate emergency'.

Opposition members refused to be drawn before Kitching's funeral. Journalists were not so squeamish. An unedifying competition to background journalists on opposing versions of events followed. Dutton called for an investigation, describing Kitching as a 'dear friend'. Nicolle Flint, who had cited parliamentary culture as a reason for her retirement, alleged that Albanese had 'failed to support and protect her in her workplace'. The day before her death, Kitching had been warned that her Senate pre-selection was not guaranteed. Labor's Victorian division was as dysfunctional as the Liberals' in New South Wales. One of Albanese's first jobs as opposition leader was to try to clean things up there. Shorten had ensured Kitching's nomination to fill a casual vacancy, which hardly recommended her to Albanese loyalists. Albanese could certainly have influenced a decision about her pre-selection. To attempt to silence Kitching over critical comments she had made about China, his office was backgrounding journalists that her pre-selection was not a fait accompli.

Marles floundered while taking questions from journalists about his role. Albanese was forced to address the issue more directly. 'I received no complaints about the treatment of Senator Kitching,' he said. Perhaps he preferred it that way. 'Politics can be a robust business,' he added, as though that were a defence of bullying.

Morrison drew the longest of bows: 'If Anthony Albanese cannot stand up to the bullies in his own party, then how on earth is he going to have the strength to stand up to the bullies in our own region,' he asked. So concerned was the PM that he campaigned in Brisbane on the day of Kitching's funeral. Liberals expected this messy business to neutralise Morrison's so-called 'woman problem'. While the government couldn't resist piling on to Labor's internal problems, it was inevitable that scrutiny would return to the government.

News Corp tabloids revelled in the Kitching story. The *Herald Sun* summed up the allegations of a friend of Kitching in a giant front-page headline as 'Bullied, Broken and Wrecked by Labor'. When we asked Albanese if he felt like his detractors in the party and the media took pleasure in his discomfort at that time, he flatly refused to dwell on what he called a sad and devastating time for the Kitching family. Albanese had steered clear of Kevin Rudd's suggestion of a Murdoch Royal Commission. Albanese disagreed with some Labor figures who wanted to blackball hostile media outlets. News Corp in Australia benefited from Labor's media ownership rules from the 1980s. Election winners tend to be less concerned about such factors than the losers.

An election budget

Bringing forward the 2022 budget to late March was supposed to put the focus on the economy, and the centrality of economic debate should have allowed Frydenberg, a less compromised figure than his leader, to come to the fore. Frydenberg's budgets during the pandemic were highly policy-focused — playing a vital role in stabilising the economy and providing income support. The COVID recession also transformed the debate about the tax cuts announced in the 2019 budget, which helped catapult the Coalition to an unlikely election win. Many in the Coalition considered the tax cuts unsustainable — something that an incoming Labor government would be responsible for wrestling with.

Labor played to its strengths. 'A Labor government will lower the cost of living' was a prominent line in social media. That's quite a claim, in an area over which the government of the day has limited control, especially when interest rates were likely to rise steadily through the life of the next parliamentary term. Frydenberg, having been slow to incorporate anti-inflationary policies into his rhetoric, was listening. 'It's the number-one topic around the kitchen tables of Australia,' he said. Having to play catch-up on inflation was a poor showing for a government usually attuned to public opinion. There was no surprise that inflationary pressures asserting themselves in the United States throughout 2021 would reach Australia.

The usual pre-Budget leaks came in February. The most prominent salve for cash-strapped households was to be a temporary fuel excise cut. Chalmers foreshadowed support, guaranteeing that Labor would preside over concomitant increases in fuel prices after a few months if it won the election. 'We want to see that responsible cost of living relief but we also want to see a plan for the future,' he said. 'Not just a plan for an election campaign.' The relief was far from responsible of course — arbitrary in scope, length and cost. There was little sign voters would see the fuel excise cut as anything other than a gimmick from a desperate government. Yet, opposing the measure would risk making Labor the issue. Bipartisanship on the fuel excise cut extended to silence on the viability of that revenue source. During the campaign, both sides would promise support for electric cars but had nothing to say over the prospect of a road user charge. This will become an equity as well as a budget and environmental question as the middle class takes up electric vehicles leaving lower income earners to pay fuel taxes. The equity problem becomes more acute with Labor's promise to discount taxes on electric cars.

In part to avoid the question of how Labor would have managed fiscal policy differently during the pandemic, Chalmers had emphasised the fact that debt had ballooned prior to the big deficits associated with pandemic spending. 'A trillion dollars in debt' became a refrain. It was easy enough for Labor to remind voters of then Shadow Treasurer Joe Hockey promising in 2013 that the conservatives would deliver a long line of surpluses. However, COVID rescued the government from its own boasting about a surplus announced but not delivered in 2019–20. The very terms of this debate showed the poor quality of economic discourse engaged in by the major parties. When a balanced budget was out of the question, our political leaders barely had the language to explain the fiscal impact on the economy. Not all the pre-budget argy-bargy went the government's way, though. Veterans Affairs' Minister Andrew Gee had to threaten to resign to get a fair shake for his department. It was a sign of just how much news was around that this wasn't a bigger story.

On budget day, 29 March, the Treasurer had to compete for news space with yet another character assessment of the Prime Minister from a member of his government. In a speech in the upper house, New South Wales Senator Concetta Fierravanti-Wells called him an 'autocrat and a bully' who is 'unfit' to lead the nation. She referred to Hawke as Morrison's 'consigliore'. 'In my public life I have met ruthless people. Morrison tops the list, followed closely by Hawke,' she concluded, apparently meaning this last description as a criticism. The senator may have had more credibility had she not just been demoted to an unwinnable position on the Coalition Senate ticket, declining to run at the election after losing her pre-selection fight. Nevertheless, such moments are a useful corrective to the endless contrived photo opportunities of Morrison's family life and stage-managed meetings with the citizenry.

Fierravanti-Welles recounted the story of Michael Towke, who had been validly pre-selected as the Liberal candidate for Cook for the 2007 election. Towke's clear win against blue-blood opponents in the pre-selection was a shock for party insiders. The result had to be overturned, they decided. The response from the party establishment had been brutal: they backgrounded false claims about Towke and his qualifications and targeted his ethnicity. Towke was replaced as candidate by Scott Morrison. Fierravanti-Welles alleged, as did Towke, that Morrison had tried to use Towke's Lebanese heritage against him in lily-white Cook. The furore forced Morrison to cancel his long-scheduled interview on *7.30*. Concetta Fierravanti-Welles — tactical genius.

Wrestling with the spotty media attention to the budget, the government justified its loose fiscal policy as a reward for the hard work of Australians over three years. 'They've been dealing with pandemics, with floods, with fires,' Morrison said. 'Australians have made great sacrifices.' Announcements on some budget goodies were reserved for the campaign. One such announcement, quickly matched by Labor, was to lower the income threshold for the Seniors Health Card, coming with a permanent cost that embodies the budget problem: if people on good incomes make such demands on the budget, where does the money come from?

Chalmers had a lower profile than Albanese during budget week, taking on the attack dog role and leaving the budget reply speech to his leader, as is tradition. 'Glib, incoherent, in denial of reality and silent on the future,' was Chalmers' appraisal of the final Coalition Budget — also a succinct summary of the government over its nine years. There was little pressure on Labor to foreshadow fiscal tightening; and little sign they would have the stomach to do it in office. Both sides were hoping for strong growth to repair the budget. In other words, taxes would increase arbitrarily through bracket creep rather than any rational policy. Asked about funding increased spending on health and aged care, Albanese emphasised cutting waste, highlighting consultants and government advertising. These things have a habit of building up over the life of any government like plaque building up on sclerotic arteries. While there is plenty of scope for a new government to reorient priorities, particularly following a government with so little appetite to make tough decisions, Labor could have done better to insulate itself from criticism of its future budgets by nominating some programs for the axe prior to the election. 'There is a task to deal with the stupendous waste and rorts that we've seen in the budget,' Albanese said in his budget reply.

Albanese's comparatively modest announcement on aged care funding sparked something approaching a real policy debate, even though it was well short of the sorts of policy change that might be expected for a sector in deep crisis. Albanese's rhetoric was good enough in the interim, though. 'Is the Coalition actually saying we can't afford to give older Australians decent food and decent care?' he asked. Few voters would be across the detail of what was on offer in aged care or childcare, but those directly affected know the weaknesses of the respective systems and didn't see anything in the budget that would fix them.

Albanese accused the government of 'underspending' on the National Disability Insurance Scheme, implying that Labor had work to do in that area as well. Questions from journalists about where the extra NDIS money would come from were easy enough to ignore for the time being. The decision to make aged care the focal point in the budget reply speech came after considering running with either Medicare or housing policies instead. They were held back for the campaign. Aged care was chosen both because it was in crisis and spending more money on the sector would be hard to criticise.

The budget became a victim of its own political nature. Labor's attack line that it was 'a plan for an election, not a plan for Australia's future' was so self-evidently true that even by the time of Albanese's reply two days later, the document generated few major headlines. Weekend newspaper think pieces looked ahead to the election campaign. The budget had sunk without a trace. The Essential poll found that the budget did nothing to win back those disaffected from the government and flirting with minor parties and independents. That was true at least at the level of national politics. Budgets also provide a lot of measures for individual MPs and candidates to promote in their local campaigns.

It wasn't as though the government was doing nothing in the big-spending areas identified by Labor. But this, the major political document prior to the campaign, concentrated on the spending measures Labor was prepared to match — killing the news cycle on those issues. The ABC's Laura Tingle pointed out that this was part of a larger pattern in the PM's media appearances in the months prior to the election. He simply wasn't engaging on the issues that were set to dominate the campaign. His appearances were so tightly targeted to spending- and other election-related announcements that he was vacating the field in vital policy areas other than economic management. Even when it came to economic policy, saying the word 'plan' hundreds of times (something Chalmers was also wont to do) does not actually convey the sense that you do indeed have a plan. Expensive government advertising promoting the supposed 'plan for a stronger future' was even more bereft of substance than usual. This lack of strategy was especially true in an election year in which the budget was designed to hide, not enhance, any semblance of fiscal strategy that might imply higher taxes and spending cuts that seem inevitable. It was to those issues, not the detail of the budget, that journalists' questions quickly returned.

Having planted in voters' minds that there would be more attention from Labor on its signature issues during the campaign, the opposition was quick to pivot back to inflation. Albanese dismissed the budget forecast for rising wages, pointing out that government expectations of wages growth were consistently wide of the mark, and that there was no policy reason for wages to suddenly grow faster. 'This is a government that attacks penalty rates, that supports insecure work, supports small casualisation, that won't even say when we've asked them in the parliament if they support people getting the minimum wage. The response to that is "it's complicated". Well, it's not complicated. It's not complicated, at all.' Actually, yes it is. But Labor didn't want to complicate its own messaging, seeking instead to cut through.

The budget forecast for wages was based on continuing low unemployment, which Albanese also dismissed since so much employment was part time and insecure. 'What we see is growth in the gig economy, a growth of casualisation, the growth of contracting out and labour hire companies. What we don't see is a growth in secure work,' he said. As is often the case, workplace relations provided sharp policy contrasts. Labor had long foreshadowed a crackdown on labour hire firms, changes to the Fair Work Commission to limit casualisation, and increasing the supply of labour through training and childcare, with an announcement on gender pay equity to come during the campaign launch.

Stoking the culture wars

The final weeks before calling the election provided some reminders of the Coalition's priorities. Acting Education Minister Stuart Robert tried to reignite education culture wars in a speech, which would have been cleared by the PMO, comparing the quality of teachers in public schools unfavourably with those in independent schools. Australia needed to 'stop pussyfooting around the fact that the problem is the protection of teachers who don't want to be there, who aren't up to the right standard,' he said. He also provided a reminder that the government would not approve the national schools curriculum until that document recognised Australia's 'Christian heritage' and removed some anti-racism content.

Home Affairs Minister Karen Andrews announced a deal for hundreds of asylum seekers who arrived by boat to be relocated from detention to New Zealand. Lest anyone think the government had suddenly located its heart or was shamed by the worldwide attention given to long-term detainees during the Australian Open visa wrangle, Senator Jacqui Lambie was quick to reveal that accepting New Zealand's long-standing offer to take refugees was part of a deal with the government over Medevac legislation in 2018.

Sussan Ley refused to release the State of the Environment Report, having received it months earlier. She also signed off on the removal of programs to protect 176 threatened animals, plants and habitats. Angus Taylor had a final tilt at requiring the Australian Renewable Energy Agency to fund carbon sequestration. And just in case the election was lost, lucrative Administrative Appeals Tribunal and other appointments flowed thick and fast. According to the *Guardian Australia*, thirty Coalition-aligned figures were given government jobs in the final months of the parliament.

Morrison visited Western Australia in mid-March to announce support for mining refinery projects, emphasising his willingness to cooperate with the popular McGowan after the election. He showed the power of incumbency then by making a joint announcement with the Premier on Perth-based construction projects. 'I got on well with him,' McGowan says. 'I actually didn't mind him at a personal level even though we are very different people.' Morrison was greeted with a poll showing numerous Coalition-held seats under water. He also tried to rewrite history by claiming to have been 'very supportive' of WA's COVID measures. 'He totally misunderstood the effectiveness of our policy and the public mood,' McGowan reflected. 'It cost them dearly. He just didn't get it.'

Nearly 70 per cent of Western Australians supported McGowan's decision to extend the border closure in early 2022. Albanese supported his Labor colleague. He was on the first flight to Perth when the borders opened in March, visiting Pearce and Hasluck and blitzing local media, reminding voters of Morrison's decision to back Clive Palmer's court challenge to the border closure. Doing so, the brainchild of senior Western Australian ministers Mathias Cormann and Christian Porter, was quickly revealed to be political poison in their home state. The COVID-induced return of federalism would have its impact on national politics. WA's tough border controls were an irritant to Morrison but popular in the state. Just before the campaign began, McGowan addressed concerns that Albanese remained an unknown quantity. 'I actually think he's quite well known. He's been in Parliament significantly longer than the Prime Minister,' he said, restating the mystery rather than solving it.

Plenty of rumours surfaced that Albanese and McGowan didn't like each other, but as McGowan told us, that was a beat-up built on people's failure to understand that, as premier, he had a job to do looking after the interests of WA. Indeed, McGowan was even more bullish about Labor's chances in his state than Albanese was, tipping the opposition to pick up Swan, Pearce, Hasluck and Tangney. The latter was not thought to be in play by either campaign.

The phoney campaign descended into farce in the days before Morrison, on 10 April, named the date for election day: Saturday 21 May. The budget, just a week old, seemed a distant memory. The leaders traded barbs. Albanese claimed the PM was running scared; Morrison accused his opponent of playing games. 'They are not going to skate into an election,' Morrison said when quizzed about the campaign. 'It will give Australians the opportunity to have a good look. They know who we are. They know what we have achieved. They know what our plans are. They don't know anything about Labor, because Labor haven't told them.' He released a video to social media touting his government's record during times of war, flood and plague.

Days before he visited the Governor-General to advise the issuing of election writs, Morrison's stage-managed visit to a Newcastle pub was interrupted by a disability pensioner, Ray Drury, angry that Morrison's 'have a go to get a go' rhetoric didn't apply to him. He was determined to have his say about the rate at which benefits are cut when recipients earn other income. A viral video emerged from the same event of a woman taking a selfie with Morrison, telling a smiling Prime Minister, 'Congratulations on being the worst prime minister we've ever had.'

Perhaps more telling for the government was Drury's mention of the government's failure to produce an anti-corruption body. Such process-based issues rarely bother the electorate, but the sheer number of allegations against the government may have pierced the electoral noise. Morrison resisted the temptation to repeat Bob Hawke's mistake in the run-up to the 1990 election of calling an elderly heckler a 'silly old bugger'. As the only grab the national television news picked up from Morrison's phoney campaign stop, the Drury incident was a reminder, though, that three years on from his 2019 miracle, campaigning with a record of governing through tough times would be an even greater challenge than coming from behind to beat Shorten. And the most effective attacks were coming from inside his government, not from random discontented voters on the campaign trail.

Morrison had a major hand in finalising New South Wales pre-selections, boasting about the number of women he was promoting. Warringah Liberal candidate Katherine Deves was one. In the final week before the campaign, it was reported that she had referred in a since-deleted tweet to transgender children being 'surgically mutilated and sterilised'. Once again, Morrison had been too smart by half, his strategy of delaying pre-selection contests until his faction was in a better position to compete had guaranteed insufficiently vetted candidates. Some Australian politicians on the right had imported, along with toxic cultural politics, the American tactic of sending out fundraising emails off the back of this type of controversy. However successful this may be for an individual, the more centralised Australian party structure inevitably tars the party as a whole with the controversial views of any member.

The PM attempted to steer the debate to ground on which he was more comfortable — the status of trans women in sport — and speculated about supporting a private member's bill from one of his backbenchers. He seemed to know, when backing her pre-selection, about Deves' position on trans women and sport but not some of her tackier statements. Moderate Simon Birmingham poured cold water on the idea of a ban on trans athletes, underlining divisions in the government. Queensland LNP Senator Gerard Rennick said it was not an area where parliament should take action. 'I hate identity politics, we shouldn't be using it to score points,' he said. New South Wales Treasurer Matt Kean called for Deves to be disendorsed.

Morrison later tried to link Deves' treatment by the media to so-called cancel culture, even though it was his campaign that encouraged the candidate to cancel her social media history and restricted her interaction with journalists. The issue didn't wedge Labor since their position on leaving the sports issue to individual organisations working within the *Sex Discrimination Act* was already clear. Deves apologised for her language but was far from finished hogging the limelight. Hirst was shaking his head. Deves became a rare point of disagreement between Morrison and Hirst. She might have been popular on *Sky After Dark*, but she was poison not just in the inner-city seats threatened by independents but everywhere. It was going to be a long election campaign.

Part 2

The campaign

Chapter 5

Week 1: Gotcha!

Morrison made the obligatory visit to Yarralumla on Palm Sunday, the day on the Christian calendar when Jesus returned to Jerusalem on a donkey. Morrison's journey that day was from Sydney to Canberra to make the announcement. There were no palms but there were a few Hawaiian shirts among the protestors lining the streets as he made his way to the Governor-General's residence. The campaign would be a six-week marathon, designed to bridge the sizeable gap the Coalition's internal polling showed the government was facing. Morrison was attempting to emulate Howard in 2004 when the latter came from behind to chase down Mark Latham over a campaign of identical length. Albanese, however, was no Latham. 'The budget hadn't been the game changer the way the 2019 budget was,' Erickson told us. 'Which meant we knew it would come down to the six-week campaign.'

A week before the announcement of the election date, Labor had started what would become its most important weekly meeting: the Sunday afternoon strategy phone hook-up. The daily meetings were tactical, the Sunday session taking a wider view: a chance to review the state of play, look to the full week ahead, where Labor wanted to be, what issues were contentious, and how it should organise the mix between media appearances and paid advertising. The daily morning ritual started with a 5.30 a.m. staff call about media. It included Erickson, Liz Fitch from Albanese's office and the media group within CHQ in Sydney. At 6.15 a.m. the politicians would join the conversation: Albanese when he wasn't already travelling or doing morning media; Marles, Wong, Keneally, Farrell, Chalmers, Gallagher, campaign spokesperson Jason Clare, Butler, Bowen and Burke. Bowen's inclusion was a sign of Albanese's respect for him even though they were not close. From time to time Stephen Smith, a former foreign minister who sometimes travelled with Albanese to advise him on national security, would join the call. Erickson would chair the discussions and, depending on the issues discussed, staffers in CHQ would contribute their areas of expertise. These calls could last anywhere from ten to twenty minutes, establishing consistency on the daily priorities, and the events and media appearances. The meetings weren't a chance to debate decisions already locked in. At 8 a.m. there would be a larger video hook-up with all staff across CHQ and on the road when they were available, chaired variously by Marles' chief of staff Lidija Ivanovski or the assistant national secretary, Jen Light, who was in charge of the key seats strategy. Erickson would jump out of this meeting for the 8.15 a.m. track polling update, which included Madigan, who was continually crafting the advertising messages.

The Coalition had a similar morning routine, starting with the previous day's tracking polls ready for discussion at 5.30 a.m., with Hirst at CHQ in Brisbane, campaign spokesperson Birmingham, Morrison's chief of staff John Kunkel, National Party federal director Jonathan Hawkes and pollster Mike Turner. Other senior staff would join when not on the road. Morrison and his principal private secretary Yaron Finkelstein, and Special Minister of State Ben Morton, who travelled with the PM, would dial in at 6.10 a.m., with the Nationals leadership on a separate call. At 6.30 a.m., a wider group including Dutton, Frydenberg, Marise Payne, Michaelia Cash, and Nationals Joyce, David Littleproud and Bridget McKenzie would be briefed on the plan for the day.

Labor's weekly Sunday call included the same staff who would join their daily 6.15 a.m. conference call. Erickson would generally start with a five-minute report on the state of play before the discussion would open up for around another twenty minutes. The Coalition didn't have an equivalent meeting to Labor's weekly one, but Hirst and state directors would catch up once a week.

That Ben Morton was constantly on the road with Morrison would prove to be consequential. Among the Western Australian seats McGowan had predicted Labor would win in December was Morton's seat of Tangney on the south side of the Swan River. Morton was from New South Wales, an old friend of Morrison. He had been state director in Western Australia, winning Tangney in 2016 and becoming Morrison's assistant minister after the 2019 win. He became a close confidant. Given his friendship with Morrison, it was thought that Morton was the best senior figure to travel with the PM in what would be a trying and lengthy campaign. The last thing the government needed was a leader under pressure making mistakes that might have led to a landslide for Labor. The press secretaries and assorted campaign staff who travel with the leaders lacked the authority to have a quiet word with Morrison when things got tough the way Morton could. 'Mood monitoring' is how campaigns refer to this role. They spent time having a drink together after the day's events. Morton would return to Perth on the occasional weekend as well as when Morrison was in town. The margin in Tangney was 9.5 per cent. They were either unaware of the storm brewing there or a decision was made to keep Morton on the road even if that put his seat at risk. Perhaps Morton was unconcerned about losing his seat if Morrison lost the prime ministership. He would never be closer to a leader again, never more in the loop. The Labor candidate, former police officer Sam Lim, was an energetic campaigner, with connections in the electorate's Malaysian and Chinese communities. 'I thought at Christmas we might win that one,' McGowan told us. 'It swung so big at the state election in that area I thought it would be in play.'

Out of the blocks

Both leaders took interviews with most of the major media outlets on the Sunday evening the election was called or the following morning. In his initial pitch, Morrison's delivery was weak, constantly reading from his notes to get the lines right. It wasn't very polished, showing that game-day nerves affect everyone.

'This election is a choice between a government that you know, and that has been delivering, and a Labor opposition that you don't,' he said. 'Others will seek to make this election about me. It's actually about the people who are watching this right now. It's about them.' Watching Morrison's speech, Albanese knew that last line was a dig at him and Labor's planned strategy to make the election a referendum on Morrison's popularity. By the time the election was called, Morrison's strong personal approval ratings from the early days of the pandemic were long gone, replaced by net negative satisfaction ratings according to Newspoll. He was only marginally in front of Albanese on the better prime minister ratings — not where an incumbent seeking a fourth term wants to be.

Albanese was stronger with his rehearsed lines but struggled with some predictable questions. 'Today I say to my fellow Australians this is our time,' he said. 'I am ready, we are ready, and Australia is ready for a better future. This government doesn't have an agenda for today, let alone a vision for tomorrow.' Most of Albanese's interviewers canvassed the question of why such an experienced politician was largely unknown to the electorate. 'I am who I am,' was his unhelpful response more than once. The *West Australian* editorialised that 'Mr Albanese cannot expect to sneak into office just by saying he is not Scott Morrison'. While that would be an unfair characterisation of Labor's campaign strategy, it was certainly their approach to the leadership contest. Hirst thought Albanese's performance was messy. Effectively offering to take unlimited questions at pressers wasn't sustainable in his view. Labor hard heads agreed, shutting the approach down as soon as they had the chance. They faced a stubborn Albo at first; he was used to running his own race. But events soon opened his mind to their prudent advice.

Albanese appeared with partner, Jodie, and cute puppies at Sydney's Royal Easter Show. Morrison's later Easter Show appearance with his family was one of his few 'free range' public appearances of the campaign. Most of his events were in controlled areas guarded by burly security staff. Labor knew it had the advantage when it came to getting among 'real voters'. Morrison needed stage-managed events to avoid the sort of blowback he had copped in Newcastle.

The campaign started with Erickson stuck in isolation with COVID. He thinks he might have caught it at the budget reply event in Canberra. Wayne Swan and Jen Light also think they got it there. Erickson woke up sick the following Monday morning, six days before Morrison called the election. What very few outside the inner circle knew was just how serious his symptoms were. By Thursday, three days before the election was called, Erickson was in Royal Prince Alfred Hospital and on a drip, suffering from acute dehydration with his throat sore to the point at which it was becoming hard to swallow. He recovered at the B&B he was staying at in Sydney's inner east during the campaign.

The first Newspoll, based on interviews prior to the campaign, showed a slight tightening, signalling very little but adding to the narrative of a testing time ahead for the Opposition Leader. Both parties' primary vote was higher in this poll compared to where it would end up — Coalition 37 per cent, Labor 36 per cent — as other voices were heard during the campaign, and the two principals hammered away at each other with negative advertising. Labor's track poll started two weeks before Morrison announced the election, giving Albanese some solid seat-by-seat data to help steer the decision-making for his early movements. It showed the opposition with a six-point lead: 53–47. Labor's track would break down to two-party figures; the Liberals tended to focus on primary numbers.

Indigenous leaders were quick out of the blocks urging a referendum on a Voice to Parliament. Albanese had already indicated support but wasn't looking to make that a theme early on. Labor's key policy messages were encapsulated by tweets from Albanese (with other Labor MPs using much the same formulation): 'More secure jobs. Stronger Medicare. Cheaper childcare. Making our future here. That's my plan.' Something was missing from this formula. There were plenty of other candidates prepared to talk climate change if Labor wouldn't.

It was revealed that Rachelle Miller was negotiating a settlement of as much as half a million dollars with the Department of Finance. How was such a payment warranted if Tudge had been cleared of breaching ministerial standards? Morrison pointed to the arms-length negotiation process to deny any knowledge. Later in the week, Miller said she was happy to release the Commonwealth from the burden of secrecy, a freedom the government didn't rush to embrace.

Meanwhile, Morrison managed to confuse everyone, including himself, with the cabinet status of Alan Tudge. While Tudge's portfolio responsibilities were being fulfilled by Stuart Robert, Tudge was still, the PM claimed, part of his cabinet — 'technically' at least. Tudge and Morrison had come to a private agreement: Tudge would formally remain in cabinet and therefore run at the election in his Victorian seat of Aston. There was concern within Team Morrison that if he was dumped from cabinet for optics — which Tudge felt would be unfair and unjustified given the report findings — he might just resign from parliament, putting his seat at greater risk. The Liberals hadn't been polling his seat, so couldn't be sure if a new candidate could hold it. For strategists, Tudge remaining in cabinet without portfolio duties was an unwelcome distraction. Questions about Deves and Tudge dominated Morrison's brief visit to Adelaide on 11 April. Tudge, said Morrison, had taken leave. He hadn't been stood down, leading to questions of whether he was still receiving the salary of a cabinet minister. As journalist Samantha Maiden pointed out, it was classic Scott Morrison. 'This is why you need to ask him very careful questions,' she tweeted. Morrison's evasions would have been the story of the first full day of the campaign — if only Anthony Albanese had known the unemployment rate.

Two steps back

It was a confident start to the day for Albanese, with a round of television and radio interviews and a successful event for the cameras at Launceston in Bass. At the following press conference, he was underlining Labor's credentials on cost-of-living pressures when Network Ten's Stela Todorovic asked him what the Reserve Bank cash rate was. 'We can do the old Q and A stuff over fifty different figures,' he retorted, commenting on the general direction of rates when Todorovic interrupted him to repeat her question. Albanese moved on. 'I know about those things that affect ordinary people,' he said in answer to a question about whether leaders should know this stuff, especially since the cash rate had been unchanged for eighteen months. By then, the reporters were hunting as a pack.

Sky News Political Editor Andrew Clennell took his opportunity when the briefest of silences ensued, asking what the national unemployment rate was. Clennell thought the national rate was something the alternative prime minister should know. Albanese didn't have the presence of mind to fire back at the reporters this time. He was rattled and briefly poked out his tongue. 'Five point, uh, four ...' It was 4 per cent. Albanese later told us, 'I had in my head that I was told that I was going to get a question about the relative unemployment rates between Liberal and Labor, which is 5.7 versus 5.1, so I had the five figure in my head. I started with five and then stopped and said four because I knew it was four. I knew there'd been a mistake once I'd said it.' Time stood still. Bass Labor candidate Ross Hart stared into the distance. Albanese shook his head, and conceded, 'I'm not sure what it is,' sounding like he wanted to curl up into the foetal position.

'I thought he'd lost the election,' Clennell told us. 'I was clearly wrong — such was the distaste of the public towards Morrison that Albanese not knowing simple facts most Australians would know did not determine the final outcome. However, I believe that exchange affected Labor's primary vote.'

Erickson, fresh out of isolation, was walking into campaign headquarters for the first time in a week when he saw his team crowded around a television. He asked CHQ deputy director of communications Josh Lloyd what had just happened. Lloyd explained. Erickson decided to watch it in his office. CHQ insisted on ensuring their transcript implied that Albanese was correcting himself in saying five, then four, not five point four, the Tasmanian unemployment rate, which is what some thought Albanese was remembering. On a quickly convened conference call, Erickson, Gartrell, Fitch and Albanese agreed he had to stand up again and take responsibility, owning the mistake. 'Morrison's key weakness isn't just that he makes mistakes, it is that he never takes responsibility,' Erickson told Albanese. There was no argument.

Treasurer Josh Frydenberg had gloated about the low unemployment rate repeatedly during his budget speech right before the campaign started, with Albanese sitting directly opposite him. It was closely tied to what was becoming Labor's signature issue: the cost of living. Trying to guess the number was a bad look, seemingly out by so much just appalling. Briefly sticking out his tongue when he realised he had stuffed up showed a momentary loss of composure.

Finance spokesperson Katy Gallagher knew what was coming when she was asked to step forward for questions. She could either push back at the journalists for asking impertinent questions — which is what Albanese should have done — or show up her leader by reeling off the numbers he couldn't recall. Like an annoying schoolchild, she had both figures learned rote. Her sharpness was an awful contrast with Albanese's meltdown. She couldn't win.

Reflecting on that day, Albanese told us, 'It was a tough day. I'd done multiple interviews in the morning that had gone well, we'd done an event with Cochlear implants for kids so I had that in my head. It was what it was — a whole bunch of people yelling questions at the one time. I knew the answer, which I found frustrating.' He prides himself on his memory for figures. 'I have a memory for how much every road cost I ever funded [as infrastructure minister]. I can tell you any rugby league grand final score. It was done and I knew it was an issue and made the decision very quickly to just own it. I told [senior media adviser] Alex [Cramb] I'll do a doorstop at the next event. Colleagues were good.' Queensland Premier Annastacia Palaszczuk hadn't known the rate of the GST in her first election campaign in 2015. She gave her support. Albanese told us, 'I had messages saying, "Don't worry about it." [CFMEU national secretary] Michael O'Connor rang me. He said, "Mate, you've got this."' Franklin rang and told him, 'You've never been gifted anything in your life. This is no different. Just keep fighting.' Albanese knew there would be media heat led by News Corp tabloids. 'I was surprised not by the extent of that pile-on but the media during the campaign, some of it was over the top. I was surprised by some of the tone with which the campaign was run but we dealt with it. The pile-on emboldened me. I had journalists asking about my academic record. There was an absurd article about staffing in Uren's office.'

Later in the day, Albanese fronted the cameras with a statement designed to provide some context for nightly news reports set to be dominated by his lapse. 'Earlier today I made a mistake. I'm human,' he said. 'When I make a mistake, I'll 'fess up to it,' he continued, turning the issue back onto the Prime Minister's character. That was an effective performance but unlike most such gaffes, this one wasn't lost in the news cycle after a day. The government released quick and dirty social media advertising, replayed extensively on television and radio, linking Albanese's performance to their 'it won't be easy under Albanese' line. Were the journalists on the scene wrong to ask such questions? In the context of the full press conference, the questions were fair. Reporters ask the leaders a lot of questions every day. They don't make the call as to what becomes the most prominent issue for publication. They certainly don't make the call as to how a fairly innocuous mistake becomes the story of the full first week of the campaign. That takes editorial judgement, and media outlets willing to compromise their editorial standards by latching on to government campaign themes. The Saturday tabloids capped off the week by highlighting (anonymous) criticism of Albanese from within Labor, some of it likely crowing from Shorten supporters.

'The stumbles became a bigger issue for the media than it did for the voters,' Erickson told us. 'But there's no denying that they had an impact. Initially, the biggest effect was reinforcing what people already thought. If you were leaning Labor, you saw Anthony owning the mistake and apologising as confirmation he's authentic and honest. If you were leaning Liberal, it probably reinforced existing doubts about Labor. What it didn't do was shift votes back from Labor to the Liberals.' There was debate in the senior ranks of Labor CHQ as to whether it needed to rejig its planned negative ads attacking Morrison for making too many mistakes. Dee Madigan argued against the push, claiming that the way the ads were being crafted — including the line that people make mistakes but Morrison makes too many mistakes — dovetail with the responses coming back from focus groups when asked about the day one gaffe.

There were good reasons why this wasn't just another lapse of memory. Qualitative polling for both parties showed swinging voters were fed up with Morrison but waiting to see about the Opposition Leader. An unusually high number of voters had no opinion on Albanese's performance as opposition leader. The point of the Labor campaign was to bring that number down. To his minders, Albanese's opening blunder represented a real risk, given the leader's tendency to run his own race. Would he be open to changing his approach? It wasn't just the unemployment mistake. It was a lack of composure and judgement as well. Was this the real Albo? He admitted to colleagues it was not a good start, privately tearing strips off himself for giving the Coalition an early win. His contrition on the morning call the next day, owning the error and promising to learn from it and do better, was much discussed afterwards by those on the call. There was universal agreement that his reaction to the mistake was a positive sign.

That night, Labor held drinks for the media at the Silo Hotel in Launceston, where the journos were staying. It was a private, off-the-record event, as spelled out to the group and by Labor media staff one by one to journalists they worried might not get the message. The beer was out of its use-by date, a fact not lost on the cameramen who happily drank it anyway.

Albanese gave a short speech towards the end of the function, telling journalists they were on the fun side of the campaign, before heading back to his room for briefings on the next day's events. It took some effort to pep himself up for the event after the day he'd had.

The incident brought the leader and his treasury spokesman closer because Albanese knew he'd need to rely on Chalmers more to cover off such issues. And to Chalmers' credit he stepped up, as he had been doing over the previous years. It was no surprise to the 'mean girls', who felt that in their time of need Chalmers had also been important, a sign he'd matured in the job. 'He [Albanese] turned it into a point of difference: one leader who can admit it when he stuffs up and another who can't,' Chalmers told us. 'It was like getting smacked in the mouth in the first minute of the first round of a title fight. The dislodged mouth guard and the taste of blood was good for him.' Dee Madigan agrees: 'It certainly brought him to attention. The mea culpa was very real and he managed to turn a negative into a positive,' she claims. 'Unlike Morrison he owned the mistake.'

There was renewed hope in Liberal circles that Labor could be chased down on the campaign trail. Hirst saw it as a chance for his troops to stay positive, but he knew it was at best step number one in a long process to cement doubt in voters' minds about Labor and its leader. Hirst was across the internal polling, and knew how much ground had to be made up in six weeks. It provided an opportunity for any voters seriously looking at Albanese for the first time to think twice. It at least helped balance the strong dislike of Morrison showing up in Liberal research.

'It kept us in the race,' Hirst told colleagues, also believing it contributed to Labor's low primary vote. Labor Party research showed the stuff-up ultimately had more resonance in Bass than elsewhere, because that was where the gaffe happened, although Liberal research didn't pick that up. Hirst ensured he had the financial reserves to take advantage if there was another gaffe.

There would be no more press conferences where Albanese would answer all questions. Franklin tried to convince the gallery that he had only meant answering all questions on day one, but to no avail. The first time Albanese left a doorstop without answering all questions journalists called out his broken promise, increasing their volume as he departed. Several retired journalists became increasingly critical of the coverage of Albanese as the campaign unfolded. Social media amplified this criticism. In response, the ABC's Patricia Karvelas tweeted about 'over the top targeting of journalists and hyper-partisanship I have not witnessed before'.

Labor's focus groups showed that the unemployment rate stumble was widely noticed and people agreed he should have been across the detail. There was a sense, however, that we all make mistakes but at least Albanese owned up to it. 'It definitely wasn't a deal breaker,' Erickson told us. The doubts it raised were as much about Labor and managing the economy as whether Albo was up to the job.

This was the first of many occasions the journalists following the leaders became as big a part of the campaign story as their subjects. The discussion among the journalists on the campaign bus and in the air was that Albanese wasn't up to the rigours of a campaign. Franklin rang around senior bureau chiefs, who rarely travel with the leader, asking them to counsel their younger journos travelling with Albanese. They were not doing themselves any favours were Labor to win, he warned them. However, having observed the day's events, those younger journos hoping to make a name for themselves had spotted an opportunity.

The following day, shadow ministers were parroting the agreed line: 'It's a leadership test, not a memory test.' Chalmers and Plibersek were prominent. Plibersek couldn't win. Whereas Albanese's team was impressed by Chalmers having the leader's back, Plibersek, they thought, was just enjoying cleaning up her rival's mess. Greens leader Adam Bandt had a better formulation, telling a journalist at the National Press Club trying to catch him out over a statistic he had referred to in his speech, 'Google it, mate,' receiving laughter and applause. Of course, minor party leaders aren't put under anywhere near the same level of scrutiny as major party leaders.

While Albanese's testy relationship with the journalists around him became a constant feature of the campaign, it was mostly confined to discussion among political insiders. Over a six-week campaign, given that this would turn out to be the low point, it was better to have a mistake happen early and have plenty of time to improve his performance. Arguably, it was Morrison's day that proved more fateful, being continually asked about Tudge and Deves throughout the week and at regular intervals during the campaign. Having once pointed towards a private member's bill introduced by Senator Claire Chandler on trans athletes as a way of containing the Deves controversy, he now distanced himself from it.

Morrison made an appearance in Gilmore with Andrew Constance, who as New South Wales Member for Bega had been critical of Morrison over his handling of the bushfires. It was a gutsy choice on the first full day of campaigning. Morrison was conciliatory, conceding that, as state MP, Constance was right about the Prime Minster deserving the hostile welcome he received at the time. His team were alive to the need not to have a repeat of such scenes. However, colour was provided by a protestor in a Hawaiian shirt with a ukulele singing 'April Sun in Cuba' as Morrison had recently done in a *60 Minutes* interview. And, of course, Morrison could recite the cash and unemployment rates, a point he was at pains to make.

Morrison rolled out one of the more vacuous promises in all of politics, vowing to create 1.3 million new jobs in five years. 'We've got the runs on the board and the proven plans to deliver these jobs,' the PM enthused. It sounded impressive, but the figure was merely the number of jobs the economy would normally produce in the absence of a recession. The announcement was made in a beer cannery. The advance team set up a gimmick with cans featuring the label 'ScoMo's Strong Economy: creating more jobs and local manufacturing'. The cans, like the jobs promise, were empty. He was never going to outflank his opponent on this front given that a microbrewery in Albanese's seat had named a beer after him — the Albo Pale Ale. The canned version has a picture of 'hot Albo', a photo from his youth which became a social media meme. Morrison backed up with another factory visit to spruik his jobs pledge on day two. The Rheem

Australia plant at Rydalmere in the seat of Parramatta was the venue. Unfortunately, it soon emerged that the factory was in the middle of offshoring jobs to Vietnam. Poor staff work had failed to unearth the news.

Alcohol was a bit of a theme early in the campaign. Pauline Hanson, struggling for publicity against Clive Palmer, was flogging 'Please Explain Aussie Spirit' gin at just under $100 a bottle. But it came with a catch — anyone buying the over-priced product had to provide full contact details to help One Nation bother them down the track with campaign messages. They would need that gin. Five thousand bottles were produced. It's likely there's still a lot of that gin in a warehouse somewhere.

Having quit the Nationals and retired from his North Queensland seat, George Christensen jumped ship to One Nation. Running third on their Senate ticket seemed to show that his change of party was just about getting his six-month and six-figure salary payout as a losing current MP rather than demonstrating a continued thirst for politics. Retiring with dignity at the election wouldn't allow such a windfall. The disingenuous stunt was well called out by the media and resoundingly so on social media.

The importance of social media increases with every election. It is at once indispensable for understanding all dimensions of an election campaign and a conduit for pointless speculation and conspiracy theories. Twitter had busied itself with speculation that the PM might call a half-Senate election — the first since 1970 — as a stand-alone poll in order to allow him to delay the House election until September. That was at least more interesting than whether a prime ministerial chicken curry, as pictured on his Facebook page, had been properly cooked. 'I can reassure you, the chicken was cooked,' Morrison said on Facebook. It didn't look like it. He had long since lost the trust of the foodie community. Morrison and Albanese both subjected themselves to lengthy interviews with Leo Puglisi, a fourteen-year-old high school student and founder of the *6 News* YouTube network. Social media also made life more complicated for the Australian Electoral Commission, which had to make sure campaign material, such as TikTok videos from third parties such as unions, was properly identified.

So, too, was the complicated impact of catch-up television and digital radio on broadcast advertising. The data viewers provide when registering for a catch-up site like *TenPlay* is used to target advertising. Madigan could buy advertising for individual postcodes, a much more efficient use of campaign funds. Unlike broadcast network advertising, Campaign Edge could treat the national election like a series of by-elections. You may have noticed less television advertising in 2022 if you lived in a safe seat.

Moving forward

The uninspired start to the campaign continued when it emerged that Labor would drop its 2019 promise to review the level of JobSeeker payments. The relevant shadow minister, Linda Burney, still had a petition on her website for the level to be raised. The decision had been taken months earlier to junk the pledge made at the last election, and Australian Council of Social Services head Cassandra Goldie had been quietly informed, but it wasn't public. It was Shadow Assistant Treasurer Andrew Leigh who belled the cat in a policy debate in Canberra. He said that, given the increase in the previous budget, there would be no review. Albanese pointed to the trillion dollars in debt. 'You can't repair all of the damage or do everything that you want to do immediately,' he said. It wasn't just anti-poverty advocates who criticised this decision. Journalists uncovered plenty of instances where Labor figures had called the payments cruel and inadequate. Because the decision had been taken within the leadership group and the finance team, it came as a surprise to most Labor MPs.

The Greens' promise to increase JobSeeker to the level of the Henderson poverty line now stood out from both major parties. 'Labor has just agreed with the Liberals to keep people in poverty,' Adam Bandt thundered. Labor had to run a national strategy to defeat the Liberals but their 'smart-target' approach left the door open for the Greens in inner-city seats. The Greens' primary vote was becoming large enough in some areas that they were competitive in marginal contests, not just safe seats where their main task is to get past the weaker of the major parties. Getting over a quarter of the vote made seats such as Ryan and Brisbane, held by the Liberals, or Richmond, possibilities. The Greens had announced target seats in 2021: Griffith, which overlapped with a seat won by the Greens at the state election, Brisbane and Ryan, all in Queensland; Richmond in northern New South Wales; and Macnamara in Melbourne. This largely went unnoticed in the national media at the time. They also aimed to win three more seats to take their representation in the Senate to twelve, the largest for a minor party in the two-party era. 'We set our goals early on, we shared our strategy publicly and we stuck to it,' Bandt told us. 'Others may not have picked up on it, but we were hiding in plain sight.'

Labor sought to move the conversation on from Albanese's gaffe by bringing forward the announcement of its $135 million policy to establish fifty urgent care clinics across the country. This was met with questions about how the centres would be staffed, given existing medical staff shortages. It was after this event that Albanese cut short his press conference, journalists shouting questions at him as he made his exit after taking questions for just six minutes. A few days later Labor was forced to revisit the cost of the clinics. Albanese had claimed the costings were from the Parliamentary Budget Office but had to clarify that the PBO work had 'informed' Labor's sums, whatever that meant. Health spokesman Mark Butler argued that the main consideration was changing the way the Medicare rules for GPs worked rather than any extra funding required. The opposition continued to be unconvincing on the staffing issue, though. Butler promised the new centres would be up and running quickly. When asked about staffing, though, Albanese pointed to Labor's plan to fund additional training places. Facing similar criticism about his plans to expand the aged-care workforce, he conceded that bringing in more foreign workers might be needed as a stopgap. The *West Australian* was unimpressed, splashing its front page with a question-cum-comment, 'Does he know his a*** from his Albo?'

Morrison travelled to Tasmania to announce on 14 April a $220 million forestry package at a timber mill in Launceston, with money for skills training and research and development. A similar package helped the Howard government take Bass and Braddon from Labor back in 2004. The PM said the package would 'turbocharge this twenty-three-billion-dollar industry'. Taking to native forests with a turbo-charged chainsaw was possibly not to everybody's taste, but party research had shown that local issues were crucial in both Bass and Braddon. However, the message such an announcement sent to voters in the teal seats, as well as a seat like Brisbane, was more problematic. An even bigger problem outside the targeted seats was that already in week one of a six-week campaign, media cynicism about such promises was just as prominent as the announcements themselves. Sky News referred to the forestry announcement as a 'cash splash', a term used continually in the media since leaks about the budget began in February. Samantha Maiden got her hands on Coalition talking points for one government announcement anticipating questions on whether the spend was pork-barrelling. 'No,' came the advice from the geniuses in Coalition communications. 'This is a grants program.'

Morrison avoided the teal seats but couldn't avoid marginal-seat MPs with whom he'd had run-ins or tensions: Reid with Fiona Martin, and in Bass with Bridget Archer. Campaigns are presidential, you have to go everywhere, every state. It was the job of those on the road to prep and deal with anyone Morrison was visiting who was a concern or could lead to adverse media. Tassie was important, so Morrison went there a lot. 'He had to take it on,' Hirst told colleagues. For example, Morrison held a press conference with Archer in Launceston, their double act on the introduction of a corruption commission was challenged by journalists but probably had the desired effect in the seat. Archer breezed past journalists' repeated invitations to contradict her leader while making her anti-corruption stance clear. Local media matters more in Tasmania, helping to overcome national impressions. The same is true, albeit to a lesser extent, in other smaller states. It was the national implications that would flow through until election day.

One of the reasons Morrison was under pressure about his election promises was that one of his 2019 promises — introducing legislation for such a commission — was still on his to-do list. Yet, he maintained that Labor was to blame. 'We have a detailed piece of legislation, which I did table in parliament, and our view has been the same. When Labor is prepared to support that legislation in that form, we will proceed.' Porter, the legislation's designer, now out of politics, conceded that he designed a deliberately weak body because he had profound concerns with the way such a body could become a 'kangaroo court'. Morrison picked up that rhetoric the pair had used privately on a few occasions when Porter was still attorney-general and subsequently used it publicly. He would only introduce his proposed bill to parliament if his toothless model had Labor's support. For Labor, this nonsensical government position had the bonus of allowing Albanese to rattle off the long list of questionable decisions and programs over the life of the government.

While in Tasmania, part of the Prime Minister's security team was involved in a collision and ran off the road, causing the afternoon's event to be cancelled. Elsewhere in Tasmania,

Eric Abetz cut a forlorn figure campaigning for himself from the unwinnable third spot on the Liberals' Senate ticket. He needed Tasmanians to vote for their favourite senator below the line. It turned out his personal vote was underwhelming.

One of Albanese's early tasks was to shore up the New South Wales coal-mining seat of Hunter, under challenge from the Nationals. He visited a coal mine and posed back-to-back for a photograph with Labor's two-metre-tall candidate for Hunter, Dan Repacholi. The optics of a tour of a coal mine were interesting for Albanese, especially since climate change was not yet front and centre in Labor's messaging. During a Sky News debate between candidates for Hunter, Repacholi insisted coal jobs were not under threat. This was despite the fact that Bowen had not ruled out coal mines being affected by Labor's changes to the Safeguard Mechanism, which would apply to the highest carbon emitters. Asked whether he would follow Fitzgibbon's example of criticising Labor's climate change policy he said, 'I'm willing to do whatever we need to do to make sure that we don't get left behind for the Hunter.' This was written up in *The Australian* as 'ALP candidate threatens revolt on climate'. It wouldn't be the last time Labor struggled with this policy. 'Climate ended up being really simple at the election,' Erickson told us. 'Broadly its positive for us, and voters knew if we get elected more action will follow. But we did enough on the jobs front not to lose support in constituencies that could have been more worrying.'

It went largely unnoticed, including by Albanese, on week one of the campaign trail that some of the nation's largest employer organisations had come out in *The Australian* claiming that Labor's secure jobs plan could cost business and hurt the economy. The plan would increase protections for casual and gig economy workers. The Australian Industry Group, the Business Council of Australia and Master Builders Australia led the charge. Labor expected such organisations to do it no favours, but it was surprising that they were prepared to be so vocal given the long-held view they would soon be dealing with a Labor government. The employer groups had been egged on to intervene by Liberals talking up their chances after Albanese had stumbled.

Regardless of his rhetoric about consultation, Albanese doesn't forget things like that. In contrast to Shorten's attacks on 'the big end of town' — largely blunted by the change of prime ministership from Turnbull to Morrison — Albanese told journalist Jacob Gerber as the campaign neared that he was 'comfortable in the boardrooms as well as the pub'. The *AFR Magazine*'s well-heeled readership was probably still suspicious of his left-wing pedigree in spite of the ditched tax policies. Yet, Albanese told us he has 'at least as good a relationship with the business community as any leader'.

The Easter break couldn't come quickly enough for the opposition. It entered the campaign well in front according to all the polls but week one had not gone as planned. 'It was a difficult week,' Albanese told us. 'But it was one in which we were finding our line and length. I was a first-time candidate up against a prime minister who had three years to prepare. We had a new national director who had just had COVID and was down. I'd lost my media director [Liz Fitch] with COVID.

I was always confident about the three-year plan and I thought it was a big mistake to run a six-week campaign. I still don't know why he did that. I found some solace with that.' Old hands were remembering Shorten badly handling questions on climate change policy in 2019 right before Easter. After a tough first week, they feared a replay.

Chapter 6

Week 2: Finding momentum

Labor's weekly strategy meeting fell on Easter Sunday, 17 April. Erickson said that the economy was showing up as the number-one issue, health number two. He noticed that health had tracked up as soon as Labor started talking about it in the first week. He thought that was a good sign because it suggested voters were listening. A few on the call quietly wondered if voters paying attention really was a good thing after the week Albanese had just had. Erickson said there was no meaningful change in the tracking results after the gaffe, but not everyone was buying that. The raw data was kept tightly in the hands of the national secretary. Even Albanese only received briefings. He did admit that there was a softening in support for Albo personally. Some people had moved from positive to unsure as they took a closer look at him. Morrison's disapproval rating remained high — still in the mid-fifties, and consistent with the public polls.

Erickson wanted to flick the switch to negative advertising to tap into voter sentiment about Morrison. Madigan thought the ads had to reinforce three things: that Morrison makes excuses, makes mistakes, and that he is a 'future risk'. The first two are usually enough. 'Voters will elect a dickhead or an incompetent but not an incompetent dickhead,' she told us. Between repeating the lines 'I don't hold a hose mate' and reminding voters about the botched vaccine rollout, these were well covered. But COVID had created a unique environment. In case voters were inclined to give Morrison the benefit of the doubt about his management of the pandemic, Madigan wanted to emphasise that he was also a threat to the future. Ads featuring Morrison saying 'that's not my job' again and again were designed to achieve this.

These themes fitted with the messaging Albanese had been deploying for years, so he was quickly on board. There had been a burst of positive ads about Albo in the first half of the first week. 'There was still five weeks to go in the campaign but we made a big decision at that [Sunday] meeting to come back on the air in a week's time, with high rotation negative attack ads,' Erickson told us. They would run all the way to the broadcast media advertising blackout. It was the national secretary's job to ensure he had the resources to sustain that level of airtime. Chris Bowen pointed out that while he agreed with the decision to turn on the negative ads as suggested, it was important they also returned to a positive theme later in the campaign. The pre-campaign two-week track poll was expensive, and Labor hadn't planned for a six-week campaign. More fundraising would be required. Erickson was very conscious of what happened in 2019 when Labor didn't match high-rotation Coalition attack ads at the back end of the campaign. Madigan had created a batch of negative ads for this campaign during the first half of April. Erickson told the meeting they couldn't just assume the hatred towards Morrison that was showing up in the research would translate into a vote for Labor. 'We need to make sure character is front of mind,' he told the meeting. Digital ads became negative almost immediately and the first negative TV ad ran the day after the first leaders' debate.

The pace of campaigning slowed during the Easter break, and there was little television advertising. However, both parties calculated that voters would tolerate some politics along with their chocolate eggs. In Sydney, Albanese and Jenny Morrison attended the same Good Friday service at St Charbel's Monastery in Tony Burke's electorate. Albanese's official Easter message was both spiritual and temporal: 'That feeling of hope inspires us all as we begin to emerge from the pandemic and look towards a better future,' he said. Scott Morrison was in Melbourne at a Baptist church in Chisholm. Liberal candidate Gladys Liu created a minor stir by handing out bags of Easter eggs with her branding — but without the authorisation required by the Electoral Commission.

To take advantage of Morrison's self-inflicted wounds on corruption, Labor released their integrity policy. While there were no surprises on the shape of Labor's preferred anti-corruption commission — broad jurisdiction, retrospectivity and capacity for public hearings — promising to legislate the body by the end of 2022 signalled some intent. 'I am proud to announce that a national anti-corruption commission would be one of the first priorities of a government I lead,' the Opposition Leader said. Morrison dismissed Labor's plan as a 'two-page fluff sheet'. Sound principles don't take up much space.

In poor health

On Easter Sunday, Morrison went to a hospital in Parramatta to announce that South Australian Senator Anne Ruston would replace Greg Hunt as health minister if the government was returned. There was a telling moment when Hunt almost made the announcement himself until Morrison interrupted, going on to claim that Hunt was Australia's best ever health minister. 'Neal Blewett might have something to say about that,' new Labor Health Minister Mark Butler told us, referring to the Hawke government health minister who established Medicare.

Labor sought to revive its 2016 'Mediscare' campaign armed with a quote from Ruston from 2014 that she thought Medicare was 'unsustainable'. Ruston had been defending an Abbott government policy for GP co-payments. She pointed out that the government had kept Medicare in place since then, but Labor already had its headline and lots of quotes from the health minister-designate to circulate on social media. Ruston sought to keep that formulation when asked by journalists in subsequent interviews about possible cuts to Medicare until the Prime Minister put an end to the debate by ruling out cuts. At first, however, a rattled PM started referring to Network Ten journalist Chloe Bouras as 'Mr Speaker' while brushing away questions about Ruston, only realising it after the third mistake. This provided a laugh for all and predictably launched a thousand Twitter rants about how the media was soft on Morrison compared to his opponent. The Prime Minister then flew to Western Australia, where he would remain until preparations for the first leaders' debate on Wednesday 20 April.

The Liberals also had Ruston, this time in her current social security portfolio, to thank for a scare campaign by Labor about the cashless debit card being extended to all pensioners. This was an example of an issue bubbling up to the forefront of the campaign without the leader being implicated. It appears to have started innocently enough with genuine confusion on the part of a voter about the government's position, which was picked up by one of Labor's social media brawlers, Victorian MP Julian Hill. Labor figures from backbencher Justine Elliot to Deputy Leader Marles had made versions of the claim in 2021. Elliot claimed on her website that '80 per cent of your pension will be put on a card and the government can then control where you spend your own pension'. She chaired something called the Protecting Pensioners Taskforce. Elliot had plenty of quotations from Ruston and other government MPs, including the Prime Minister, talking up the functionality of the card in a way that suggested universal use for recipients of social security was possible. The ads received hundreds of thousands of page views. However, Ruston had only specifically mentioned moving recipients already on other types of income management to the cashless debit card. Just like Labor had to deny plans for death duties in 2019, the government would need a firm denial in this case. Ruston had been denying the claims for months. It took Morrison a few days to intervene. Fact-checkers had diligently pointed out that there was no basis to the claims, underlining the limited use of such an approach to misinformation. The danger in addressing lies is that a denial only amplifies them. Morrison went on the attack. 'The Labor Party should stop frightening pensioners,' he said, before doing the same when suggesting Labor managing money should scare everyone. 'It is an out and out disgusting lie,' Morrison thundered. Labor's own position was less ambiguous. 'Labor will abolish the cashless debit card,' Chalmers reiterated.

Albanese attended an Easter Sunday service at Cairns Cathedral. There was another stumble when he had to correct his party's position on border protection after trying to dismiss a journalist's question too quickly. He gave a one-word answer 'yes' when the detail of the question had asked if Labor would bring back temporary protection visas, contrary to Labor policy. There were actually two questions, one on Operation Sovereign Borders and one specifically about TPVs. Albanese claimed not to have heard all the reporter said. He hastily took to the cameras again after the short presser outside the cathedral to clarify his position. In isolation, it was nothing, especially since it came on the same day as Morrison's own senior's moment. After Albanese's first week, though, it caused an intake of breath inside the campaign.

Albanese headed to the Byron Bay Blues Festival where he received a rock star welcome. Later in the night when he took to the stage to introduce Jimmy Barnes there were audible boos from the crowd, which the media made a big deal about. It became a point of contention because Jimmy's son David Campbell — a media personality in his own right — tweeted that only a small group close to the crowd mic had booed, and in fact the broader reception was positive. This became part of the debate over whether Albanese was receiving fair treatment from the media. The confusion made it a poor example either way. It was an advance team error, though, not to have Albo on stage with Jimmy when introducing him, which would have guaranteed a positive reception.

At Liberal CHQ, watching the reporting of the event, there was speculation about whether COVID contagion would be a consequence of Albanese's attendance. It seemed likely.

Albanese headed back to the seat of Brisbane to take advantage of Ruston's hesitancy to rule out cuts to Medicare. 'The Prime Minister's hand-picked health minister was given multiple opportunities this morning to rule out further cuts to Medicare and she couldn't do it. Medicare is not safe under Scott Morrison and Anne Ruston,' Albanese said. When he later toured flood-ravaged areas, he continued the theme of Morrison only being motivated by short-term political pressures: 'We saw again a political response, rather than a human response, rather than looking at people who were going through a really tough time and saying, "What can we do to help?"' Chalmers joined his leader on the campaign trail, a sign that Albanese increasingly saw his Shadow Treasurer as a political asset. They had to make their comments in the backyard of a house after the original venue, a nearby park, was occupied by a gaggle of Young Liberals carrying placards including a 'cheat sheet' for Albo on the cash and unemployment rates. Albanese also visited the seat of Ryan where the Greens were quietly mounting a monumental door-knocking campaign. It was looming as a three-cornered contest.

Morrison's battlers

In his first press conference in Perth, Morrison reached straight for border protection, promising funding for two new patrol boats to be built locally. He later promised to force foreign-born criminals to pay for the cost of their detention. From the other side of the country, Albanese played defence. 'Mr Morrison had a choice between Mark McGowan and Clive Palmer and he chose Clive Palmer,' he said. 'I know what side I'm on. I'm on the side of Mark McGowan,' Albanese added. McGowan told us, 'I had a number of calls with him [Morrison] where he was adamant they were going to win in the High Court. Actually he and Porter were quite arrogant about it.' Labor ran anti-Palmer ads in WA throughout the campaign, capitalising on Morrison's misstep. 'The only ad I can remember is the Palmer one. It was on high rotation,' McGowan recalls. 'He always tried to have a one-size-fits-all approach for the entire country. It was a very east coast outlook.'

Protestors dressed as cavemen greeted Morrison in Cowan in Perth's northern suburbs, referencing a comment Morrison had made about Western Australia's approach to the pandemic in 2021, and admirably staying in character when asked by journalists for comment. That the PM's first visit to a seat in Western Australia was the Labor-held marginal of Cowan is a reminder that the Coalition had little idea at the beginning of the campaign of the storm to come from the west. Even on the eve of the election, armed with its track polling throughout the campaign, Liberals believed with a little luck they could hold all their seats, or they could lose the three obvious ones — Swan, Pearce and Hasluck — if circumstances conspired against them. The size and breadth of the swing in WA was an election night shock for team Morrison.

Travelling east to Pearce, Morrison was asked about cost-of-living increases. In part of his answer, he referred to an increase in JobSeeker payments but he cited the rate at $46 per week instead of per day. Social media erupted, of course, with claims that the slip of the tongue wasn't treated the same way as Albo's unemployment gaffe. A lot of this social media activity was simply 'working the ref' — putting pressure on journalists to be more guarded. Journalists already had a more promising angle, asking the PM at his next event if the error showed he was out of touch with welfare recipients.

Yet more bigoted comments from Deves emerged, among them a spurious link between transvestism and sexual predation. Morrison disingenuously claimed that the criticism of Deves was a reaction to the issue of sport, not her more incendiary comments. 'I think Australians are getting pretty fed-up with having to walk on eggshells every day because they may or may not say something one day that's going to upset someone,' he said. The party of free speech banned the media from a politics-at-the-pub event featuring Deves. She was attending in conjunction with Falinski, Liberal MP for the neighbouring seat of Mackellar. Why a moderate MP under threat from a teal independent thought it was a good idea to headline an event with Deves was beyond anyone's comprehension.

More Liberals were calling for Deves' disendorsement. Morrison held firm. Among the cavalcade of stupid she had unleashed on the trans issue over the years, Deves suffered from delusions of grandeur, comparing her crusade to resistance against Nazi Germany. Samantha Maiden published an email from the president of one of the Liberal Party branches in Warringah to the New South Wales Liberal state director, Chris Stone, urging him to intervene. Marise Payne's performance on ABC's *Insiders* on 17 April illustrated the problem facing moderate MPs in seats targeted by teal independents. Payne distanced herself from Deves' comments but said that preselection was a matter for the party organisation. Moderates claimed that voting against them would only weaken the moderate voices in the Liberal Party on climate change, accountability and gender equality. Where, though, were those moderate voices? When the senior leadership sets a conservative tone, even leading moderates struggle to put a different point of view. Zimmerman briefed journalists that he was lobbying for Deves' disendorsement. These quiet Australians were behaving just the way Morrison expected.

The first two weeks of the campaign confirmed Hirst's fears that the Prime Minister would not be able to resist commenting on what Hirst considered a distraction from the main campaign strategy. Rather, Morrison was targeting his messages at the outer metropolitan electorates he needed to win against Labor: both Coalition-held seats and others he was trying to win, such as Macquarie, Parramatta and Greenway in Sydney's west. This came at the expense of the seats under threat from the teal independents. Irrespective of how many, if any, of the non-incumbent independent candidates ultimately won, their credible threat drained money and human capital from the wider Coalition campaign. These traditionally safe seats usually would be expected to raise funds to be distributed among the outer metro marginal seat campaigns, with inner-city Liberals also expected to use Google Maps to find their way to the marginals to help campaign. All of that couldn't happen because of the challenges in those soon-to-be teal seats.

Morrison's willingness to defend Deves also raised questions among journalists about the extent to which the Coalition was imitating the British Conservative Party's 'red wall' strategy. Boris Johnson had retained his prime ministership in 2019 in part by winning more seats from Labour in the north of England than it lost in London and the Conservative England heartland. This was in part due to the proximity of the election to the Brexit campaign, which also relied on a populist pitch, and a Labour leader more in tune with middle-class than working-class concerns. 'We never saw any evidence that the red wall strategy was a threat,' Erickson told us. It's not as though Morrison was offering working-class Australian conservatives much when it came to wages growth and tax cuts, just endless culture wars.

On the final Thursday before the election, Erickson texted journalists rejecting the assertion a red-wall strategy was realistic. Morrison's team had been putting it about that they were chasing Labor-held seats to offset losses. Erickson wasn't buying it, believing it was a tactic to appear competitive. This is the text he sent:

Last week they were closing the gap in Parramatta. Then earlier this week he visited Blair, and they said they were confident of McEwen. Oh, and they're putting more resources in Eden-Monaro and Dobell. Today it's Werriwa.

Does that mean they've given up on all of the others? Or are they making 6 gains? If they're making 6 gains they're in a majority even with teal losses; are they saying they're on 51–52% nationally?

He was calling bullshit.

Australian parties are well versed in tailoring imported campaign strategies to local conditions, but what we saw in 2022 is really just part of a long-term realignment. Conservative parties have always needed the votes of at least a few socially conservative blue-collar workers, just as Labor has always needed the votes of white-collar workers. Labor's inroads into the professional middle classes since Whitlam and his state colleagues such as Don Dunstan sharpened this trend. John Howard's school education policies, in particular, were aimed at making inroads into the Catholic vote. It seems unlikely that a political party would simply wave goodbye to some of its safest seats in pursuit of an unproven strategy. It wasn't a coordinated strategy, as some would speculate; it was just Morrison's approach. The challenge was how to fight on two fronts. The cultural politics that Howard pioneered was now dividing Coalition supporters. What issue do all Australians have in common? House prices, of course.

The budget had foreshadowed an increase in the number of places available in the Home Guarantee Scheme, which tops up home deposits. Morrison announced how this was to work, with the maximum value of the house qualifying for the scheme increasing depending on the condition of the market in each state. This was the first of several housing measures announced during the campaign that addressed the demand side of the housing market but not the supply side. Increasing the caps was a perfect illustration of the fact that with such schemes the government is only adding to the problem. Finding ways to help homebuyers who haven't been able to save a large enough deposit, in some cases only 2 per cent, into ever larger loans when interest rates were about to rise seemed particularly irresponsible.

The Pacific family

The first two major opinion polls of the campaign showed the primary vote of the major parties slipping, a strong vote for the Greens, and Albanese slipping behind as preferred prime minister after his unsteady start to the campaign. Liberal polling was showing the teals as a real threat. Both leaders were asked about whether they would deal with crossbenchers in the event of a hung parliament. They both said that they wouldn't and they were both unconvincing. There was speculation that Rebekha Sharkie would support the government. Albanese was given an opportunity to put some distance between his party and the Greens. Greens senator Jordon Steele-John had claimed that China was not a military threat to Australia. China had moved quietly towards establishing a military presence in the Solomon Islands, filling the gap in Australia's inconsistent diplomatic efforts in the region. As politicians from all sides had noted, as a sovereign country, the Solomon Islands can do whatever it wishes. Steele-John went a step further in criticising the alarm the issue had raised. 'It is a racist, paternalistic double standard that needs to be called out,' he said. *The Australian* gave Liberals the opportunity to refer to Steele-John's comments and link them to Labor and the prospect of a minority government. Former diplomat Dave Sharma took his cue. 'Adam Bandt has been saying he's going to form part of a Labor–Greens Government,' he said. 'These views they've expressed are alarming.'

Albanese was the wrong Labor leader to try this nonsense against. He had bitter memories of wrestling with Greens candidates in Grayndler. He had been against the Gillard government negotiating with the Greens in 2010. As Rudd's deputy on his return in 2013 he shut down Greens attempts to renegotiate their previous deal with Gillard. In any event, Labor was confident throughout the campaign that the worst result for them would see them miss majority government only marginally. The Greens would be one of several options for confidence motions and passing legislation. No need to mollify them during the campaign. Morrison had a different problem, with suggestions that, were the teal independents successful, another leader might be required to negotiate in a hung parliament. Another sign of Coalition desperation came from reports of push-polling from the National Party linking independent candidates to Labor or the Greens.

When the Solomons deal, the first of its kind between China and a Pacific state, was announced, it became a rare instance of a foreign policy issue becoming a major talking point in an Australian election campaign. A draft of the agreement had been leaked, but the announcement that a deal had been signed appeared to take the Australian government by surprise, sparking the kind of megaphone diplomacy that Pacific leaders despise, despite Morrison underlining the sovereign choices of the Pacific nation. The Solomons' Prime Minister, Manasseh Sogavare, said he had 'learned of the Aukus treaty in the media' and 'one would expect that as a member of the Pacific family, Solomon Islands and members of the Pacific should have been consulted to ensure that this Aukus treaty is transparent, since it will affect the Pacific family by allowing nuclear submarines in Pacific waters'. Sogavare went on to say he realised Australia was 'a sovereign country, and that it can enter into any treaty that it wants to, transparently or not — which is exactly what they did with [the] Aukus treaty'. Morrison couldn't help himself, claiming 'there's a remarkable similarity between those statements and those of the Chinese government'.

Unhelpful discussion of 'red lines' followed. Zed Seselja, the Minister for International Development and the Pacific — notably not the Minister for Foreign Affairs — was dispatched to Honiara to ... well, it's not clear what he was expected to achieve after the event. Evidence of action perhaps. Peter Dutton made his usual insinuations that bribery was involved. Home Affairs Minister Karen Andrews suggested that the timing showed China interfering in the election, implicitly in Labor's favour. Later, on the final day of campaigning, Payne's 2021 cabinet submission to increase Pacific aid funding specifically to head off China's empire-building in the region, was leaked. The proposal was reportedly rejected because ministers were not convinced there would be any specific commitment from Pacific nations.

Most foreign policy is bipartisan. Yet, there is a longstanding advantage to the Coalition on national security as a general issue. Shadow Foreign Affairs Minister Penny Wong wove her response into Labor's campaign theme against Morrison. 'Yet again Mr Morrison has gone missing and might talk a tough game, but what we are seeing on his watch is the worst Australian foreign policy blunder in the Pacific since the end of World War Two,' she told ABC Radio. There was a unanimous view across the campaign leadership group that the Coalition were going to try to create a divisive and partisan argument over national security. 'When the Solomon Islands security pact became public, what became clear in our nightly research was that voters were worried about the news of the pact and worried that the government had dropped the ball,' Erickson told us. 'So it became clear that national security became a positive for us.'

On 18 April, Morrison addressed a WA Minerals Council meeting at a breakfast, announcing a $250-million package for the sector. Paul Everingham, a former WA Liberal Party state director, was the Council's chief executive. Morrison announced hydrogen hubs in Perth and the Pilbara, which would create 5000 jobs. In his speech, Morrison riffed on a Liberal Party advertisement. 'It certainly won't be easy under Mr Albanese, especially if your job depends on our resources industry,' he said. Later in the day, Senator Cash joined journalists on Morrison's bus. This charm offensive failed to charm. Once Morrison had left Perth, Cash also tried to quietly kill off claims the Coalition would make further reforms in workplace relations, ruling out changes to the *Fair Work Act*'s Better Off Overall Test. Yet, a week later employer groups used *The Australian* to call for more reform. Of all the interest groups in Australian politics, employers are the most useless when it comes to election campaigns.

On 19 April, in Dutton's Brisbane seat of Dickson, before moving on to Griffith to visit an electric charging station manufacturer, Albanese continued to trade barbs with the PM from opposite sides of the continent. With Tony Burke in tow, Albanese was responding to a spurious Coalition calculation about energy prices under Labor's policies. 'The market is choosing clean energy and renewables for new energy growth,' he said. 'That is something that is happening in spite of the government, not because of the government.' Mark Riley pivoted the line of questioning to ask Albanese about the government underestimating him: 'Well, I've been underestimated my whole life,' he responded. Later, Albanese told us, 'I used that in my own head to motivate me.'

He left the campaign trail early to prepare for the debate the following day. With no more events that afternoon or evening, journalists were left to their own devices, sharing photos of themselves relaxing in various pubs and restaurants replete with messages such as 'Campaigning is easy with Albanese'. It was a catchy slogan. Morrison made a point of saying that he didn't need to hunker down for the debate. 'My approach is not to lock myself away in rooms before having these things,' he said, although he had plenty of time to prepare on the plane from Perth to Adelaide, where he dropped into Boothby, before flying on to Brisbane. Close to Adelaide Airport, Boothby lent itself to flying visits for a quick announcement and some local media coverage. Albanese thought Morrison's claim about not needing to prepare was ridiculous.

Be prepared for anything

Chalmers joined Albanese as he prepared for the debate, which included mock debates with the Shadow Treasurer playing the role of Morrison. They practised in a conference room overlooking the tennis courts at the Brisbane Hilton, both the afternoon before the day of the debate and the morning of. Also present for the preparations were Tony Burke, Stephen Smith and Albanese's staffer Katie Connolly, who ran the prep for all three debates. They had already held a mock debate weeks out from the election being called, to help Albanese hone his skills. 'He approached his prep for them seriously, with a bit of humility, never underestimating Morrison's cunning,' Chalmers told us. Albanese played tennis to clear his head between sessions. Practice included Chalmers trying to put Albo off his game, standing up close and over him like Morrison had to Shorten in one of the 2019 debates. There were lots of Jenny references in the mock debates. Burke was very influential in these sessions. A former university debater and responsible for Labor tactics on the floor of parliament, he was good at stripping away the irrelevant distractions to get to the core things Albo needed to get right. The group were happy with his prep, laughing off Morrison's attempt to suggest too much preparation was a sign of weakness.

Chalmers felt like Albanese was well placed to win the debate. He had all the words he needed, he just needed time to arrange them ahead of the showdown. He was left to himself to quietly prepare after the session. Before the debate started on 20 April, Marles, Burke and Chalmers joined Albanese and Liz Fitch at the venue, a conference room at The Gabba.

Marles stayed in the room for the debate, a friendly face for the wannabe PM at this important outing. Chalmers and Burke stayed in the Green Room where they nervously paced up and down. It was better they remained hidden from view or their nervous energy might have rubbed off. There were no TVs there, so they had to watch the debate on Fitch's iPad.

The format for the debate on Sky News was a community forum with questions coming directly from audience members. The audience was made up of self-described undecided voters. This format allowed only limited interaction between the two leaders. Albanese showed his confidence in a media conference prior to the debate, hitting Morrison hard over aged care and the government's failures in the Pacific. The former chief of staff to Bill Shorten, Cameron Milner, wrote in *The Australian* before the formal campaign that the small-target strategy was 'myopic' and he wanted to see the 'real Albo' provide a genuine alternative to the government. The electorate, this argument runs, wants a new approach and the small-target strategy risks missing an opportunity to promote widespread policy reform. Milner was full of praise for Albanese as a genuine reformer but criticised unnamed strategists for the conservative approach. As we have seen, though, Albanese was primarily responsible for Labor's electoral strategy.

The more interesting question was whether there was a 'real Albo' waiting to govern as a reformer. This presented a communications challenge in that any hint that he had policies up his sleeve to bring out in government would be pounced upon by the government and journalists. Morrison enjoyed this bind. 'He's not a small target, he's a complete blank page,' the Prime Minister goaded his opponent. Albanese tried to address this in the first leaders' debate. Despite a slip-up over asylum policy, which Morrison seemed almost too eager to jump all over, Albanese performed well. He seemed to address the question of how he would govern by making much of what previous Labor governments have done. 'It's always Labor that does the big changes that make a difference to people's lives,' he said, echoing Paul Keating. He could wrap himself in Labor values without promising many specifics. Madigan and Erickson discussed what they saw as a permanent challenge for Labor throughout the campaign: they had to make a case for change without too much change. They were happy with the line Albanese walked in the first debate.

Morrison's preparation — of course he also prepped — focused on the interaction with the audience since his campaign was organised around him not coming into contact with unscreened citizens, especially after his experience with the angry pensioner in Newcastle. In fact, he had handled that incident as well as he could have. Especially considering, as we saw throughout the parliamentary term, showing empathy is not his strongest feature as a political leader. The audience questions were a good mix, favouring Albanese as they dwelt on health, the cost of living and integrity. It was a question about the NDIS reducing funding to a disabled child that tripped Morrison up. He responded with an aside that he and Jenny had been 'blessed' to have two daughters without disability. He seemed to know that was the wrong formulation. 'And so for parents with children who are disabled. I can only try and understand your aspirations for those children,' he continued. Condemnation followed quickly, which was fair enough but helped obscure the underlying issue of the way the NDIS operates.

Morrison sought absolution from Australian of the Year Dylan Alcott, who had shown his class by tweeting that he had woken up 'feeling pretty blessed to be disabled'. Morrison called Alcott to apologise. Former Australian of the Year Grace Tame took the opportunity to post a photograph of her giving the PM the side-eye, with the caption: 'Autism blesses those of us who have it with the ability to spot fakes from a mile off.' Americans have a term for this sort of mistake. A 'Kinsley gaffe', named after the journalist who coined the term, is when a politician reveals the truth by accident.

Albanese was widely judged to have won the debate. 'Because we had issues in week one, the first debate was more important than it should have been,' Albanese told us. 'There aren't five million swinging voters watching the debates, but in terms of perception and the way it's reported, it showed that the fact I won all three debates, and they were his choice of venue and timing, was pretty good.' This might have been cold comfort since Shorten won all the debates in 2019. However, in addition to the conventional wisdom that an opposition leader benefits from debates simply by sharing the stage with the incumbent and looking reasonably intelligent, Albanese had clearly steadied the ship after an uncertain first week. 'It wasn't a shock to us that he did so well in the debates, especially that first one,' Chalmers recalled for us. The team who had helped prep him for the debate hugged their leader one by one, giving him a warm congrats on his performance.

Richard Marles made the point on the morning call the next day that when it was up to voters to ask questions, rather than journalists, they asked about all the issues Labor was seeking to talk about. He felt it validated the advice being given about what was motivating them coming up in the Labor research. Penny Wong said that the audience questions on national security confirmed, in her mind, the Labor strategy of muscling up to the Coalition on that issue was working: 'That's when I knew we'd made the right decision,' she told us.

The debate was an interesting example of just how many different dimensions there are to an election campaign. One might see Albanese's performance as a turning point of the campaign — at least, of the national campaign, which the nightly television news and the major newspapers focus on. Yet, for Labor this part of the campaign saw their best asset — the leader — deployed up and down the Queensland coast for days at a time. Albanese visited the seats of Flynn, Hinkler, Leichhardt, Brisbane, Ryan, Dickson and Griffith, all of which Labor ended up losing.

The Prime Minister, meanwhile, lingered in Queensland after the debate. There was mixed news from Liberal CHQ. Morrison was buoyed by internal research showing that there were still enough undecided voters for him to pull off a win. However, the extent of the teals' challenge was underlined with the realisation that Kate Chaney could win in Curtin against Celia Hammond, showing it wasn't just the boys under threat from the independents. The Liberals' failure to change their internal processes, policies and attitudes towards women now saw them spending millions of dollars trying to stave off challenges from a well-funded and motivated collection of women in their safest electorates. The teal movement has a broader base, but the 2022 incarnation was the direct result of Liberal Party failures on gender politics.

Much of the sniping directed at the teals simply didn't ring true. No amount of sledging from the Liberal candidates or News Corp papers seemed to harm them, and probably helped. Front-page stories about the contests, even those supportive of their opponents, probably only had the effect of raising their profile. Journalists scouring social media didn't come up with much. Monique Ryan was accused by the *Herald Sun* of calling Peter Dutton a 'toxic potato-head' in a Facebook post. Why that would be a problem in Kooyong wasn't clear. Most importantly, whether their opponents accused them of being under the thumb of Holmes à Court, Labor or the Greens, the teals were different enough from each other to appear independent. If the economy was the major issue, for example, they probably wouldn't assemble under a single banner. They came across as reasonable in the face of over-the-top attacks. The idea that a hung parliament would lead to chaos with the teals in power was absurd. Indeed, knowing their audience, they were more likely to refer to the Business Council of Australia on climate policy than any environmental group. Holmes à Court often claimed that donations from Climate 200 came with 'no strings attached'. Yet, the teals know what will be required of them to receive that funding again. That's simply how power works.

The teals' ability to engage the electorate on nationally focused issues in a network, rather than making the usual independent complaints about local resourcing, garnered more attention in the state and national media. They also appealed to an educated electorate unimpressed by the culture war noises designed for suburban and regional electorates. Other issues raised by these candidates include political donations reform, Steggall having endured a scandal about how a disclosure from a mining millionaire had been handled.

Morrison campaigned in Longman at a retirement village after the debate, which guaranteed that he would have to address the cashless debit card scare after his photo-op trying out lawn bowls. He made yet another defence announcement in nearby Bonner and pledged more community facilities in Petrie, but the day was dominated by responses to his comments on disability. The best he could offer was that Labor had twisted his comments. Labor strategists didn't mind that — more of Morrison not taking responsibility, they thought.

Still in Queensland, Morrison kept up his pattern of announcing goodies for the locals while addressing national issues with the travelling press. An attempt to whip up a coffee in a café went wrong when Morrison managed to spray hot milk on himself. He addressed defence and veterans' issues in the seats of Blair and Forde. With Marles set to take a higher profile, he revisited his attack on the Deputy Leader, deflecting attacks on his government's failures in the Pacific by alleging that Marles had encouraged China's growing influence in the region. The week had barely touched on Morrison's preferred ground: the economy.

The Coalition's fortunes were best summed up by an irate voter who delivered an expletive-ridden spray to Barnaby Joyce at a roadside stop in his New England electorate. Joyce's AFP security detail was forced to intervene and arrest the man. 'He was aggressive, but I held my ground,' Joyce told us.

Albanese followed up his post-debate visit to Gilmore with a relaxing coffee in Sydney's Bennelong with Labor's candidate Jerome Laxale and some locals. He needed a PCR test because he was going to Perth the next day. 'I went home, got tested at a quarter past four and it came through at 5.51 p.m. that I'd tested positive,' Albanese told us.

It seems likely that some on the Opposition Leader's bus had caught COVID at the Byron Bay Music Festival event, and subsequently so had Albanese. The irony was that Labor had much stricter COVID protocols than the Liberal Party, requiring triple vaccination and masks at all times on the campaign bus — no exceptions. Yet he'd had no inkling that he had COVID. He had climbed six flights of stairs at the Manildra ethanol plant with no ill effects and felt energised enough to add the trip to Bennelong to an already long day. 'I rang Tim [Gartrell] and Paul [Erickson] and quickly told them. I was conscious of the six o'clock news. The campaign launch is in nine days' time and I need to be in iso for the week.'

Those staffers who had given Albanese congratulatory hugs after his debate performance reflected on their closeness to him at a time when he'd undoubtedly been positive.

The response had been gamed out prior to the campaign. 'We had war-gamed the scenario and it just clicked into gear,' Albanese told us. 'We got the statement out within half an hour. The phone went nuts. Nathan was on the exercise bike. I yelled out to him. "Mate, you gotta go! You should go to your mum's." Then it was just me and the dog. I felt okay the next day, then really unwell on days three and four.' Albanese wasn't surprised that his opponent would try to take advantage of his illness. 'It was bizarre' that Morrison bragged about working through COVID in March. 'The other thing that Morrison did was try to get all the debates in the following week when I had Q+A. There was argy-bargy about that. That was clearly designed to have a pile-on after COVID,' Albanese claims.

Erickson was supposed to go to a Midnight Oil concert that night but had to miss it as the Labor team put plans in place late into the night to keep the campaign going. In a call with Gartrell and Fitch, they agreed that Jason Clare would stand up the following day as part of the main act. Erickson rang Swan and Smith to discuss the week ahead — what, if anything, needed to be done to ensure the party stayed upbeat — and believed things were under control. The idea was to have the whole of the team up across the week, but also have consistency within that — Wong and Marles focusing on national security and Anzac Day. The finance team took centre stage when the CPI figures came out later in the week. Erickson felt it was important that it wasn't just one person replacing Albo. 'It had to be the team.' The depth of Labor's bench was about to be tested, just when CHQ was confident things were back on track.

Chapter 7

Week 3: No Albo, no worries

The timing of Albanese's week in isolation couldn't have been better. 'It was absolutely the perfect time,' he told us.

> I'd won the debate, I'd done Gilmore. I'd been up to Bennelong. I had a trip to Perth planned, but importantly I was not out for the launch. It gave me that week to work on not just the launch speech but a speech I gave to the Australian Chamber of Commerce and Industry the following Thursday and to just really spend time planning the rest of the campaign without the pressure of jumping around on planes. That made me feel quite good.

Hirst also reflected after the election to colleagues that Labor couldn't have timed it better. A week earlier and Albo goes into iso with a bloody nose, a week later and he would have missed the Labor launch unless it was delayed. 'Anthony getting COVID and having to isolate at home for a week made him more relatable to voters,' Erickson says. 'So many Australians had contracted the virus, become unwell, self-isolated for a week and had to manage working from home whilst being sick.'

Albanese agrees: 'If it had happened the day before the debate and I'd cancelled the debate that would have been a problem, given the pile-on that was happening from the media,' he recalled. 'Even when I won the debate, the page one of the tabloids didn't represent that in Sydney or Melbourne.' He went into isolation late on the Thursday of the second week of the campaign. A shorter campaign also might have made things dicey.

The contrast with Morrison had been anticipated. 'We had thought that through. If I go down, we want to focus on Morrison, show that I'm the captain of the team and we want a different style of leadership,' Albanese told us. 'We don't want someone who is the captain, the front row, the halfback, the fullback, the centre, the second row because no one will run for him. He's gotta do everything himself, make every tackle because he hasn't got a team.' (For those in southern states, these are the key positions on a rugby league team.) 'Given that it did happen, we were comfortable that it would be okay.'

At the strategy meeting on Sunday 24 April, Erickson reported that voters had certainly noticed Albo had COVID, even though it was only revealed days earlier. They also noticed that both campaigns had flicked the switch to negative. The fact that the Liberals ramped up their negative ads only confirmed in Erickson's mind that the team had made the right call to do the same at the previous Sunday's meeting. The leaders' debate wasn't watched by most voters, but the research showed that word was getting around that Albanese had won it. It helped send a stabilising message, especially significant now that Albanese was in iso. Marles reiterated what he'd said the day after the debate: that voters, when asked directly, identified issues Labor, not the government, were focused on. Erickson updated the group on the track polling, which had tightened. The lead was now four points, not six. The election was still in the balance. We were told there was no panic in response to that by a number of meeting attendees, which might be a case of rose-coloured glasses looking back from a position of victory.

Fully sick

Albanese got sicker than Labor ever let on. And the after-effects were also worse than the public was told. Having had a severe bout of COVID himself, Erickson pushed back at the bosses at Channels Seven and Nine as they sought to strong-arm Labor about holding election debates as soon as Albo was out of iso. Erickson reminded them that COVID was a serious illness and they were being unreasonable. He had to be careful that argument didn't result in news stories to follow which might imply Albanese's health wasn't up to becoming PM. A silly extension to be sure, but the media circus was already in full swing. The practicalities of isolation were trying. 'I was setting everything up by myself,' Albanese told us. I had the computer set up in the kitchen, but we had to get a teleprompter app and proper mic as well. I didn't do much television because the internet was unreliable. There wasn't much food in the house so someone had to pick my groceries up at Woolworths.' Labor had prepared for a possible COVID election which might have required Albanese to spend more time in Canberra. They built a mock office at National Headquarters, which was used for the first round of behind-the-desk television ads shot in December 2021. But despite putting contingency plans in place to campaign without Albanese, little was done to ready him for life stuck at home.

The removal of the leader from the travelling campaign had several flow-on effects. It sharpened the focus on Morrison, whose own mistakes had been overshadowed by Albanese's rough start. And it would test Labor's leadership team. 'We had a rolling roster of people out there,' Albanese told us. 'We wouldn't allow my disruption to have follow-on effects on other members of the team who already had an itinerary.' Albanese did conduct occasional radio and television interviews, in a much more controlled environment than the conferences on the campaign trail. 'There was a particular interview with [talkback radio host] Ray Hadley where he went hard and the good thing about not feeling well is I would have reacted more if I wasn't, because he was just yelling down the phone at me. I wasn't well so I was dealing with it in a much more passive way with some of his assertions that were just wrong.'

Albanese had time to recalibrate and think about the remainder of the campaign. By the time he came out of isolation, he was immediately on a plane to Perth for the formal launch, which would provide momentum and increase his confidence. The election became a campaign of two halves — the first almost irrelevant to what followed. Early on, Albanese had not been at his best and had been found wanting. Having formal events at Easter and Anzac Day, overlapping with school holidays, brought some milestones to a marathon effort.

If Albanese caught COVID at the perfect time, the same can't be said for Liberal federal director Andrew Hirst. On the Tuesday of week three of the campaign, he tested positive, as the virus swept through the Coalition campaign headquarters. Frydenberg's chief media adviser was also working in CHQ and went down, along with several others. Hirst was knocked around by the virus for forty-eight hours, but was still phoning into the morning meetings. On one call someone told him he sounded like Darth Vader. Coalition CHQ was operating with a reduced staff right at the time Labor's team were doing well in Albo's absence and the focus was squarely on Morrison.

The PM was campaigning on the Central Coast of New South Wales, servicing both coastal seats with a promise of support for fishing and boating activities, a retread of a successful program from 2019. With no Albanese press conference, Morrison didn't risk one of his own, which was bound to be dominated by criticism of his performance on the Solomon Islands issue. He couldn't win, though, with his failure to front-up widely reported. Labor noticed the PM avoiding a presser on Albanese's first full day in isolation. The team quickly realised this contrast could be very politically useful — putting closer singular attention on an unpopular PM in a presidential-style contest was manna from heaven for the opposition. Jenny joined her husband to attend a candlelit Greek Orthodox midnight mass in Sydney, as the Prime Minister conducted a bit of mid-campaign diplomacy with a visiting Greek minister. Locals enjoyed the PM's woeful attempt to say a few words in Greek after the mass. Frydenberg attended a similar event in Kooyong, having been forced, earlier in the campaign, to change some posters featuring him interacting with Scouts after one of them objected to being included.

Labor research showed that people had been reserving judgement but, to the extent they were beginning to pay attention in week three while the Opposition Leader was partially inaccessible, something interesting happened. Showing unusual depth for a modern election campaign, Labor's team was attracting widespread praise. Campaign spokesman Jason Clare delivered zinger after zinger, capturing the attention of the media. His authoritative voice during pressers in Sydney was complemented by the cutting lines. These had been practised on the morning calls, and James Jeffrey, who travelled with the leader throughout the campaign, was texting through ideas. 'Scott Morrison talks about his team, where are they?' Clare asked. 'Most of them are in hiding. Some of them are in witness protection. I don't think Scooby Doo could find Alan Tudge at the moment.' These could easily have been received in the same vein as Morrison's groan-inducing dad jokes. Instead, Clare's Cary Grant routine became one of the few viral moments of the campaign. He handled gotcha questions with ease. Clare had been touted as a future leader in his early years in parliament, but his star faded in opposition. His return was spectacular, his charm and wit being new to most observers. Before the campaign, Clare's head had been on the front-bench chopping block. After this performance, he would instead be rewarded with a promotion into the Education portfolio. Labor had other good lines about Tudge being in hiding, though their attacks would have been more effective if they'd had an education policy worth talking about. With Australian students falling in international achievement rankings, Plibersek pointed out the continued favouring of private schools by the Commonwealth but wasn't promising to do much about it.

With half the media contingent dropping off with the leader not present, Wong, Marles and Chalmers were able to take the lead on the campaign trail under less pressure. Marles wasn't at his best, or at least not at what should be a par performance for a deputy leader, and there were news stories questioning his capacity, brought on by Morrison's attacks, but for most voters that was inside-the-bubble stuff. Marles may have been a loyal deputy but he wasn't a great campaigner; one of those parliamentarians better at government than opposition; a better administrator than media performer. He was fine answering questions about a speech he had made in China since the government had been peppering him about that for months. On climate policy, though, he floundered, Chalmers stepping in to help him. Journalist Jonathan Lea from Sky insisted that since Marles was substituting for the leader, he should have been able to handle questions about policy detail. This was probably the silliest objection journalists had to the way the opposition conducted itself. Having shadow ministers answer specialised questions seems perfectly sensible. Again, Chalmers' steadiness impressed Albanese. Some of those asked to do more were outside Albanese's circle of mates. Husic joined the election trail. Plibersek got more responsibility than she otherwise might have, but journalists noticed that she wasn't facing press conferences in Albanese's absence. The services of Shorten, though, were not required.

Who might have stepped up if it had been Morrison with COVID? The Coalition already had to keep Morrison and Joyce — the Prime Minister and his Deputy — away from a host of seats as well as each other, given those texts from Joyce labelling the PM a liar. The Treasurer was under threat in his own seat and increasingly focused only on that contest. Would we have seen more of Dutton's belligerence? Marise Payne's timidity? Stuart Robert's vacuousness? More likely, we would have seen the first election campaign run entirely by Zoom from a leader's lounge room.

A different sort of leader might have been threatened by the media praise for their lieutenants. For the future PM, though, having to rely on more than a core group taught Albanese to both widen his arc of trust and rely even more on his inner group. Chalmers was impressed with this aspect of his leader. 'I think it showcased what are typically under-appreciated leadership traits,' he told us. 'The ability to build a team, empower the people in it, and let them do their jobs. He was grateful for and gracious in acknowledging the effort put in in his absence. Australians got a little glimpse of a leader who genuinely values and appreciates his team, isn't a one-man band, and I think they liked it.'

This process of trusting a wider circle of colleagues had begun after the day-one stumble when Albo needed to rely more on Chalmers than he had planned to. On his return, Albanese was noticeably more praiseworthy of those around him, partly because he was genuinely thankful to them and partly to draw comparisons with the hollowed-out government team. A prime minister can't be a lone wolf.

Chalmers foreshadowed Labor's budget principles. 'We've made it clear we do need to trim spending,' he said, adding, 'We are not proposing any tax reforms beyond the proposals we will shortly make about multinational tax reform.' He accused Morrison of walking away from supporting the OECD's proposed global crackdown on multinational corporations' tax avoidance because of his no-new-taxes pledge. To press this perceived advantage, new Coalition television and press ads promoted its economic record, supposedly bettering Labor's, comparing electricity prices, unemployment rates, interest rates and balanced budgets. The ads were full of spurious comparisons, statistical tricks and selective memory. Welcome to the largely unregulated theatre of political advertising. The comparative ad ended with what would become a campaign staple in Liberal ads — 'It won't be easy under Albanese', with a dollar symbol instead of the 'S'. Over time that dollar sign would crack in the updated ads.

The Prime Minister headed to Alice Springs, the Coalition targeting both Northern Territory seats: Lingiari and Solomon. Lingiari was the primary target, with long-time Labor MP Warren Snowdon retiring. Morrison promised $14 million locally to reduce crime, via early intervention and increased patrols. Anti-fracking protestors' chants distracted at the presser, which gave the PM the chance to talk about loud voices drowning out the quiet Australians. Both campaigns were in the Territory ahead of Anzac Day, when the campaign would be suspended for the day. Wong promoted Labor's Indigenous health policy in Alice Springs with Butler and Labor's candidate for Lingiari, Marion Scrymgour. Referencing the difficulty of the minister to win adequate funding in the budget earlier in the year, Wong also announced a $500 million veterans' health and pensions policy. 'We will fix the crisis in Veterans' Affairs,' Wong boldly declared. Yet with the leader away, this important announcement didn't get the attention it deserved — in Darwin, Morrison was announcing a $300 million gift to the gas industry. It stole the spotlight. Such is the way of things, a much smaller sum along with a leader photo opportunity gets more attention, particularly from television. Politics can be a depressingly superficial business at times.

Morrison attacked Labor ads in the Chisholm contest which asked, 'What do we know about Liberal Gladys Liu?' The ads made tough but fair claims about Liu's 2019 campaign but, wrapped up in the vaguely sinister tagline, they came across as dog whistling. Labor was never seriously questioned about it.

Deves hogged attention again, claiming on SBS that she had received death threats and sent her family away because of the tumult. 'My safety has been threatened,' she said. 'My family are away out of Sydney because I don't want them to witness what I am going through and nor do I want their safety put at risk.' Police said they knew nothing about such threats and the Deves family's flight coincided with school holidays. She was hardly the only MP (or journalist) working over school holidays on the campaign while the rest of the family took a break. After an event headlined by the Prime Minister, Deves refused to answer any questions. She was pursued by journalists into a lift. The journos were blocked from joining the candidate by security guards almost as wide as the lift doors. The Victorian premier, Dan Andrews, had had enough of the 'cruel' dialogue around trans issues, commenting that he had been in parliament twenty years without schools raising this issue with him. 'I've never had parents come to me, I've never had a teacher come to me and raise this issue,' he said. 'What is the problem we're trying to solve here?'

Dutton popped his head up on Anzac Day to declare that war, presumably against China, could be imminent. 'We have to be realistic that people like Hitler and others aren't just a figment of our imagination or that they're consigned to history,' he said. 'The only way you can preserve peace is to prepare for war and be strong as a country.' This was in light of Morrison's touting of mysterious 'red lines' over the Solomon Islands deal with China, the Prime Minister also bringing back his 'arc of autocracy' line from earlier in the year. Albanese released an Anzac Day video from home, conveying a message remarkably similar to Dutton's but with the grace and restraint the defence minister congenitally lacked. 'Darkness,' he said, 'has not been vanquished from the world.'

Labor questioned Dutton's timing as well as his assessment of regional security. Marles, rehearsing for the Defence portfolio in government, wasn't going to be lectured to by a government so incompetent on national security. 'This is a government which beats its chest,' he pointed out. 'When it comes to actually delivering, and doing what needs to be done, it's a government which repeatedly fails.' It was a marginal call on whether drawing attention to security was wise in the middle of the Solomons affair, which the government had mishandled. Being seen to politicise Anzac Day made the exchange a net negative for the government, reinforced when Morrison was caught texting during a service. He claimed the service was already over, but the vision showed the people surrounding him clapping, cuing the PM to briefly join them, before getting back to his important text. What was it about? Just logistics for his next event. The Dawn Service had interfered with his morning campaign calls.

More public polls showed a steady race, something that was reflected in the parties' tracking polls, and a contrast to 2019 when the public polls bounced around. The Coalition wasn't making up the ground it needed to, which had begun to worry campaign headquarters. The Coalition track showed the contest tightening each week, just not quickly enough to overhaul Labor's lead. Labor was speculating about a change of tactics from the government even though orthodox tactics are to stick to your game plan because it can take weeks for messages to bite, and when they do the gap closes more quickly.

To capitalise on the government's failures on Pacific security, Labor pledged to dramatically increase foreign aid in the region if elected, in order to stave off the influence of China. Payne argued that there was no difference between the two major party policies, but it was too late to depoliticise foreign policy. Morrison characterised Labor's policy, which included restoring Australian radio broadcasts to the Pacific, as 'send in the ABC'. Recalling an advertising campaign featuring Lara Bingle from when Morrison was Tourism Australia chief,

Clare asked the PM 'Where the bloody hell were you?' when Australian leadership was required in the Pacific. The zingers didn't stop.

An outbreak of climate scepticism disrupted the Coalition campaign for two days. The Nationals candidate in Flynn, Colin Boyce, claimed there was 'wiggle room' around the net zero target. Senator Matt Canavan chimed in saying, 'the net zero thing is sort of dead anyway', referring to alleged backsliding in Europe. Visiting Rockhampton, Morrison did his usual trick of turning a question about Canavan's intervention into a related attack on Labor. As it increasingly did, though, this came across as a failure of leadership, in this case a failure to defend his own party's hard-fought position on carbon emissions when some of his MPs were struggling to defend their seats from the teal independents. Member for Capricornia Michelle Landry was having none of this. Having been part of that hard fight over policy, and with no shortage of coal-mining jobs in her electorate, she was not going to let colleagues undermine her (and Morrison's) position. Standing alongside Morrison, she gave him a lesson in political courage, joining fellow Nationals in telling Canavan, 'Pull your head in, Matt.'

The usual scaremongering

Climate change became the subject of extensive debate. There was the usual Coalition scaremongering about Labor's policy, not helped by various shadow ministers making a poor fist of explaining the nuance. However, having extracted a pound of flesh to sign up to net zero emissions, Nationals members and candidates — but not Barnaby Joyce — questioned whether other countries were serious about achieving the targets. Serial offender Matt Canavan was joined by a few less blunt tools in the National Party trying to narrowcast their message by emphasising support for coal and gas. While the leadership sought to explain all this away as debate over methods rather than targets, it was nothing of the sort. It was a reminder that the Coalition has simply never accepted the need for urgent policy action. Both Labor and the teal independents relished the discussion. Neither of the major parties was paying enough attention to the Greens.

The government could only make serious claims about Labor's policy by drawing attention to the weaknesses in its own existing frameworks. For example, the Safeguard Mechanism put in place when the government axed the carbon tax was designed to limit the emissions of big polluters. However, it had been continually watered down to appease those same polluters. With Labor threatening to run the Safeguard Mechanism as the government designed it — as a de facto carbon price — Coalition figures screamed blue murder. In a splash in *The Australian* on 26 April, the chief executive of Whitehaven Coal, Paul Flynn, claimed that Labor was planning a 'carbon levy by stealth'. Morrison accused Labor of wanting to introduce a 'sneaky carbon tax'. This is one of the most longstanding and important principles in emissions reduction. Whether you call the policy a tax, a price, emissions trading or (if you are into pointless acronyms) a CPRS, Carbon Pollution Reduction Scheme, serious reductions require government to make emissions more costly over time. Anything else is window dressing. Concerns that governments around the world will get squeamish about screwing up the price of carbon when faced with rising energy costs are real but beside the point. And being beside the point is where Scott Morrison resides.

On 27 April, for the first time in the campaign, the PM caught up with the man who had described him as a hypocrite and a fraud: Barnaby Joyce. They eschewed a joint media conference in Rockhampton to avoid the obvious questions. Instead, Morrison gave his deputy a shout-out in his speech to the Capricornia Chamber of Commerce. 'Barnaby and I have a very strong working partnership,' he enthused without a hint of shame. Joyce had a better analogy. 'It's a business partnership, not a marriage,' he said. Morrison made a modified version of his jobs pledge. 'We commit to 450,000 more jobs in rural and regional Australia,' he said. When a journalist asked Joyce at the event, 'Why are you having separate press conferences today?' Joyce replied, 'Look I don't even know the program and how it works,' before dashing away. At one of the pic facs (aka photo ops), a member of the public selected by advancers to sit around a table chewing the fat with the PM and others over coffee said, 'I applaud you for being able to get out of bed every morning and face up to the world.' The PM felt that way some mornings when he got the update on the previous night's track polling. The gap just wasn't closing quickly enough. He would need another miracle.

Morrison moved on to Townsville to announce a $70 million hydrogen hub. At the factory where the policy was announced, a safety sign read, 'If you mess up, fess up'. Coalition advancers covered the sign with a high-vis vest so the PM wouldn't be caught by the cameras standing near it. Of course, this had the effect of bringing attention to the problem. Eagle-eyed gallery types are always on the lookout for such opportunities.

Perhaps feeling the pressure on the Solomons deal, all of a sudden the PM sought the security of bipartisanship on foreign policy, claiming that Labor's attacks on the government could only benefit China. 'They are playing politics with the Pacific and the only ones who are benefiting from Labor's attacks on the government is the Chinese government,' he said with a straight face.

Coalition strategists wanted to pivot back to the economy after a week's worth of national security focus to meet the return of Albanese from isolation. The release of quarterly inflation figures did the trick but not in the way the government had hoped. The biggest inflation spike in twenty-one years played to Labor's strengths and turned attention to inevitable interest rate rises. Treasurer Josh Frydenberg blamed international volatility, briefly popping his head up for a national audience beyond Kooyong. In Cairns to help shore up the seat of Leichhardt for long-time member Warren Entsch, Morrison denied responsibility. He continued his ongoing seminar on Australia's economic performance compared to the rest of the world. 'There are inflationary pressures in all the major economies around the world,' he said, holding up a graph showing inflation in Australia lower than elsewhere, asking whether Labor could be trusted in a deteriorating global economy. This was cold comfort to those feeling the squeeze, who aren't in the habit of comparing their cost of living with people residing overseas. 'This government has dropped the ball on inflation,' Chalmers claimed. 'When things are going well in the economy Scott Morrison takes all of the credit. But when times are tough for Australians, he takes none of the responsibility.' Morrison referred back to the $250 announced in the budget paid to around six million Australians on pension and other support payments.

Chalmers released Labor's budget principles in Canberra, including the commitment that 'not one cent' in revenue or spending cuts would be paid for by ordinary Australians. The tax on multinational corporations, projected to raise a modest amount of revenue, was the sort of policy recommended by the election review — a statement of values and part of Labor's narrative. It was also enough for Chalmers to return serve on government claims about 'no new taxes' under the Coalition: that it isn't realistic to expect to retain spending on services without some increases in revenue. It's just a matter of who pays. Chalmers' own language pointed to modest savings: 'trim' spending on 'contractors, consultants and labour hire'. Just as importantly, while there may be good reason to bring this capacity back into the public sector, the cost will offset any savings and rebuilding will take time.

Morrison returned to Tasmania on 29 April, tasting some whisky early in the morning while promising funding for a distillery in the seat of Lyons. 'Wow, it's going to be a good day,' he said in response to a warning that the booze was 63 per cent ABV. Moving, inevitably, to Bass, he announced another $70 million hydrogen hub, this time for Bell Bay. The Coalition pledged to cut PBS medicines by $10. Labor suggested that Morrison was getting in ahead of its plans to do something similar. In one day, the PM traversed four of Tasmania's five lower-house seats. Journalists wanted to know about the price of lettuce, which had become emblematic of the soaring inflation rate. 'On every shelf in every shop in every suburb is a reminder of Scott Morrison's cost of living crisis,' Chalmers noted.

As news organisations revealed just how much money the Coalition was promising to marginal seats, the government tried to make the distinction between investment — 'Australia capital' was the formulation used by the Nationals' David Littleproud — and recurrent spending. This line of argument was weakened by the reluctance of the government to use its own resources to test the business case of most of the pork-barrelling prior to their announcements.

The day he escaped isolation, Albanese failed to join a scheduled media conference before heading to Perth — instead, releasing a video of himself playing with his dog at the local park. The footage had to be replaced because Albanese's mobile number was visible on Toto's collar.

Week three of the campaign ended with the Opposition Leader doing some pre-campaign launch events in WA. The media plane was delayed in Adelaide with a mechanical fault. They needed to switch planes, the press pack getting into Perth late Friday night and rather angry. Fresh out of iso, and having flown into Perth separately earlier on the Friday afternoon, Albanese held an event in a bus depot on the Saturday to announce a $250 million commitment in conjunction with the WA state government to build more electric buses. Shorten announced funding for Labor's long-foreshadowed Royal Commission into Robodebt, and joked with journalists about his low profile on the campaign trail. Albanese also joined Anne Aly, MP for Cowan, in her electorate later that day. He looked cool in sunnies, chinos and shirt without a tie as he sizzled some democracy sausages at a community barbeque and posed for selfies. With the biggest moment of his political life less than a day away, he was taking it all in his stride.

Chapter 8

Week 4: Ready to launch

It was the night before the Labor launch and all through the Hilton in Perth it was anything but quiet. The Labor Party arranged drinks for the assembled media pack and for the Labor shadow ministers who had flown in to accompany Anthony Albanese the following morning. Keneally, Clare and Wong led the way, chatting freely with those who had been following and heckling the Opposition Leader for weeks. The various television and print political editors flew in separately from the traveling media pack. Missing the campaign launches was not an option. The veneer of friendship abounded, but there was no Albo in sight. He was preparing for his most important moment of the campaign: his speech the next day, Sunday 1 May, at Optus Stadium, proclaiming the need for a Labor government. There was no strategy meeting scheduled for the afternoon of the launch because when it was over most participants were catching planes.

The launch had been set down for Perth more than a year earlier when Labor's brains trust sat down to plan what it hoped would be a winning campaign. 'I had come up with doing it in Perth when we were war-gaming for an October 2021 election,' Albanese recalled. Some were worried about the cost and logistics. Albanese had identified Western Australia as important even prior to McGowan's landslide. 'I felt that it would have cut-through in WA, that it would really draw their attention and it did. Doing it at Optus Stadium was the iconic venue. You feel like you're out of the bubble, out of the norm.'

'We had the opportunity to ask voters, do you think this is as good as it gets and if the answer is no then think about voting Labor. That was what the launch was all about,' Erickson reflected. This wasn't the first election at which high hopes existed for a return to equilibrium in the west. Three years earlier, Bill Shorten had been hopeful on election night that close seats on the east coast coupled with a WA landslide could save his prime ministerial dream. It wasn't to be. Albanese was leaving nothing to chance. This was the first major party launch in the west. But the Opposition Leader was still feeling the after-effects of COVID. 'Sometimes I felt fine but when I did the campaign launch in Perth I was still a bit ordinary so I was doing hydrolytes,' he recalled for us.

The pitch

Perhaps surprisingly, Erickson had never been to a campaign launch. As an organiser he was always the guy who stayed back at CHQ keeping things ticking along. Albanese was 'super interested' in the launch. Yes, it's the baby of the national secretary, but Albo was invested. He had been thinking about the launch for a solid eighteen months. It was earlier in the campaign than usual, partly to take advantage of early postal voting, which Erickson was cognisant was being increasingly used by voters, as was pre-poll voting — he liked the idea of getting the launch done a week before postal votes opened so the glow of the launch could permeate for a few days before people started voting. Albanese agreed. 'The whole event really told the story about the case for change, allowing Anthony to stand up and give his policy speech about how things would be different under us,' Erickson says. 'We were really happy with it. It's rare for a launch to be as pivotal to a campaign as the 2022 launch was. Campaign launches are always important, but this one was more than ever. Not by design but because of Anthony being sick it was genuinely the moment we had to re-launch our campaign.'

As well as running through the familiar roll call of premiers and former prime ministers, Albanese at the launch gave a prominent role to the candidate for Swan, Zaneta Mascarenhas. Mascarenhas embodied one of Labor's dilemmas — in that she had both worked in the mining industry and led climate action. She was a neat contrast with her Liberal opponent, Kristy McSweeney, a regular on *Sky After Dark*.

Penny Wong gave a warm tribute to Albanese. 'The most steadfast of friends. The toughest of fighters. And the kindest of hearts.' Some in the audience not on the list of friends of the next prime minister wondered which of those qualities they would face in the scramble for jobs after the election. Wong also highlighted her leader's 'compassion and integrity'. It was the right time for an opposition leader with those strengths, so lacking in the government but so often found in the qualities of the second-place runners in Australian politics. As journalist Katharine Murphy wrote in response to Albanese's speech, his lack of the hallmarks of toxic masculinity may signal a different style of politics.

Jason Clare's status as a potential star of a Labor government was confirmed with his speech attacking the Prime Minister, although his best lines had already been used during the time when he had stepped into Albanese's absence from the campaign trail. It was telling just how many apt one-liners such as Clare's 'all tinsel no tree' Morrison had collected in just four years as prime minister. Interviewers had started picking up on the theme, meeting any evasion from Morrison with the 'not your job?' line.

The video preview for the leader was voiced by Russell Crowe — lined up personally by Albanese with his fellow South Sydney supporter and kept secret even inside the campaign so as not to leak. 'I was at the Souths–St George game just after the budget. I said, "Mate, do you reckon you could do us a favour?"' Albanese recalled. He told Erickson about Crowe — asking him and Madigan to come up with the rough script before sending it to Albanese to play with, then he sent it on to Crowe. Crowe didn't want to do an ad, but would do this for his fellow South Sydney man. 'I sent him the draft when he was shooting outside London. He played around with it, had suggestions.' This was while Albanese was in isolation. 'We had to work out how to get the sound file back. We didn't want it to be the story.' The Crowe video was part of the positive pitch, but it also hit some negative notes, targeting Coalition failures. Running a minute long it wasn't used in broadcast advertising, as requested by Crowe, but the social and digital teams certainly pushed it online. Introduced by McGowan, Albanese climbed to the stage with GANGgajang's 'Sounds of Then' in the background — a song more bittersweet than its alternate title 'This is Australia' suggests, which is what the campaign wanted picked up by broadcasters.

The speech was delivered in the now practised Albo style, with passion if not eloquence. Asked if he was nervous at the beginning he said, 'I probably was. It was a big deal! I was two days out of iso. I was not one hundred per cent.' The headline rhetoric — 'you can vote for a better future' — masked as much as it revealed. This was underlined by the modest policy announcements saved for the campaign launch. The centrepiece of his speech — a policy pledge to help low- and middle-income earners buy a home through shared equity, had been fed to media on the Saturday. 'A plan that puts more Australians onto the path to the life that they dream about,' Albanese enthused. Well, 10,000 more Australians at most. Once again, the small-target platform was designed to maximise the contrast with the government. 'Today I announce that Labor will make gender pay equity an objective of the *Fair Work Act*,' he said to loud applause. He also trumped Morrison's announcement on the PBS, promising a larger cut in prices than the government's.

Even Albanese's supporters had their doubts that their man had the discipline to build the Labor narrative recommended by the 2019 campaign review. After a faltering start to the campaign, he was finding the right lines to balance his limited number of specific commitments with the 'vibe' that a Labor government would actually improve things in its signature areas. His speechwriters needed words to paper over the lack of policy change he was foreshadowing: 'dignity and respect' when it comes to aged care. This was buttressed by a line of argument he began in the first debate: that only Labor makes the big reforms and an Albanese government could be trusted to bring the principles of universal, affordable and quality service to childcare and to aged care.

Reluctant to guarantee spending levels or rule out cuts, Albanese stuck with a formula to situate Labor between the government and the minor parties: 'Labor will always be better on health, education and NDIS' had been a common refrain on social media. He drew some more points of contrast over principles:

Vote for an Australia that recognises the privilege of sharing our vast continent with the oldest continuous culture on earth. Vote for a country that celebrates our success as a multicultural nation. Vote for an Australia that believes the doors of opportunity should be open to every Australian, no matter where you live, who you pray to or who you love.

Words that shouldn't be controversial yet would not cross Morrison's lips. Then, the contrast more directly with the Prime Minister: 'Vote for hope and optimism over fear and division.'

Making a virtue of his strategy, Albanese said he wanted to 'under-promise and over-deliver'. He got the under-promising part right. Then came the lines that revealed how confident Labor was becoming that this line of attack was resonating strongly in the electorate: 'I think people know all about Scott Morrison, they have worked him out … we cannot bet our future on three more years of a prime minister who looks at every challenge facing our country and says, "That is not my job."' There are many moments from a campaign that help build momentum towards a win. 'That was one of them,' Albanese told us.

With the published polls indicating that Labor's lead was steady at 6 to 8 per cent of the two-party preferred indicator, there was an air of confidence among spokespeople in the days following the launch. Yet, even with Newspoll at 53–47 to Labor, there would still be a danger of minority government. Such is the attention on each side's launch that the day's national media attention is usually forfeited to the other side, the Coalition concentrating on local events in each seat. In Sydney, Dave Sharma won what would be his only gold medal of the campaign — a ten-kilometre fun run as a fundraiser for the Women's and Girls' Emergency Centre at Centennial Park. He is an avid runner known to clock four-minute kilometres on long runs. Not bad, although Liberal insiders wished he'd put such energy to good use with more doorknocking during the campaign.

Josh Frydenberg joined a thousand supporters by the banks of the Yarra, describing himself as the underdog in his battle to retain Kooyong. Frydenberg's calm, measured manner is useful in a treasurer, not so much for a local MP under threat from an insurgent independent. He told the story of opponent Monique

Ryan's mother-in-law privately declaring to the Treasurer that she would be voting for him because he is a nice young man. Putting that label to the test he outed the conversation to crowd laughter, only to see the yarn backfire in the coming days as he was accused of picking on an elderly lady and not respecting her right to privacy as family of a political candidate. Frydenberg refused to apologise. Many voters would have sympathised with an in-law not always coming to one's defence.

Ryan drew the top spot on the ballot. In a sign that he realised the depth of his predicament, Frydenberg agreed to debate her in the electorate. This was a no-win situation for the Treasurer. He was either seen to be running away from a contest or he raised his opponent's profile in a forum in which she would — and did — perform perfectly well. Not needing to dumb down her rhetoric, Ryan condemned 'the toxic miasma of division' that was the Morrison government. Guide Dogs Victoria was forced to launch an investigation after its CEO, Karen Hayes, endorsed the Treasurer in campaign material distributed as part of Frydenberg's bid to save his seat, which featured prominent Melburnians supporting him. From New York, Turnbull, the former Member for Wentworth — Sharma's electorate — would not confirm he was going to vote for the Liberals, saying he understood the appeal of the teals. There were inevitable calls for him to quit the party or be kicked out. It was a distraction for the Liberals. Some Liberals seem to pride themselves on forcing dissident former prime ministers out of the party.

Albanese flew out of Perth almost immediately after the launch, heading to Brisbane to attend a Labour Day rally.

It included various loud union demands being yelled by the crowd, but not during Albanese's speech. That didn't stop Liberal 'spies' taking their own video footage from other sections of the march featuring signs such as 'Smash Capitalism' for the PMO to send out to any media takers to run, which Network Ten did. Albanese spent his media conference highlighting the various housing industry associations supporting Labor's home equity scheme.

Morrison started the week in Parramatta. He received mixed reviews for his appearance at Eid prayers marking the end of Ramadan. 'Australia is like a rope with many different strands that weave together to make it incredibly strong,' he said in his speech.

'All the dogs are here for their bones,' one of the locals told *The Guardian*, although there were other possible retorts to Morrison's rope metaphor. Kevin Rudd also breezed into Parramatta to support the Labor candidate, his one-time economic adviser, Andrew Charlton. Morrison's attack on Labor's housing policy — 'Labor wants the government to own your home' — was as unsurprising as it was hypocritical. When he was shadow housing minister he had promoted a private sector version of shared equity that had been developed by the Menzies Research Centre, a Liberal think tank. Morrison emphasised the difference between a private and a public scheme, but the core critique of shared equity — that the homeowner misses out on a big chunk of the capital gain — is the same.

Albanese promoted his housing policy in Gosford with the candidates for Dobell and Robertson, also dropping into a pharmacy to promote Labor's promise for cheaper pharmaceuticals. The Central Coast is a mix of retirees and young couples seeking relief from Sydney housing prices. Questions from journalists about the home equity policy centred on whether it would have an impact on prices, paying the opposition the compliment that the measure was large enough to affect the broader market.

In the Victorian seat of Corangamite, Morrison announced plans to extend Seniors Health Card eligibility to 50,000 more elderly people, as he also searched for votes in retiree-rich seats. 'They want that independence they've worked hard for,' he said. Passive welfare to some is well-earned independence to others. Labor quickly pledged to match the expansion, one of the benefits of debt no longer mattering. Morrison appeared to be readying the ground for the announcement of an interest rate rise, telling anyone still listening that it was 'not about me'. And he had some advice for reporters: 'I mean, sometimes you guys always see things through a totally political lens. I don't. And Australians don't.'

Triple whammy

On 3 May, the Reserve Bank raised interest rates for the first time in over a decade and for the first time during an election campaign since 2007. It brought cost of living issues centre stage. 'It became an election-defining issue and it was to our benefit because of the really strong arguments the front bench had developed,' Erickson told us. The government feared the timing of the rate rise, but hoped that the issue would at least return the economy to the forefront of the campaign. Morrison visited a supermarket in Dunkley, photographed next to some of those expensive lettuces, dismissing journalists' claims that he likes taking credit for good economic news but not the tough stuff. Chalmers highlighted the 'triple whammy' of interest rates, inflation and dismal wages growth. 'This is a full-blown cost-of-living crisis on Scott Morrison's watch and now interest rate rises are about to be part of the pain,' he said. Albanese outlined the range of policies Labor would use to deal with inflation: 'Cheaper childcare, cheaper electricity prices, investing in new industries, making sure that we have our National Reconstruction, … new energy apprenticeships, … additional university places.' As Erickson told us, 'We felt comfortable going into that debate.'

Moving on to Adelaide, the Prime Minister argued that the Reserve Bank needed to raise rates because the economy was so strong. He described his government as a 'shield' against global economic threats, launching a slew of metaphors on social media — some complimentary, some not. The line had tested well in focus groups the weekend before. This was part of a shift of tactics during the campaign to accept that economic times were difficult and that Australia had fared better emerging from the pandemic than many comparable countries. The 'shield' metaphor would be part of Morrison's armoury right up to election day. In Boothby, he announced a freeze on the deeming rate on savings affecting social security payments to help with the cost of living. 'The big challenge for us was framing the debate about the economy in terms of kitchen table economics,' Erickson notes.

The Australian had reported that Plibersek would join Albanese on the campaign trail that week for the first time. The education spokesperson wasn't at the launch on Sunday, instead launching her own campaign in her electorate of Sydney that same day. Despite claims there was no issue between the pair, insiders knew better. Holding back this encounter until the fourth week only guaranteed it would become more of a distraction. At the much-anticipated event in Melbourne, where there was more smiling and nodding than seems natural in normal human interaction, the two sat down for coffee with candidate Carina Garland and hand-picked locals in Chisholm to talk education. There were no questions on education from the press, though. 'Have you been shafted from the official Labor election campaign?' Sky's Julia Bradley wanted to know, 'And is your appearance here today an effort to put those rumours to bed?' Tellingly, Albanese thought this was pretty funny. Plibersek showed good grace, explaining with a smile that she had been all over the country campaigning for a Labor win. Just not with the alternative prime minister.

On 4 May, at the National Press Club debate between the Treasurer and his shadow, neither man was able to say how they would address the structural budget deficit. Frydenberg either didn't hear or just ignored the question. 'We're prepared to say we will continue to cut taxes. The Labor Party will never say that,' was his response. Chalmers was no more forthcoming: 'What we need to be able to do is to flick the switch in the budget not to austerity but to quality,' he explained, 'so we can fund the things that we care the most about.' Pressed by journalists on whether there were more substantial savings to be found, Frydenberg and his shadow found themselves on a unity ticket where the Commonwealth oversees council responsibilities like dog parks, provided they are in marginal seats. The best Chalmers could offer was 'maximum bang for buck' (or should that be 'bark'?). The biggest blow landed in the debate was Chalmers telling Frydenberg the Treasurer was living in the past for trying to lay into his shadow for supporting tax increases at the 2019 campaign. Let bygones be bygones.

Morrison had re-announced its 'lower tax guarantee', a pointless policy designed purely to focus attention on economic management. Committing to a tax-to-GDP ratio of no higher than 23.9 per cent (the 0.9 is a nice touch) when spending is already much higher, means that structural deficits will be a fact of life until spending comes down. However, Australians don't want spending cuts — quite the opposite when it comes to areas such as aged care and childcare. Tellingly, there was no tax reform to go with the guarantee. Australia needs a serious debate about the future of the tax system given that both sides are foreshadowing higher spending.

The announcement was accompanied by a glossy brochure, with the headline on the cover: 'Lower Taxes'. It was an example of the impoverished nature of the debate about the economy under the Coalition. If it were to be taken seriously, it would be a recipe for endless budget deficits. Fortunately, few took it seriously, which is a pity since while the debate about taxation levels gave Chalmers some easy marks about just which side of politics taxes the highest, he and his leader were not drawn into a more extensive debate about size of government. Chalmers would have none of the government's claims to be the party of low tax. He was withering during the debate with Frydenberg.

'In the history of this nation, that tax cap has been breached four times,' he said. 'Every single time it was a Liberal government. Every single time. No Labor government has got anywhere near breaching the current tax-to-GDP cap. Let's have some facts about this on the table. This government is the second highest taxing government of the last thirty years, and the highest taxing was John Howard's. So enough of this rubbish about tax.' As we have seen, though, Labor struggles with the ideological and policy consequences of this sort of rhetoric. Shouldn't a Labor government responsible for fixing everything from childcare to aged care aspire to smash that purely artificial cap? This is not a debate they will be able to avoid in office.

In an interview with the *Sydney Morning Herald*, Morrison doubled down on his 'kangaroo court' criticism of the NSW Independent Commission Against Corruption, which had been touted as a model for a federal integrity commission. 'I am trying to prevent a massive mistake,' he said. Australia could become a 'public autocracy' with 'faceless officials'. Surely it was better to say nothing on the issue at this point other than that Labor hadn't supported the bill? His comments were pointedly rejected by Perrottet. Pressed to match his prime minister's description, Frydenberg demurred. 'I would use different words,' he said. ICAC commissioner Stephen Rushton described those who labelled the commission as a kangaroo court 'buffoons'. His more measured words were largely overlooked: 'To make an uninformed comment that this commission is a kangaroo court has a real capacity to undermine the commission's work, and just as importantly, public confidence in public administration.'

Albanese dodged questions about whether it was appropriate for politicians to appear in secret at corruption commissions, while standing next to Dan Andrews, suggesting that such bodies should not take directions from politicians and avoiding the question of what his legislation might require. It was an awkward moment, given that Andrews would soon be giving evidence behind closed doors to Victoria's Independent Broad-based Anti-corruption Commission.

Gotcha covered

Albanese attended a clean energy conference in Sydney before appearing on *Q+A*. At his presser on Thursday 5 May, he was asked by Nine's Jonathan Kearsley what the six points of Labor's NDIS plan were. With a knowing smile, Albanese started to talk about the policy generally without addressing the question. Kearsley interrupted to ask about the six points, growing louder in his insistence as Albanese ploughed on. Other journalists piled on. Albanese reached for his notes. Journalists asked why he needed to refer to notes. In *The Guardian*, veteran campaign correspondent Malcolm Farr called this 'rudeness journalism', something that captured the occasional intensity of the journos following the leaders when they hunted as a pack. Albanese had been nowhere to be seen when Shorten launched Labor's NDIS policy a fortnight earlier. In fact, with no support from the campaign, Shorten had to do his own ring-around to get attention. Given what was to come for the leader, this sign of a disconnect between the campaign and a shadow minister in a vital area looked like a case of taking personal animosity too far.

Journalists demanding that the Opposition Leader elaborate on his six points was more defensible, given that it had been Albanese who first mentioned it, than the newsreaders dutifully reading from their teleprompters the shocking story that a politician needed to speak from notes. And the extent to which the whole story was amplified by the usual newspapers suggested that the fairly substantial two weeks of debate after Albanese's isolation had been too much substance for some. Morrison's confusion of daily and fortnightly rates of JobSeeker payments had been widely reported but quickly lost in the news cycle. The NDIS exchange coincided with the Coalition making their personal criticism of Labor and the independents, clearly frustrated with their lack of inroads based on policy debate.

The NDIS 'gaffe' came on the same day Albanese delivered the economic speech he told us he'd used his time in isolation to pull together. But it was overshadowed by the coverage given to his inability to recite the six NDIS points. The NDIS incident clearly bugged Albanese, who accused reporters the next day of playing word games when asked whether colleagues were unimpressed with his knowledge of policy detail. Showing less irritation with this kind of treatment was one of the things Albanese had worked on since becoming leader. 'Let me tell you what the NDIS is about,' he thundered. 'It is not about gotcha questions.' He launched into a passionate defence of the NDIS based on the experience of his disabled mother. It was authentic Albo.

Albanese dropped into Labor CHQ that afternoon to do some filming for new ads for the campaign. He chatted to everyone, personally thanking them for their work. 'In campaigns things will happen, there will be mistakes, there has never been a mistake-free campaign,' Erickson told us. 'It is how you respond to them, not keeping a scoreboard. He put in a really strong performance the next day, showing he wasn't going to be rattled.' The ads cut on the Friday were the last positive ones for the campaign — making the point Albanese didn't want Australia to miss out on big opportunities, and only a change of government would ensure that. Investing in renewables, local manufacturing and creating more jobs was the theme. 'It was his best performance in an ad,' Erickson claims. Albanese missed the Souths game against the Broncos to make it to the ABC studio for his *Q+A* appearance. Host David Speers was roundly criticised on Twitter, including by Rudd, for — wait for it — interrupting a politician. Albanese did fine. At this point, he had a talking point for every conceivable question and was experienced enough to adapt them to the format. Why supporters thought they needed to work the ref when the candidate was performing well was a mystery.

The Prime Minister was also in Sydney, making another visit to Parramatta to sell his five-year plan to bring down overhead costs for small businesses. 'You can't run the economy like Harry Potter,' he said, seemingly not noticing the magical qualities in his claim that the vacuous policy would 'help create business conditions' to support 400,000 new enterprises. Morrison then returned to Western Australia to announce support for training in the defence manufacturing and technology sector. At a business lunch, he put his faith in the mining sector to provide the innovation necessary to cut greenhouse gas emissions. 'Australia has a major opportunity to crack this technology and be the energy and technology exporter into the world,' he said. The next day, trying to defend the seat of Hasluck, he promised more tourism dollars for WA while tasting wine in the Swan Valley.

Labor's internal polling showed they were competitive in Tasmania but not set to pick up seats. Albanese headed to Bass, where his task was made more difficult by the Jacqui Lambie Network, which announced it was directing preferences to Bridget Archer. *The Australian* splashed with a story about Labor running up an extra $10 billion of debt across the forward estimates. In a sign of how hard it was for the Coalition to campaign on the risk Labor poses to debt and deficits, with total government debt projected to hit $1 trillion in the coming years, it just didn't resonate with voters as an attack. Albanese denied the report, but when Labor released its costings in the final week of the campaign, the figure wasn't far off. Morrison fought hard to claim more debt puts more pressure on inflation and interest rates, but given his debt-fuelled budgets that was weak tea. Chalmers said Labor would unveil a second budget for the year, in October, to recalibrate spending priorities. *The Australian* tried again a few days later, with a front-page claim that Labor's off-budget spending plans would see national debt 'balloon' by $52 billion to pay for its climate change and housing policies. The story claimed it would also add $3 billion to the interest bill. The article, by political editor Simon Benson, quoted

Finance Minister Simon Birmingham condemning Labor, and it had comments from Albanese defending himself and a campaign spokesperson saying they wouldn't take lectures from a wasteful government. But the story had no source for its analysis, leaving readers to assume it must have been done in-house by the government or the paper.

Outflanked

Frydenberg was required to spend more and more time defending his electorate instead of helping to sandbag similar seats under threat from independents, as well as holding press conferences in response to major economic news and policy announcements. He took the risk of joining in the attacks on his opponent that had been left to staffers. Frydenberg looked spent halfway through the campaign. It was a reminder that, if nothing else, Morrison brings tremendous energy to campaigning. 'Keep Josh' became the main slogan in Kooyong, plastered in every vacant shop window. It's rather difficult for a treasurer to differentiate himself from his own government.

In nearby Goldstein, public polling showed Tim Wilson tied on the primary vote with Zoe Daniel, which would see him tipped out of parliament. The campaign was exposing the fact that the Liberal MPs in safe seats were not experienced grass roots campaigners. Wilson had made a career out of showy adversarialism — not the right approach to take on an eminently reasonable journalist like Daniel. *Crikey*'s Guy Rundle noted Wilson's 'gamut of emotions appears to run from the perfunctory to the insincere to the dismissive and contemptuous'.

Polls can become self-fulfilling. In the case of Allegra Spender, the candidate in Wentworth, they landed her a coveted spot on *Insiders*. A high profile was vital also to remind potential swing voters that Labor needed to run third for an independent to win. Journalists sometimes struggled to get hold of the Labor candidates in these seats. The teal campaign also naturally attracted some fire, most notably from News — *The Australian*'s Paul Kelly accusing them of dishonesty in the way they present themselves as independents. Conservative interests could live with a small-target Labor government. A hung parliament not so much. Some of the criticism of the teal independents was counterproductive. 'They're not independents, they're anti-Liberal groupies,' John Howard told a friendly crowd in Sydney, in a clear reference to Holmes à Court's role.

Simon Holmes à Court thought the teals had a secret weapon. 'I've heard people say this before but now I absolutely see how the Murdoch media is the PR arm of the Liberal Party,' he told *Crikey* after the campaign. 'There were stories that were definitely fed to them by Andrew Bragg and Jason Falinski that they would magnify with innuendo and bullshit. Then it would be printed and within seconds the MPs would tweet the articles out again and that would be turned into a derivative story on Sky, but stripped of any of the context.' Holmes à Court said the News attacks would always cause a spike in donations to Climate 200.

Not all parties showed their wares on familiar advertising venues. The Brisbane Greens candidate Stephen Bates promoted his campaign on the gay dating app Grindr. Facebook allows geographic targeting, ideal for the independent candidates, who spent the lion's share of their budgets on that platform. It is also one of the most cost-effective platforms for the minor parties trying to jag a Senate spot. United Australia Party's millions were spread fairly widely, its extensive Google spend pushing ads onto familiar platforms like YouTube but also to in-game ads. While social media allows greater demographic targeting, effectiveness depends a lot on understanding how each demographic uses the platform. The Greens had some success on TikTok. The major parties less so. Morrison's accounts do not allow comments. Some platforms banned political advertising after the Cambridge Analytica scandal. Breakout success on Instagram or TikTok requires a kind of naturalism that is the antithesis of politics. Unless posts are widely shared, social media accounts simply bounce around within their networks, which isn't really campaigning at all. That energy would be better off spent on more targeted promotion. Indeed, social media works better organically, when users spontaneously share content. For example, TikTok account *Gen Z for Albo* had gained 2.9 million likes by the end of the campaign, slightly more than the official ALP account, and with a presence on Instagram and Twitter as well. One of the most popular posts adapted a meme featuring British actress Miriam Margolyes in a swimsuit, swearing profusely. Superimposed is the text, 'Labor getting into govt and seeing the mess tht Scott Morrison left [sic]'. Not something an ad agency would recommend but effective on social media nonetheless.

Social media outreach is one area where the major parties lose out in replacing mass party membership with the party machine. Professionalised politics was effective during the mass media era. Using broadcast methods on social media is much less effective. It is widely understood that the major parties have fewer 'rusted-on' voters, giving greater space to minor parties and independents. Within this overall trend of declining party identification, though, is an even sharper downward trend in strong supporters. These are the activists who will endure branch meetings, hand out how-to-vote cards, or, if they are young and talented enough, create viral TikTok videos. Labor reportedly hired a consultancy firm to pay for good social media posts, but this approach is unlikely to uncover the right sort of content. Instead, it's left to the parties themselves to come up with lame videos of leaders with their dogs or their latest culinary creation, or simply repeating their focus-group-tested lines. Liberal Senator Jane Hume made an Instagram video post in which she touted the government's economic record, then, after a suspicious edit, walked up to a golf tee and hit a nice drive in her heels. Lame, certainly, but widely shared. We were treated to a live comparison between the way Twitter covered the war in Ukraine and the election campaign. Coverage of the war served up lengthy high-quality analysis of the fast-moving events, ideal for the platform. Election Twitter threw up more in the way of third-rate media criticism than policy analysis.

The Coalition campaign was becoming increasingly frank about Morrison being the main issue in the election. The election 'is not a popularity contest' the PM told Channel Seven's *Sunrise* and sundry other media outlets. He was struggling to control the agenda, still receiving questions about the status of Tudge and what had gone wrong with the Solomon Islands relationship. The pandemic all but disappeared from the issue agenda in spite of the daily double-digit death toll, and Australia at one point having the highest level of cumulative cases per capita in the OECD. Yet getting through the pandemic remained central to Morrison's pitch. Labor promised a royal commission into the handling of the pandemic. On issue after issue, Morrison followed his instinct to double down. A misinterpretation of John Howard winning success through strong leadership was on show. Howard could back-flip with the best of them — not least in the lead-up to an election — if the politics demanded it. Morrison, instead, proved himself a one-trick pony.

Albanese encouraged voters to deny the Coalition a fourth term. Such longevity, he said, never ends well. 'Nothing good happens in a fourth term of government.' This didn't pay a lot of respect to Paul Keating's only full term as prime minister, during which Albanese mounted his first campaign for his seat. When Albanese made a similar suggestion in 2019, Keating had sent a detailed rebuttal to *The Australian*'s Troy Bramston.

Despite the NDIS hiccup, the week was a momentum builder for Labor. The party's research was suggesting voters were tiring of the media obsession with gotcha questions, which only helped Albo's growing confidence as he pushed back at media conferences. The leader was feeling good. He said of his visit to CHQ, 'I went into the campaign office one day and all these people who were friends, a dozen of them who had worked for me were there. I didn't even know they were volunteering. That motivated me.'

Chapter 9

Week 5: The bulldozer versus the builder

With less than two weeks until polling day, and early voting set to open, Coalition strategists were sweating on the bad news their focus groups and internal polling were telling them: the Prime Minister is unpopular and voters are inclined to throw him and the government out of office. What to do? Andrew Hirst knew he would need to brief the Prime Minister that a change in direction might be necessary. It was the only way to address the evidence coming through that the PM was seen as not listening to people and not able to respond to concerns in a nuanced way. The danger of a mid-campaign reset was that it might only draw attention to the problem. Julia Gillard's attempt to reintroduce herself to voters in 2010 as 'Real Julia', instead of the leader taking too much advice from PR flacks, was a debacle. Nevertheless, something had to change for Morrison. Newspoll published a gender breakdown of its

54–46 per cent result in favour of Labor, the largest of the campaign to that point. The primary vote among women was 45–38 per cent, with male voters evenly split. Morrison's lead as preferred prime minister, boosted by Albanese's poor start to the campaign, had all but disappeared. Focus groups were revealing that while Morrison was 'experienced' and good on the economy, swinging voters hadn't enjoyed their experience with him, using words like 'arrogant' and 'obnoxious'. Such descriptors are not fatal if voters think the arrogance brings results. But participants were still raising his performance during the bushfires unprompted. Labor was getting the same results, voters bringing up the bushfires and vaccine 'strollout' at every opportunity.

Morrison declared that he could and would change if re-elected. The idea was to do it late in the week ahead of the Liberal campaign launch on Sunday 15 May, less than a week out from the election. That way they hoped to send the message to undecided voters that Morrison was open to a different approach, but move on from that message quickly so that it didn't drag into the final week as a distraction. Ultimately it was a clumsily worded effort by Morrison and it came after the final two debates where the old Scott was on display.

Erickson started Labor's Sunday strategy meeting by pointing out that voting was opening the next day. Labor was starting to identify a different mix of people turning up in focus group samples — they were less engaged in politics, time poor, and didn't like Morrison. They were ready for a change of government, but still unsure about Labor. They had noticed the Labor launch and liked what they saw. Erickson let the team know that the 'that's not my job' ad Madigan had produced was biting. The previous day, the Liberals had launched their 'hole in my bucket, dear Labor' ad. It was clearly their final big attack in an advertising sense, Erickson told the team, and they were monitoring whether a response was necessary.

The big issue Labor expected to run all week was cost of living and wages, which indeed it did. The penultimate week of the campaign included two leaders' debates, on Channels Nine (Sunday 8 May) and Seven (Wednesday 11 May), where these issues took centre stage with a decent viewing audience.

Confidence player

Labor was continuing to build on the momentum of its early launch, with Albanese campaigning with renewed confidence. The media on his tail were still searching for their gotcha takedown. Mother's Day, 8 May, saw both parties pitch their policy announcements at women. Albanese talked about how important his mother was to him. She had gone to hospital on Mother's Day twenty years earlier, and never come home. Albanese spent the day in Sydney campaigning in Bennelong with an $11 million early childhood learning announcement.

The Coalition pledged $53 million towards IVF services, Morrison talking passionately about his family's difficult experience. Three years earlier, he launched his campaign on Mother's Day, with his mum on stage. This time she was treated to a trip to Victoria to help him work the marginals. Mums are always happy to help their sons, even on what is supposed to be their day. There weren't many questions for the PM on IVF. Instead, journalists wanted to know about how trans students would be protected under the *Religious Discrimination Act*, which Morrison had raised the previous day as a priority, underlining his intention to leave any changes to the *Sex Discrimination Act* for later on. Morrison denied there was any evidence of discrimination. 'Religious schools themselves don't wish to do that,' he claimed. Asked about this claim, Albanese was sceptical. 'If people don't think that young people are discriminated against and vilified because of their sexuality, then that does not reflect reality,' he said. Once again, Morrison was only bringing attention to divisions in his own party, with Katie Allen, who had crossed the floor earlier in the year, saying her position was unchanged.

Channel Nine's Sunday night debate was a messy spectacle. With Chalmers back in Brisbane for Mother's Day, Clare acted as Morrison during the debate prep for Labor. Chalmers returned for the third debate. The format in debate number two gave both leaders the chance to really get stuck into each other, but for the audience there wasn't much to be learned from prime ministerial contenders just talking over each other. It was a poor choice of staging for the two leaders, who detested each other as much as any pairing since Keating and Howard. It would have been more informative if Nine's political editor Chris Uhlmann got to moderate the affair and ask the questions all on his own, but he was one of a gaggle of journalists trying to extract information from the leaders as they continually interrupted one another. The contest did have considerable viewing reach, unlike the first one on Sky, with 1.2-million peak viewership on the main channel, with another 2 million spread across 9Now, YouTube, Facebook, Twitter and Nine's newspaper sites. Clare thought Morrison was over the top. 'All that try-hard bully-boy stuff might work in the Liberal Party, but didn't work last night,' he said. Asked whether Albanese was also overbearing, he was having none of it. 'When someone's trying to bully you or overpower you, you stand up to them,' Clare retorted.

Albanese received a rock-star welcome at his old school in central Sydney, St Mary's Cathedral School. When the school bell sounded, he quipped 'the bell tolls for the Morrison government'. His confidence was building. He took aim at the PM's comments the night before about whether people should be guaranteed to be paid the minimum wage. Morrison had hedged, pointing towards the complexity facing small business and the gig economy. It was a mirage to promise such workers a guaranteed wage rise, he argued. Albanese headed to Adelaide for the first time on the campaign trail, handing out how-to-vote cards at a pre-poll centre with South Australian Premier Peter Malinauskas. The Liberals refused to match a $400 million Labor pledge for Adelaide's Flinders Medical Centre, Finance Minister Simon Birmingham labeling it 'reckless spending'. In a sign of both policy and fiscal priorities, Morrison made another defence (re)announcement — $8 billion for new helicopters — in Gilmore, New South Wales, home to the Navy's air arm.

Happy to keep the focus on wages and living costs, Albanese said the minimum wage should rise to meet inflation. This became a major theme right up until the Liberals' launch. 'These are people who are earning $20.33 an hour,' Albanese said. 'We think no one should go backwards.' Asked if he would support a rise of 5.1 per cent — the latest inflation reading — to keep up with the cost of living, Albanese didn't hesitate. 'Absolutely,' he replied, allowing the journalist to put words in his mouth. Labor had avoided putting a number to its policy. 'We'd said that from day one of the campaign,' Albanese recalled. 'We were trying to work out how to get wages as a bigger issue. It lifted the mobilisation of our unions, challenging the government to support a real wage cut. It was great.' Labor MPs other than Albanese, Chalmers and Burke were surprised by the leader's comments. Burke and Chalmers were working on a submission for Fair Work Australia. With Albanese, they had talked about how to 'turbo-charge' the issue but weren't going to attach a number. As it turned out, a specific question from a journalist got a specific answer. Labor's messaging wasn't quite on the mark, Keneally stating that the 5.1 per cent figure was a 'misstatement' of what the Opposition Leader had said. She wasn't inside the tent on this issue, which hadn't been canvassed in the morning briefings she was party to.

Morrison played the skinflint, accusing Albanese of making policy on the run. 'It is like throwing fuel on the fire of rising interest rates and rising cost of living,' he said. Parsing of Albanese's position followed, with Labor pointing out that the Fair Work Commission would make the decision. This point cut both ways, though, since a Labor government could therefore not guarantee that real wages would not go backwards. It turned out the FWC ruled the minimum wage should be raised by even more — 5.2 per cent, in the election's aftermath. Campaigning in regional Queensland, Albanese held up a dollar coin to emphasise the modest hourly wage increase he was supporting for the lowest-paid workers. 'To voters struggling under cost of living pressures, it seemed reasonable,' Madigan argues. That's what Labor's focus groups were clearly showing. Team Albanese was confident the government had missed the political mark on this issue.

The Prime Minister accused the Opposition Leader of being a 'loose unit on the economy', another focus group line he'd been briefed on. Albanese retorted that Morrison is 'loose with the truth'. Labor made a TikTok video featuring the 'loose unit' line, showing that they thought it reflected poorly on the PM. Meanwhile, Indigenous Affairs Minister Ken Wyatt was talking about wages that were quite a bit higher than the minimum, reaffirming his view that MPs deserve a wage rise. They probably do, but timing is everything. No wonder he lost his seat.

Ten News obtained leaked internal Liberal Party polling that showed Liberals trailing in Bennelong, Roberston, Reid, Gilmore and Parramatta. Morrison's communications director Andrew Carswell was incensed, convinced Bragg was behind the leaks and aware that the senator had commissioned research from ReachTel. More leaked Liberal polling was to follow, this time out of Victoria. The New South Wales senator couldn't be blamed for that; now the PMO wondered if it was state divisions doing the leaking. The leak showed Goldstein, Kooyong and Higgins all in trouble. Every one of these seats mentioned was lost by the Coalition at the election.

Happy with his 'loose unit' line, Morrison used it in the final debate on Seven. This debate was a more orderly affair, making host Mark Riley as much a star as the two contestants. At the end of the debate, Riley asked the two leaders to say something complimentary about their opponent. Albanese pointed to Morrison's commitment to supporting mental health. Morrison said he admired the way Albanese never forgot where he comes from, but quickly pivoted to familiar criticisms of the Opposition Leader. He later claimed disingenuously that he may have misunderstood the question. Albanese won the Seven debate 'pub test' of undecided voters spread across marginal seats throughout the country. Scuttlebutt that the questions being asked in the debate were leaked was just that.

In Bass with Bridget Archer, the Prime Minister announced a $55 million mental health partnership with the Tasmanian government, a happy coincidence after the debate praise Albo chose for Morrison, but the positive angle on the mental health focus didn't last long for Morrison. Archer spoke movingly about her own struggle with anxiety. The previous day, Sky News's Chris Kenny had found Deves on the campaign trail in Warringah. Whereas her interview with SBS had been authorised, she wasn't supposed to talk to any other media. Perhaps dropping her guard with a friendly face, perhaps meeting Kenny and his cameraman on the campaign hustings was more than coincidental, she walked back her apology from prior to the campaign. 'I apologise for my language. I do not resile from my position,' she said. In case anyone was in doubt about that position, she had claimed 'mutilation' is the correct medical term. Journalists inevitably asked about the mental health of trans youth, testing whether Morrison and Archer would remain on the same page. Morrison emphasised his government's record on mental health funding. Archer was diplomatic. 'We could all do better,' she said. The spectre of Deves had already derailed Morrison's earlier announcements on online safety to protect children's mental health — the young journalists following the leaders were well versed in the high suicide rate of trans youth.

A Bass constituent and former diplomat tried to approach the PM to ask about the Solomon Islands at another of his tightly controlled events. The constituent was man-handled by security, prompting questions about whether the Prime Minister was being protected by taxpayer-funded goons from threats or from political embarrassment. To show that defence, not just foreign policy, was ripe for politicisation, Dutton labelled the presence of a Chinese spy ship off the Western Australian coast 'an aggressive act'. This was a new posture towards such on-water matters. 'They have every right to be there under international maritime law, just like we have every right to be in the South China Sea,' had been Morrison's response to a similar incident months earlier. In response, McGowan described Dutton as 'the biggest threat to national security'.

Reset take two

Labor advertising featuring Morrison's 'I don't hold a hose, mate' and 'that's not my job' lines were on high rotation. The tagline was 'No more mistakes, no more excuses, no more Morrison'. The Liberals took the unwise step of running online responses putting his comments in context to try to refute the ads, only drawing attention to the central charge, with the exchange featuring in news stories — free publicity for Labor's central theme, even though the 'job' quotations were indeed ripped out of their context. Hopefully, Labor's proposed truth in advertising laws will prevent such misleading Labor ads in future. There could be no clearer sign that Morrison was issue number one in the campaign.

The Prime Minister dropped his willingness to change into the middle of his daily press conference. 'As we go into this next period on the other side of this election, I know there are things that are going to have to change with the way I do things,' he said. It sounded like something a bloke says to save a relationship. He was mocked for it, but strategists had told him he needed to get some sort of message like that through. Morrison said it was not polling that led to his change of tack but listening to people all over the country. 'It's very important to be listening to Australians and I have done that all across my political career. And, you know, over the last three years and particularly the last two, what Australians have needed from me going through this pandemic has been strength and resilience.' He continued:

Now, I admit that hasn't enabled Australians to see a lot of other gears in the way I work. And I know Australians know that I can be a bit of a bulldozer when it comes to issues, and I suspect you guys know that too … You've got to be pretty determined to be able to land those sorts of things but that doesn't mean— Because as we go into this next period on the other side of this election, I know there are things that are going to have to change with the way I do things. Because we are moving into a different time.

He knew that Australians think he can be 'a bit of a bulldozer' because focus groups had said so. Looking on as the PM sought to use the research to maximum effect to rebrand his image, Coalition campaign headquarters thought he could have done so in a less ham-fisted way. He was basically reading straight from what the research showed rather than finessing the message. The attempted reset pretty neatly reflected what the problem was rather than becoming part of the solution.

Albanese was in Cairns at the time. 'I couldn't say it then but I thought, "They're cooked!" They had spent four weeks saying, "You know us, stick with us, stick with what you know," and then they said, two weeks out "Ignore all that, I'm going to be somebody else." They just walked away from their whole campaign.' The bulldozer reference 'just perfectly played into my space. He was going to be nice but it reminded everybody that he wasn't nice, that he wasn't a builder, that he was rude. It reinforced the perception that he couldn't be trusted.'

Erickson adds, 'It's never a good sign if you're having to change your message and direction with eight days to go. I could not have predicted that. We were watching it at CHQ and thought this was a real turning point. He was conceding that his personal style turned off a lot of voters. That's not the act of a campaign that thinks it's winning.'

The next day, 14 May, Morrison was still talking about changing instead of just … changing. He was asked about mistakes he had made as prime minister. It had the air of a valedictory speech instead of an election campaign:

My father, my brother and I, we go in and fix things. And sometimes … people can get the impression that perhaps we are not as aware of many of the sensitivities that can be around these issues. We see a crisis, we see a problem, we see a need. I know that sometimes that makes it look like I am just pressing on, but as a prime minister, you've got to get the stuff done. You've got to get the stuff done. I will seek to be and to explain my motives and my concerns and empathise a lot more, but I tell you what, at the end of the day, what matters most is that I get the job done.

Given there's some level of self-awareness on display here, we wonder whether, had Morrison made such an adjustment over some months instead of just announcing, a week out from polling day, that he would change, would the election have been closer? On the other hand, given the framing as something his wife told him, the lines seemed road-tested to appeal to the female demographic he had just spent a year alienating. As Chalmers quipped, 'Scott Morrison started this campaign saying people know who I am. It's only now that it's dawned on him that that's the problem.' There was one last chance for Morrison to change the momentum of the campaign in its dying days: the Coalition's official launch.

Privately, Albanese was contemptuous of Morrison's strategy. 'Using the template of 2019, bringing the budget forward, having the campaign launch six days out, it being about housing, doing the photo-ops during the campaign but no real policy substance, the ads about expenditure when you've got a trillion dollars of debt, even the use of my name like "the Bill you can't afford", it was like they were trying to recreate 2019 and the circumstances were totally different,' he told us. Madigan thought the 2019 ads were powerful because they tapped into voter dislike of Shorten and concerns over economic management. The 2022 'life won't be easy' version directed at Albanese, on the other hand, wrongly assumed Albanese was unpopular and only drew attention to the fact that life already wasn't easy under Morrison's prime ministership. 'Scott only dealt with the fire at his feet,' Morrison's closest friend in the parliament, Stuart Robert, told us. 'He couldn't project forward.' That was exactly where Labor's advertising strategy was hoping to lead voters to.

Albanese kept his confidence in check. 'It's hard for Labor to win from opposition,' he said, trying to avoid complacency. 'If you don't shape the future, the future will shape you,' he told us. 'And the future caught up with him.'

Chapter 10

Week 6: The future caught up with him

The Coalition campaign launch was set for Brisbane on the final Sunday of the campaign. Scott Morrison and Andrew Hirst were in agreement that just like the previous election they should launch in Brisbane, doing so with one week left to try and steal the momentum late. With the Liberals launching in Brisbane, Labor would have a rally there as well. Albanese didn't buy into the idea of Morrison as a great campaigner. 'He's very predictable. He has people around him who are good at lining up photo-ops if you weren't known for photo-ops, if it was seen as genuine. Once it was seen as opportunistic, it's value just dissipated completely and indeed it reinforced his negatives.' The Liberal Party's own polling suggested that power was slipping away. It would take a few days for public polling to register a bounce from the launch, so Hirst was desperate for any sign of momentum. Record numbers of Australians were voting early, though, to avoid exposing themselves to COVID. Some tightening was perhaps inevitable given the historical reluctance to give Labor the sort of majority that the mid-campaign polls were pointing towards.

At the beginning of the final week a Channel Nine poll had Labor ahead by just two points: 51–49. Essential was rumoured, wrongly as it turned out, to have a similar number. Hirst was hoping for a bandwagon effect from tighter public polling. He reminded colleagues of former Liberal pollster Mark Textor's advice that it's better to be an underdog than just a dog. But the track polling Liberals were looking at did not reflect the closeness of the Channel Nine poll. Nor did the Labor track.

'The whole way through the campaign, we were never behind. I've seen tracking polls before. I've never seen a track like this one whereby it was so consistent. I was in the zone by then,' Albanese told us. 'I had a plan to rev up, we were talking about wages, they were on the defensive about who they were. There was an argument within the campaign for me not to do so much media in the final week.' That didn't come from Erickson; it was a discussion among shadow ministers. While broadly very positive, the Labor track polling was jumping around like all track polling does. But Albanese didn't need to know that. He needed to keep his head in the game, and not be distracted by outlier results the data crunchers knew to be statistically meaningless.

Asked if his final push had been the difference between minority and majority government, Albanese says, 'Yeah, probably. We had to drive it home. The extraordinary thing was the discipline that we showed, the team. The trust that people showed in me.' By the final week the public were largely over the election. Morrison had not helped his cause with the bulldozer rhetoric. While Albanese probably overestimates the extent to which voters were hanging off his every word late in the campaign, he's right that the sense of teamwork and a consistent message stayed strong to the end.

Labor's final Sunday strategy meeting wasn't held until 8.30 p.m. in the evening, later than the usual Sunday sessions because of the rally in Brisbane designed to counter the formal Coalition launch. The Coalition had briefed the media that the theme would be housing, but it held back the sizzle — the use of superannuation to help first homebuyers to get into the market. Labor CHQ had a running joke about what to expect when the Liberals did their launch. They would say, expect it six days out with a housing announcement, same as at the last election. There was a theme developing that the government was looking for history to repeat, but that was hurting its ability to appeal to voters wanting a better future. Erickson and Labor President Wayne Swan discussed the morsels that had been thrown the media's way by the Liberals before the event kicked off. Swan said he expected super to be part of the main event. He was right. After Labor's event, Albanese flew straight to Perth. Those not in the air yet realised they needed to respond to the Coalition's proposal. Clare and Chalmers worked out the response to the policy, and Clare did the presser.

Erickson's focus was on pre-poll and postal voting. Three million Australians had already voted as of Saturday, two million via pre-poll, one million with postal ballots. Labor's track polling had asked participants whether they had already voted. It found that older voters, Labor voters and people in the capital cities were predominant. The people who hadn't voted yet were disproportionately younger outer suburban voters, and more likely to be women. Clare said on the call, 'It's not a surprise Morrison did super for housing in the last week then. They have an offer for people who haven't voted and haven't made up their minds yet.' In his post-election National Press Club address, Erickson talked about two types of voters: those up for a change of government, who Labor needed to keep motivated, and risk-adverse voters who are tired of politics. This second grouping was discussed on the strategy call. The focus of the last week needed to target them with the message that the last thing they needed was three more years of Morrison. '"Nothing will change if you vote him back in, because he won't change," that's the message,' Erickson said. Neither Erickson nor Albanese noted that Julia Gillard would be joining the campaign in Boothby in South Australia on the final Friday. They were keeping that up their sleeves.

Last chance express

Albanese again fronted an ABC program that Morrison had dodged, this time *Insiders*, and talked up an Indigenous Voice to Parliament. 'All they're asking for,' he explained, 'is a bit of politeness, basically, good manners. It says that if you have an issue that affects directly the health, education, housing, lives of First Nations people, you should consult them.' The Labor leader had revealed himself as a confidence player, clearly enjoying the campaign more as the polls stabilised in his favour.

Outwardly, though, he would only concede that Labor was competitive. His refrain that Labor had a 'mountain to climb' was as much about keeping himself focused as it was about managing expectations.

The psychological effects of a successful launch, then, were just as important as the policies to be announced or the media coverage. The timing of most campaign events was a mystery even to the travelling journalists. The Liberal launch was an exception, allowing a hundred or so protestors to make their presence felt outside the Brisbane Convention Centre. 'Raving banshees,' Joyce called them. Joyce and Frydenberg attacked Labor and their policies. 'You change the government, you change the economy,' the Treasurer claimed in a weak echo of Paul Keating.

Morrison started his speech with a reminder of just how hard things had been. 'It has been one of the most challenging times we have ever known,' he said. 'I had one focus as your prime minister — to save the country.' But the launch was always going to be a celebration of Scott Morrison's Australia. 'On almost every measure — growth, jobs, debt levels, mortality rates, vaccine rates, Australia's recovery is leading the advanced world,' he asserted again, even though these claims had been shown to be exaggerated. 'Nothing fires me up more than seeing young Australians getting jobs. Nothing.' Again, Morrison sounded like he was on a lap of honour instead of closing the deal with voters. 'I never leave anything on the field,' he said. 'It's a great privilege to serve in this role. It's the great professional privilege of my life.' A strong sense of nationalism dominated the speech; he tried to strike a balance between claiming success for his government in 'building a bridge' over global troubles and crediting Australians for their tenacity. He again said the government were not 'loose units' on the economy, an odd phrase to use in a formal speech but one that was obviously testing well. The crowd liked it. 'Three more years, three more years,' they chanted. 'Let's not turn back now,' the PM finished. Launches so late in the campaign have long been an oddity, but this was exactly what the Prime Minister needed to catapult the entire team into the final week.

On the policy front, there was something for the locals — a promise to build a new cancer treatment centre. The centrepiece of the launch was yet another policy likely to increase demand for housing. Up to 40 per cent of a superannuation account (with a cap of $50,000) could be used towards a deposit, with the money returned to the fund when the home is sold. Housing supply issues were dealt with through incentives for 'empty-nesters' to relocate to something smaller. The problem with such incentives is that they reward people for the most part for things they were going to do anyway, and in this case is another example of taxes and transfers skewing towards the elderly and wealthy.

It was inevitable that Labor would oppose this policy, although campaign spokesperson Clare struggled to explain why Coalition policies would add to demand but not supply whereas Labor's housing policy would not. Labor had promised to address supply issues through a commission but there was little concrete in the mix. The policy did earn a broadside from Keating who described it as 'a frontal assault' on the superannuation system. Albanese waxed philosophical, calling the plan 'an attack on future generations', seeking to dovetail the Coalition announcement with Labor's 'future risk' strategy around Morrison. If only future generations got a look-in during Australian elections.

The harshest criticism came from Coalition figures batting away a similar plan floated by Morrison a couple of times when he was treasurer. When it came up in 2017, Anne Ruston said it would be like 'a bucket of kerosene on a fire'. Mathias Cormann, Liberal finance minister for seven years before becoming Secretary-General of the OECD, expected it to drive prices higher, and Peter Dutton weighed in against it back then as well. Morrison had allies, though. Tim Wilson had been a long-term advocate of such a change, and such a policy would be even more helpful in his, and other, seats under assault from teal independents as it would in the outer suburbs. To underline how keen some Liberals were to further the issue, it had been revisited by a back-bench committee led by Falinski. Shortly before the election, the committee recommended using super only as collateral. Morrison would not be denied. The policy did have cut-through, though. It was one of the few substantive issues picked up in FM radio interviews with Morrison in the final week.

Morrison blitzed morning TV and radio to start the week and got plenty of questions about his housing policy. Most were implicitly critical, but he was happy to be engaging on what he perceived as a strength. Minister for Superannuation Jane Hume conceded a 'short-term bump' in house prices was likely — only she was talking the day after the campaign launch, apparently having missed the talking points. When

Hume's comments were put to Morrison, he argued that 'balancing of all of these factors means that any potential risk on that side is mitigated' — a typically kinda-true-but-misleading formulation, neatly omitting reference to higher prices in case the quote was picked up by broadcast media. He refused to release any modelling supporting his position. But the waffle on housing was bipartisan, Albanese having to respond to similar questions about the Labor housing policy.

Economist Saul Eslake asked a pertinent question: 'Why do politicians of both political persuasions, not just Coalition ones, continue to do things that disadvantage the people they say they're trying to help — namely, aspiring first-homebuyers?' It's another indictment on the standard of political and economic debate in Australia that both sides treat symptoms instead of causes in this policy area. Yet, this issue has been fairly well traversed over the last two decades since the Howard government doubled the First Home Owner Grant. If voters aren't paying attention, we get the standard of politics we deserve. Professor of Economics and former Reserve Bank board member Warwick McKibbin tweeted that the housing plan seemed to be 'designed by the same marketing focus group that designed the Australian government's climate policy'. This was the problem with any move Morrison had made all year — it was widely interpreted as politics first and policy second. The parties' respective policies did offer voters clear choices, though, not just in attitudes towards superannuation; the totality of Labor's housing effort was more progressive.

The Prime Minister visited housing display villages in Brisbane and then Darwin to meet with prospective first homebuyers who were struggling to leave the rental market. Wife Jenny became a permanent part of Morrison's campaign stunts for the final stretch. There wasn't much sign of the deep personal growth voters had been promised just days earlier. To the frustration of the travelling press pack, he only took a couple of questions in Brisbane. Asked by a persistent journalist in Darwin about the modelling for the policy, the PM's response was 'Calm down!' In a bad look for the Coalition, nobody was available for a debate on National Indigenous TV to appear with Labor's Linda Burney and Greens Senator Lidia Thorpe.

With Coalition costings to be released that day, Morrison took every question as an opportunity to attack Labor. Frydenberg emerged from Kooyong to condemn Labor's lack of costings, replete with a billboard showing twenty-two Coalition policies costed by the Treasury and zero lodged by Labor. Coalition costings revealed a small improvement in the budget across the forward estimates. The government was happy that journalists were using every opportunity to interview Albanese, Chalmers or Gallagher to ask why Labor's costings were being released so late, something that seems to exercise the minds of journalists more so than voters.

In an interview on *7.30*, his last as prime minister, Morrison drifted into commentary by suggesting the rise of the teal independents was because economic management is less important in wealthier seats. There is something to this — what political scientists call post-materialism — by which concern for things like the environment and political process become relatively more important at higher income levels. But, of course, the following day Frydenberg had to concede that economic management was 'absolutely critical' to the people of Kooyong.

Morrison received one of the tougher interviews of the campaign from Tracy Grimshaw on Channel Nine's *A Current Affair*. Grimshaw read to a clearly unimpressed Morrison a long list of his shortcomings. 'Do you think maybe you slightly over-egged the part about "I saved the country"?' she concluded, referring to his speech at the campaign launch the day before. What followed was perhaps the longest silence on record for an interview featuring Scott Morrison. 'Well,' he said with resignation, 'that's quite a long list you've been able to pull together.' The Prime Minister would have hoped that fifteen minutes with the difficult-to-reach commercial television audience — who probably tuned in for the following story on a dog that can drive a car — would have seen him on the front foot. In his wider engagements, Morrison made a course correction on wages, concerned about the way his ridicule of Albanese was perceived in the electorate. He emphasised being supportive of sustainable wage rises more so than responding to Albanese's more specific promise.

The Greens also had a late campaign launch in Brisbane, on 16 May, Bandt having attended the National Press Club crossbench panel earlier in the day in Canberra. He knew they had a good chance of picking up seats in Brisbane. 'With Labor clinging to the Liberals, there were three planks to our campaign,' Bandt told us. 'An economic alternative that addressed real cost-of-living pressures, a climate alternative that focused on stopping new coal and gas mines, and a campaign that empowered people and offered hope that politics could be different.'

The launch was held in Kevin Rudd's former seat of Griffith, held for Labor by frontbencher Terri Butler. The Greens made up for a lack of media attention compared to 2019 with a spirited ground campaign in inner-city seats. Now a veteran of the parliament, having first won his seat of Melbourne back in 2010, leader Adam Bandt cut a confident figure. His party was consistently polling around 12 to 14 per cent, tracking better than their 10 per cent in 2019 and on track towards their goal of an additional three Senate seats. They were hoping to piggy-back on the independent vote by encouraging a Greens vote in the Senate, capitalising on voter dissatisfaction with the major parties, given that the Climate 200 goals many independents had signed up to were similar those of the Greens.

Labor was mindful that while its small-target strategy had the government's measure, it left room for the Greens to increase their vote. At his party's launch, Bandt castigated the contest between a 'terrible government and a visionless opposition'. Some Labor figures played up the rather remote prospect of the Greens supporting a minority Coalition government, pointing out that such an arrangement once happened in Tasmania, which has proportional voting in the lower house. Labor's strategy also left room for other parties to take up some of the policy innovation happening on the left elsewhere in the world. The Greens announced a 'liveable income guarantee', dipping into extensive research and policy experimentation around a universal basic income. While politically it wouldn't do Albanese any harm to stay to the right of this kind of proposal in 2022, a more work-centred variant will begin to look more attractive over time. The Greens also promised to extend Medicare to dentistry services, introduce universal free childcare, eliminate student debt, and provide free NBN access to health care card holders. This would be funded by ending fossil fuel subsidies, a super-profits tax and a new tax on billionaires. Bandt wrapped these policies up, along with progress on the Uluru Statement goals, as a 'balance of power' shortlist at his campaign launch.

The closer

Husic and Marles joined Albanese in Perth to announce a $1.5 billion fund to support medical device and pharmaceutical production. Albanese had a chance to use one of his favourite lines about Australia making things again. The money was part of the off-budget manufacturing fund already announced, but it was a good chance to revisit Labor's criticism of the government during the vaccine rollout. And, given recent events, a nice line referring to the PM: 'Serious countries should be led by builders, not bulldozers,' Albanese quipped, a line from speechwriter Jeffrey.

Greg Hunt played the bulldozer this time: 'This billion-dollar sinkhole has no detail, and no plan,' he said, 'and it threatens the stability of Australia's world-class health system.' Hunt did inadvertently raise an important issue. Albanese had underlined the independent nature of the authorities that would choose projects for funding from these bodies.

The Opposition Leader wasn't going to stand for yet more journalistic haranguing about why Labor hadn't released their costings. He stormed out of a press conference in a bus manufacturing plant in Perth, cameras stalking him as he made his exit. 'You have to answer eventually,' one journalist yelled out with a self-importance familiar to those observing the journalists following Albanese. 'I took eighteen questions and then they said I was running away from questions about the costings and that went on the front page. It was crazy,' Albanese told us. After the election, McGowan gave the journalists who pursued Albanese both barrels. 'Screaming and interrupting, and rude, and insulting, intimidating and bullying,' he said. 'The sort of thing in a workplace, you'd get sacked for. They need to reflect on their behaviour. I've never seen anything like it.'

On 18 May, Albanese made a strong speech at the National Press Club, Morrison becoming the first prime minister in fifty years to skip the NPC Leader's Address. Albanese's deputy almost missed his appearance. Because of other campaign commitments Richard Marles only flew in on the morning of the speech from Sydney, but the fog in Canberra was particularly thick. After a long delay he finally made it, with little time to spare. Marles received a text from another attendee also flying in, who'd seen him seated on the flight from the non-pointy end of the plane. He asked if it was by design that the deputy was cutting it so fine, and 'surely a future deputy prime minister gets his own plane'. Marles laughed. Labor was relaxing into the anticipated election outcome.

The best part of Albanese's speech was added at the last minute, responding to the government foreshadowing yet another public service efficiency dividend as a substitute for thinking about expenditure: 'Yesterday, they said they're going to gut the public service even more. Well, you know what that leads to? Robodebt. It doesn't save money. It costs money because you take humans out of human services and it has devastating consequences for real people. It costs lives. Lives! As well as over a billion dollars to taxpayers.'

Some of the Albo mongrel was back. And more of the passion as his speech reached its crescendo with another commitment to the Uluru Statement from the Heart: 'This is the Labor Government I want to lead. This is the positive campaign I have run. Honest, real, focused on the lives and values of the Australian people. That's how I started, it's how I intend to finish. Focusing on solutions, not arguments. Taking responsibility. Treating people with respect.'

'That was bringing it home,' he later told us. 'You've gotta ramp it up!' The fourth quarter, again. The breeze was stiffening.

He even got a good write-up in *The Australian*, outlining a hundred-day plan for government. Replacing the head of the Department of Prime Minister and Cabinet, Phil Gaetjens, who had compromised his position by coming across as Morrison's errand boy, was high on the list. So, too, the relatively quick assembling of the new parliament, the sorts of policy summits Albanese had long foreshadowed, and the restructuring of government departments around the priorities of the new government, singling out energy, jobs and skills. An opposition leader needs to find a balance between looking ready for government without looking like they have already measured up the curtains at The Lodge. Albanese said Australians were tired of 'conflict fatigue' and he would bring a new leadership style to the prime ministership.

There was criticism, though, of Albanese flagging the early swearing-in of himself and Penny Wong in order to travel to the Quad Summit in Japan. The claims of arrogance, including from the Prime Minister, were silly, but it was odd that nobody else was nominated to be sworn in to become acting prime minister in Albanese's absence, an omission that was quickly corrected.

After his press club appearance, Albanese visited the Marconi Club in the seat of Fowler in western Sydney, a sign Keneally was in trouble there. He was approached by people concerned about the Coalition line 'things won't be easy under Albanese' as they had been teased about their names all their lives. Albanese fed this line back during the event, which he should have avoided as it became a national story and threatened to reinforce the government's main attack lines on him as weak. Morning television hosts badgered him about whether he thought the ads were racist. He remarked, 'If we're successful on Saturday, there will be an Albanese as the leader in the lower house and a Wong as the leader of the Labor Party in the Senate, but we still have a bit to go.'

A *Guardian Australia* analysis of media coverage found that most of the issues of highest priority for voters were well covered during the campaign. The outliers were aged care — which in fairness had been fairly extensively covered prior to the campaign, and featured heavily in Labor's advertising — and education, which reflected the lack of attention to that issue by the major parties. Another disconnect on policy was the role that attitudes to women played throughout 2021 but was mostly subtext during the campaign. Anti-domestic violence groups, for example, struggled for coverage.

One issue where media coverage outstripped voter interest was integrity. To keep that issue in the news, thirty-one former judges — including former High Court Justice Mary Gaudron — called for a robust federal anti-corruption commission. 'Nothing less than halting the serious erosion of our shared democratic principles is at stake,' the letter stated. 'Despite recent criticisms of anti-corruption commissions, the widely accepted case for a well-designed national integrity commission remains impregnable.' The judges wanted the commission to have powers that Morrison had ruled out, such as public hearings.

After a run of economic data on wages and inflation favourable to Labor, Morrison got his wish for an unemployment number with a three in front of it. The March reading came in at 3.9 per cent. The most pleasing part of the data would have been the 90,000 new full-time jobs. While such news has an agenda-setting effect during the campaign, the more important factor is how voters feel the economy is affecting them and those they care about. The cost of living trumped all other economic issues in that respect.

The PM's photo opportunities showed that even tightly controlled events retain a human factor. Having copped a stray basketball to the head in the first week of the campaign, Morrison bowled over a child while playing soccer in Devonport, providing opportunities to extend the bulldozer metaphor, which interviewers had enjoyed playing with over the intervening week. 'It should have been a penalty,' the victim, seven-year-old Luca Fauvette, told Nine's *Today* show the next morning. There's just no accountability in politics! The talent shown in his media appearances suggested that Luca may have been milking the penalty. Hirst knew the images unwantedly brought Morrison's promise to change his bulldozer ways back into focus.

Albanese chatted to Erickson that evening asking 'Surely this is showing up,' referring to the PM's close encounter. Erickson responded, 'Well it's just happened, Anthony.' But it did show up the following night, the final Thursday of the campaign, in what was Labor's final track. An accident to be sure, it still showed a PM bulldozing his way into trouble. Voters were over him, the election was over for the Coalition. Hirst picked up the same message that evening. The Liberal track showed a very gradual tightening but it was too slow and from too far back. The Coalition could not form majority government, and winning as a minority also looked extremely unlikely. When Morrison was given the final track polling results he knew it was over. While he kept his faith in miracles it was a longshot at best. He stayed as positive as he could, hoping for undecideds to break his way and deliver something.

Some interviewers noted Morrison's bulldozing style with journalists, not just children, didn't seem to have changed since his spiritual awakening the previous week. Asked about an apparent lack of empathy, he said, having first avoided addressing the question:

> What I have been able to demonstrate is the empathy that comes with action. And when you understand the pressures that Australians face, you do take action and the most important action a prime minister and, indeed, a treasurer and a government can take, is to ensure that our economy is strong and to ensure that our finances are well-managed.

This was followed by a diatribe on Labor's supposed weakness on defence and borders. It was the opposite of what was required to win back women voters — deliberately changing the subject from empathy to the policy strengths he already enjoyed with male voters.

Also not helping win back women voters was Barnaby Joyce, who had talked over Tanya Plibersek on a *Sunrise* debate about housing policy. One of the MPs who lost to a teal would later cite women in their electorate raising that exchange. Another unhappy MP claimed that 'when Barnaby Joyce became leader, he was asked to please stay out of metro media', but 'it lasted about ten days. He kept doing *Today*, *Sunrise*, and ABC24.' Joyce confirmed this to us, although he never thought it was realistic that the National Party leader could stay off national networks. Joyce had made a particularly uncompelling case for the government at the National Press Club. 'This election is a case of whether voters wish to change the curtains,' he said. 'No one has proven to us whether the replacements will keep the sun out of our eyes, the carpet from fading and stop other countries from peeking through your window to see what you're up to.' We had no access to National Party focus groups. Perhaps they were responsive to this argument.

More leaked internal Liberal polling underlined the problem, showing the biggest gender divide on record. The Liberals were still trailing in Reid, Bennelong and Parramatta. Only 38 per cent of Liberal voters were women. The PM's net satisfaction rating in Parramatta was minus 29, Bennelong minus 14, Reid minus 15.

The journalists following Albanese had one last, colossal whinge. After hounding Labor about the late release of their policy costings, Team Albo thought the journos would appreciate flying to Canberra for that event. They rebelled, thinking Albanese was hiding something. '"You say you care about the costings,"' he told us. '"We're sending you to the costings press conference in Canberra." Instead they said, "Oh that's an outrage." You want to come and watch me hand out how to vote cards in Ryan and Dickson! There weren't many journalists at the costings press conference. There was a total of one person from News Corp — the whole organisation.'

Chalmers and Gallagher's release of the opposition's policy costings created scarcely more news than had the debate about when those costings should have been released. Chalmers had already foreshadowed the scale of the larger deficit Labor was forecasting, which landed at $7.4 billion over four years, with the deficit declining as a proportion of GDP, so it all seemed a waste of breath. They also announced the winding back of some of the more controversial grant programs — a useful way of underlining their criticism of pork-barrelling. More noteworthy was the impressive pair the Treasury and Finance duo made. In government, they will at least remember the unemployment rate. We assume Albo will too. As a point of contrast, Albanese got into a barney with journalists about why he wouldn't use the words 'billion dollars' to describe the deficit increase, reminiscent of Kevin Rudd refusing to say how much net debt the government was forecasting in fighting the Global Financial Crisis. If Albanese did, he knew the grab would make the nightly news, but so did refusing. It was a no-win situation.

Exactly how many voters left their choice of candidate to the final days is difficult to say. The parties were taking no chances, though. Albanese traversed five states in the final two days and sent frontbenchers to every contested seat in a 'final sprint'. Strategists pointed out that this had worked for Kevin 07, so why not Albo? Albanese dropped into Bennelong before flying to Brisbane, even paying a visit to Peter Dutton's seat of Dickson. Erickson told Albanese that Labor's track polling most likely showed them securing a majority. On the Friday, he joined Julia Gillard in Sturt and Boothby in just his second trip to Adelaide for the campaign. They emphasised their harmonious working relationship in government. An emotional Albanese said his mum would be 'proud as punch' that he was leading the Australian Labor Party. 'The fact that young kid is now running for prime minister says a lot about her and her courage, but also says a lot about this country,' he said. Albanese smiled for selfies with students at Cabra Dominican College. He made a lightning visit to Bass in Tasmania, making an appearance at the largest early voting booth in Launceston where the Labor and Liberal candidates had been on duty. Sitting MP Archer had been expecting some competition. 'Once they start bussing the unions in, you know it's on,' she said. Albanese was in Tasmania for all of ninety minutes, arriving in Melbourne in the early evening for a round of media interviews before heading to the Woolworths warehouse in Chisholm to thank workers for their efforts during the pandemic. He retired to the hotel restaurant for a quiet dinner with Jodie. The traveling Labor staffers enjoyed a peaceful drink to celebrate the end of what had been a long campaign.

The campaign released a final video to social media featuring the leader walking the streets where he grew up. The election was about 'unlocking the potential of this great country'.

'The last thing you want to do is take your foot off the pedal in the last thirty-six hours and then fall short,' Erickson told us. He was party to the decision to slow down in 2019 after Bob Hawke died, when Shorten slackened the pace of his campaign to pay tribute to the Labor icon. Learning from what Erickson now sees as a mistake on the final day of the campaign, Albanese flew from Sydney to Adelaide, then on to Tasmania before ending up in Melbourne, from where he appeared on *7.30* that evening. 'The picture that painted for voters was we were taking nothing for granted,' Erickson says.

Not everyone closed on an optimistic note. The United Australia Party concluded its campaign with an advertising blitz (including double-page spreads across major newspapers) claiming the World Health Organization would be taking over the health departments of sovereign countries — a fitting end to Clive Palmer's political career. Pauline Hanson announced that she had tested positive to COVID. Her statement said that people who dislike her probably hoped she would drop dead. Projection?

Morrison spent his last full campaign day in Western Australia, in Swan, Pearce and Cowan, underlining WA's generous GST deal, and also visited a Sikh temple in Hasluck. His chin was up. Cowan was included in the seats visited to project a sense of optimism even though Hirst knew they had no chance of picking it up. Morrison was still spruiking his housing policy, one of the few policy announcements to outlast one day's media cycle during the campaign. Even the extensive criticism had the virtue of keeping the policy in the news. Morrison's favourite characterisation from the 2019 campaign, the 'quiet Australians', made a return in the closing days of 2022. He warned against voting for independents and minor parties, which he said would produce a 'weak' parliament where 'people are voting based on what Twitter's saying'. It's not clear who he thought would be persuaded by this. Morrison also trotted out what has now become boilerplate rhetoric in right-wing circles around the Anglo world: that the Coalition now represents the workers and Labor the elites. It was an odd claim to make on the day that the *Australian Financial Review* backed the government in its election editorial, and a report revealed just how much the nation's wealthiest private schools had rorted JobKeeper.

Newspoll ended the campaign where it started: 53–47 in favour of Labor. Hirst knew this was a closer reflection of the internal polling than published polls earlier that week, which had suggested the race had tightened to 51–49. A record five and a half million pre-poll votes had already been cast as the leaders made their final pitches. Albanese wanted to watch the count from home, rather than holed up in a hotel room at the venue where he would (hopefully) claim victory.

Part 3

Victory and aftermath

Chapter 11

The victory

Campaigning on election day has a different feel. Everything that can be done has been done. The leaders are more relaxed, and it shows. The day started with a late flurry of automated texts to voters, some misleading, some not, and a last round of leader interviews for morning radio and television. One Coalition text provided 'breaking' news that 'Border Force has intercepted an illegal boat'. Morrison's promise that he can change was still the primary theme for many interviewers, underlining why political leaders are so reluctant to offer commentary on their performance. Indeed, Johanna Nicholson reminded Morrison on ABC News 24 that his supposed propensity to rush in and fix things was hardly the problem when it came to the bushfires, vaccines and floods.

Albanese visited Higgins, handing out how-to-vote cards for the hopeful Labor candidate before flying home to vote in his own electorate. 'Wind at our backs, fourth quarter,' he said. Confidence player. 'What's the unemployment rate?'

asked a Liberal volunteer in Higgins. About to go up locally,
with another Victorian Liberal MP losing their seat, just as
Labor's national secretary had predicted. 'We're almost there,'
Albanese commented at his Marrickville booth, dog Toto in
tow, where Liberal placards were hard to spot. He'd gone inside
to cast his vote before doing a short doorstop out the front. It
was crowded and difficult at first to find a good spot to say a few
words. Eventually he knew exactly where he wanted to stand.
There is a statue out the front of the Marrickville Town Hall
where voting was taking place, 'Nike, the Goddess of Victory'.
According to the conservators' website, the original statue was
tarnished and suffering from neglect before being replaced by
the newer version, retaining all the best bits of the original
but tougher and built to last. The scene was set. He got a little
emotional talking about his electorate being representative of
Australia's diversity and what an honour it was for him to lead
the Australian Labor Party. Fired up, he turned his attention to
Morrison. 'What is there to be proud of?' he asked. 'The sort
of nonsense that we've seen of playing wedge politics against
vulnerable people that Scott Morrison's been prepared to do
during this campaign. I want to change politics.'

Morrison also started the day in Melbourne, cancelling a
visit to Chisholm in favour of McEwen where protesters were
parroting UAP's lie about the WTO. McEwen was one of the
few seats where tracking polls showed a swing towards the
government. It was Liu who had made the difference in Chisholm
in 2019, so the decision was made to leave her to win or lose
on her own merits. The track polling suggested neither seat was
really in play. Morrison was just keeping up appearances now.

He was soon back in Sydney, to vote in Cook, surrounded by his family, stopping to shake hands with kids at Lilli Pilli Public School shouting 'ScoMo, ScoMo'. A dream photo opportunity, just a little late. For old time's sake, he even got a question about the Sri Lankan vessel being intercepted before reaching Australian waters. The PMO had instructed Border Force to release the news, allowing Morrison one final comment on 'on water matters'. Albanese later accused Morrison of breaking the caretaker conventions, which would require such a decision to be made in consultation with the opposition. However, since no policy change was involved, the action was a more straightforward politicisation of the public service, something Albanese is now in a position to do something about. Still energised, or at least pretending to be, Morrison rattled off his stump speech as though it was the first time in the campaign. According to *The Guardian*, government promises were run up at the rate of $8 million an hour over the six weeks of the campaign, Labor a paltry $5 million.

Election night

Burned by their misplaced confidence that Shorten would prevail in 2019, Labor insiders were happy with the campaign but were not predicting a big win. Albanese watched the count from his house, Morrison from Kirribilli. Albanese was home by late afternoon, changing into a Newtown footy jumper. He was joined by Jodie and Nathan, Gartrell, Wong, and media advisers Liz Fitch and Katie Connolly. 'I was pretty relaxed, comfortable that I had done what I could. I thought we would win. I cooked spaghetti arrabbiata,' he told us. 'Everyone else was too nervous to eat.'

Wong told us: 'I had some! I hadn't eaten all day.'

Nathan found a website taking bets on the colour of Albo's tie for his victory speech. 'It's 13 to 1 if I wear a Bunnies tie,' an excited Albanese told Erickson, calling the busy national secretary at 6.20 p.m. just after booths had closed. 'Put some money on it,' the soon-to-be PM joked.

'Don't ring me again,' was Erickson's reply, before he abruptly hung up, according to what Albanese could remember.

'I'm glad he told you that story not me,' Erickson said when we spoke to him. 'The only booth that had come in was Norfolk Island, which had a different time zone.' Erickson was at CHQ surrounded by staffers and party officials, including ALP President Wayne Swan. When the phone rang and it was the leader, everyone went quiet as Erickson walked slightly away from the group to take the call. He doesn't recall telling Albo to not ring him again, but he does recall politely informing him that they were still working at CHQ and he should get off the phone to be able to keep an eye on the numbers as they came in. Of course, the pair were in regular contact throughout the night. Much later in the count when the election was won, Albanese rang Erickson to lament the low primary vote. The national secretary was seriously engaging with the comment when Albo interrupted him to exclaim, 'See, that's why we should have put everything we have left on me wearing a Bunnies tie to make up for the lost public funding.' (The level of public election funding depends on the number of votes received.) Erickson could see Albo was enjoying his night.

Of Labor's original hit list of twelve seats, they were only certain of taking three before the Western Australian numbers started coming in. Reid, Chisholm and Boothby were theirs, and as WA votes started to register they hoped Swan, Pearce and Hasluck would soon show good results in the early count. Flynn and Brisbane hadn't turned out how Labor had hoped, even though Queensland was one of only two states where Labor's primary vote increased, and they were in danger of losing Griffith to the Greens. Erickson wasn't expecting to win Flynn, but Albanese was more hopeful. The combination of Bridget Archer distancing herself from Morrison and some hefty pork-barrelling kept Bass in Liberal hands, but again it wasn't on Erickson's must-win list. Tasmania was the only state where the swing was towards the government. The early news about Bass, the most marginal of Labor's target seats, was one of the reasons the result was unclear for a little while. Robertson, Bennelong and Higgins were all too close to call early in the count. In fact, there were nerves in CHQ around Erickson. Early on, it was clear Kristina Keneally was in trouble in Fowler. The betting markets saw money pouring in for the Coalition, and Labor's odds were lengthening. By around 6.45 p.m., Labor was still the favourite on the betting markets, but its odds were out to $1.70. News out of Gilmore was suggesting Andrew Constance might steal the Labor seat, but it was too close to call. Erickson was telling everyone not to panic, which of course usually elicits the opposite response. Between booths closing on the east coast and the west coast the numbers slowly started to trend Labor's way. While Morrison's chances of commanding a majority were slipping away, it remained unclear for a while whether Labor would move close enough to a majority — the magic 76 seats — to be certain of victory.

The Greens were the big winners in Queensland, defying assumptions about that state's conservatism. Labor's internal track poll had it winning Brisbane, not the Greens. The Liberals were more alive to the Greens threat. In Ryan, Labor knew it was a chance but so were the Greens and Liberals. Both major parties understood that Griffith was problematic for the Labor Party, but Labor did poll it a few weeks out from election day and because they were in front it hadn't been polled after that. More resources thrown at saving Terri Butler might have got Griffith over the line. It will be hard to win back now that the Greens have it. Labor won the election despite failing to break the LNP in Queensland, and despite Albanese spending an enormous amount of time campaigning there. Margins were reduced in some seats, which could put them within striking distance next time around. 'The swing to us around the state has put more seats in realistic reach,' Chalmers told us. 'The outcome here makes us more determined and more focused on Queensland, not less.'

Victoria soon provided better hunting. Chisholm fell early, as mentioned, and Corangamite held for Labor despite a lot of Coalition talk about picking up the seat. Hirst knew that wasn't going to happen looking at his own track polling, which means the PM knew too. There was a big swing in Higgins and before long it was clear Labor would win it. Erickson had long been confident Higgins would be a Labor pick-up, but the Liberals were also alive to the threat. It sat in their second tier of at-risk seats based on their final set of tracking results. Even safe Liberal seats like Aston and Deakin, held by ministers Alan Tudge and Michael Sukkar, were in danger. Those two ended up being the only Liberals re-elected in Melbourne — not exactly a sound foundation on which to rebuild. Sukkar had to wait for days to be sure he'd be returning to Canberra. Jane Hume conceded during the Nine television coverage that the expected rebellion against the Victorian government simply didn't materialise. 'We thought there would have been a bigger Dan Andrews effect,' she said. Whoever comprised 'we' in the Victorian Liberals watches too much *Sky News After Dark*. Andrews had emerged largely unscathed from relentless criticism by News Corp papers, even though his government was far from blameless for the death toll during the 2020 lockdowns.

In New South Wales, Labor won Robertson, although the result took a while to become clear. With Bennelong and Gilmore still too close to call, Albanese needed Western Australia to deliver. McGowan looked forward to WA being decisive on federal election night for the first time in memory. When WA's results hit shortly after 8.30 p.m. east coast time confidence skyrocketed. Labor's stretch goal in the West, minister Ken Wyatt's seat of Hasluck, fell just as quickly as Swan and Pearce. Swings of more than 10 per cent against the Coalition saw prime-ministerial right-hand man Ben Morton's supposedly safe seat of Tangney fall to Labor. Moore nearly went too. Yet, the feeling at Labor CHQ was relief rather than jubilation.

Channel Nine political editor Chris Uhlmann was out of the blocks early calling the election for Labor, in a close match with author van Onselen on Network Ten. But Erickson and Hirst didn't need the musings of commentators to know the result. The figures they were looking at went close enough to matching the final Thursday track poll for each major party before anyone was chancing their arm picking a result. The tracks showed that a change of government was in the offing and so did the official figures after 7.30 p.m. Besides, they were each tuned in to the ABC's coverage to see what the oracle Antony Green had to say.

The contest between Labor and the Coalition had been decisive, Labor winning ten seats and losing nothing to the government. With the Liberals devastated by the teal independents, the only question was whether Labor would govern as a minority or majority. Underlining the extraordinary nature of their success, collectively the teals represent a tenth of the independents ever elected to the House. Tim Wilson refused to concede defeat in Goldstein on Saturday night but did manage a graceful concession the following day. Frydenberg was also slow to concede, even though the result in Kooyong was clear. Teals also picked up Wentworth, Mackellar and North Sydney in NSW and Curtin in WA. The biggest under-performer among candidates supported by Climate 200 was Dyer in Boothby, winning just 6.5 per cent of the vote despite a high-profile campaign. Deves was as classy as ever in defeat in Warringah. 'I'd like to say to my detractors that when they thought I could not withstand the storm, I am the storm,' she said. 'You haven't seen the last of me,' she added.

While the preference counts would take days to finalise, it was clear the Greens had done very well in their target seats of Griffith, Ryan, Brisbane, Richmond and Macnamara, winning the first three and making the final preference count in the others. With majority government looking difficult for Labor, Bandt hailed the 'Greenslide'. Their vote in the House was a record 11.9 per cent.

Just after 9.30 p.m., Albanese's phone rang; Morrison's name came up on the screen. Albanese showed his phone to those around him, a broad smile on his face. This was it, the concession was about to be given. He walked away and into his bedroom to take the call in private. It was a quick conversation, a pleasant enough chat, Albanese recalls. 'Thanks to you and your family for your service,' he told Morrison. Albanese wasn't interested in a tour of The Lodge. 'I wasn't going to do that!' he told us, and none was offered. No love lost between this pair. Even Keating and Howard had managed that ritual. When Albo emerged, everyone was just standing there, waiting to be told what was said. 'It's done,' Albanese told them to a few howls and clapping. Luckily for the incoming PM, Morrison took a while between conceding and starting his journey to the Liberal Party function to concede publicly. It gave Albanese time to pull together a speech. Yes, that's right, he didn't pre-empt fate by having one ready. Connolly sat on the floor, legs crossed, while Albanese dictated his victory speech from his couch. 'That's why it worked,' he told us. 'It was totally authentic and it flowed.' He took a shower then read the speech, making a few changes. 'Who will introduce you?' Wong asked him. 'You!' was Albo's response. 'Who else was going to do it?' Wong had to quickly write her own speech. On the way to Labor's victory party, he got his first international congratulatory call, from New Zealand's prime minister, Jacinda Ardern.

Morrison headed to the Fullerton Hotel in Sydney's CBD, quite some time after his call to Albanese. He gave a gracious enough concession speech, but it recycled too many of his campaign lines. It's over, ScoMo!

The crowd at the Canterbury–Hurlstone Park RSL shouted, 'Albo, Albo.' No Bunnies tie unfortunately. 'I wanted the speech to be at a local RSL,' Albanese told us. 'I didn't want it to be at a spivvy joint. It was a really good message. It's where Hawke did my parliamentary twentieth anniversary function. There was that sense of history and connection with Bob.' Albanese's AFP guard was worried about just how happy the crowd might have been to see Albo in the flesh, so they arranged for him to reach the stage without going through so many well-wishers. 'They're my people,' he told them. 'They'll be fine.' But he later told us, 'When people have been on the piss for five hours, you just don't know. For some of them it was the first time they've experienced an election win.' He agreed to let his security have their head but insisted on mixing with the crowd later.

As she had at the launch, Wong introduced her good friend. Albanese, Jodie and Nathan joined her on the stage. Spontaneously, they joined hands and lifted their arms in victory. 'People were going crazy,' Albo recalled. 'The energy was extraordinary. I'll never forget it, that sense of relief and joy.'

On stage, the emotion of the moment nearly made him burst into tears. 'I'm an emotional guy and I felt, during the campaign, enormous pressure to win because so many people desperately wanted that. I felt this great weight of responsibility,' he told us.

'Tonight, the Australian people have voted for change,' said the Prime Minister-elect, barely needing to look at the autocue. 'I am humbled by this victory.' Yet another recitation of his biography could have sounded like a cliché. Instead, Albanese gave it authenticity and emotion. 'My fellow Australians, it says a lot about our great country that a son of a single mum who was a disability pensioner, who grew up in public housing down the road in Camperdown, can stand before you tonight as Australia's Prime Minister,' he said. Then, he translated biography into governing philosophy. 'No one left behind, because we should always look after the disadvantaged and the vulnerable. But also no one held back, because we should always support aspiration and opportunity.' Easier said than done, of course. Yet, a prime minister who embodies those principles seems likelier to uphold them. He promised to respond to the 'patient, gracious call for a Voice enshrined in our Constitution' to great cheers.

The launch, the Press Club, the victory: three great speeches. Later, he told us, 'If I had more than a couple of sentences to say about my mum I would have lost it. I think it will stand the test of time pretty well.' Albanese circulated in the ecstatic crowd, meeting some of his Young Labor mates and dragging them upstairs, where they had hired the venue's conference room for a private party, and shared a beer. Erickson and Madigan, having watched the results come in at CHQ, arrived at the RSL in time to join the crowd watching Morrison concede and congratulated Albo with hugs. 'You don't make things easy, do you!' Madigan said with relief. 'It felt like he really earned it through sheer tenacity,' she told us. Unfortunately, the after-party may have become a COVID super-spreader event. Supporters, including senior media advisers Cramb and Franklin, tested positive, leaving the new prime minister short-staffed in his first week. Albanese arrived home at about 2.30 a.m., taking a late congratulatory call from Jimmy Barnes. 'It was a good night,' he said.

Final counting

The declarations of Macnamara and Gilmore took Labor's total to seventy-seven, allowing Labor to appoint a speaker and retain a majority on the floor of the House. This was the exact number Paul Erickson had predicted they would win, to author van Onselen at the end of the final parliamentary sitting week before the election. Holding Lingiari, Parramatta, Macquarie and Dobell proved crucial for Labor. The only gain for the Liberals was that of Hughes, from the UAP. Albanese privately predicted seventy-eight seats before the campaign, justifying being one seat out because he didn't pick Keneally's loss in Fowler. That result annoyed Albo, not only because he was losing the former premier from his team in government, but also because he had opposed the factional deal that saw Keneally parachuted into Fowler as the Labor candidate in the first place. 'The important thing is, Labor won the election,' Keneally graciously told us.

Clive Palmer got little value for money from the $100 million spent on UAP advertising. Palmer's own candidacy for the Senate in Queensland returned a paltry 4 per cent, although they won the lottery for the sixth Senate seat in Victoria.

Labor's new MPs were also the most ethnically diverse in history: Sally Sitou (Chinese) in Reid, Michelle Ananda-Rajah (Tamil) in Higgins, Sam Lim (Chinese–Malay) in Tangney, Zaneta Mascarenhas (Indian) in Swan, Marion Scrymgour (Indigenous Australian) in Lingiari, and Cassandra Fernando (Sri Lankan) in Holt brought a wealth of experience to the parliament. The seats with a critical mass of Chinese–Australian voters, such as Chisholm and Bennelong, swung hard for Labor. Even where the swings were not as large, such as in Parramatta, breaking down the swing to booths shows bigger moves in the suburbs with the largest Chinese–Australian populations. Labor's loss of Fowler added to this diversity. Dai Le's defeat of Keneally was a reminder that it isn't just the Liberals that need to pay more attention to candidate selection.

In the upper house, First Nations senators now make up 10 per cent of representatives in that chamber. Jana Stewart, who had replaced Kimberley Kitching in Victoria, was re-elected in May. Jacinta Nampijinpa Price won for the Country Liberal Party in the Northern Territory. Kerrynne Liddle was elected to the Senate for the Liberals in South Australia, becoming that state's first Indigenous senator. They joined Jacqui Lambie, Labor's Pat Dodson and Malarndirri McCarthy, and the Greens' Lidia Thorpe and Dorinda Cox.

The Coalition's haul of fifty-eight seats was their lowest since the House of Representatives was enlarged in 1984. Labor's primary vote of 32.6 per cent also received a lot of attention. It wasn't that long ago that the conventional wisdom was that Labor needed a primary vote above 40 per cent to win an election. While that doesn't mean a lot in a preferential system, and Labor's vote was lower because it ran dead in the teal seats, both parties will be mindful of seats where a third party or independent can be competitive.

In a speech to the National Press Club after the victory, Erickson outlined eight factors undermining the Coalition: a refusal to take responsibility for anything, incompetent management during the pandemic, partisan attacks on state governments throughout the pandemic, incompetent budget management, an incoherent and incompetent response to the cost-of-living crisis, incompetent engagement with Australia's allies and region, a lack of awareness or interest in women's experiences, and a decades-long failure to take climate change seriously. It was testament to the smart-target strategy that none of these was about what Labor did, other than reinforcing the message on these issues.

Talking to Albanese a few weeks after his victory, it was clear just how much he enjoyed beating Scott Morrison like a drum. 'There are a lot of moments that add up to an election victory,' he told us. Naturally, he adds some of his own actions and policies to Erickson's list. Albanese concedes, though, that the centrality of the former prime minister's unpopularity was key to his strategy.

Chapter 12

Aftermath

The new government wasted no time settling in. There were shades of Whitlam and his deputy, Lance Barnard, in the early swearing in of a small number of ministers so Albanese and Wong could head to Japan for a meeting of Quad leaders on 24 May. Albanese mentioned to his senior team at various times on the plane during the campaign that if they won he'd be going to the Quad, even though it was being held early in the week right after the election. He'd have to leave at lunchtime on the first Monday. Even his closest supporters thought that was a bit ambitious. There might not even be a clear outcome by then. He gave what would become Albo's gang of four (Marles, Wong, Chalmers and Gallagher) advance warning that they would need to be ready to be sworn in on Monday morning before the plane left. It was a sign of his belief in himself and Labor winning.

Although this group processed the outcome intellectually, emotionally it didn't hit most of them until they were heading along the long driveway at Yarralumla to be sworn in. Less than forty hours after polls closed, the gang of four became ministers, along with Albanese of course, collectively running the new government in advance of the full cabinet taking their oaths. The inner sanctum had a meeting after the swearing-in at the Opposition Leader's office, then they took the long walk on the blue carpet to their first press conference, there together explaining what would come next. There was another, shorter, ten-minute meeting afterwards back in the office, which was the last time Anthony Albanese was in that room. When he returned, he moved straight into the prime minister's suite.

Albanese needed a new passport. Without travelling during COVID, he hadn't realised his had expired. 'It sent a really good message about our democracy. We had an election on Saturday night. A lot of votes were still being counted.' Albanese scored a public engagement with Joe Biden after a scheduled bilateral meeting at the Quad talks. Biden remarked about the speed of the transition to the new government, a nice contrast with Trump's lingering stench back in Washington. A leak of the unsuccessful Department of Foreign Affairs and Trade cabinet submission to increase aid to Pacific states in mid-2021 allowed the new prime minister to get on the front foot. Pacific leaders noted commitments on climate change in their congratulations to Albanese.

After returning from Tokyo, he visited his mother's grave on the twentieth anniversary of her death, as a reminder of the values that drive him. He was determined that his government would be true to those traditions. He was nearly sixty, the oldest leader to win the prime ministership from opposition (something he hadn't realised until we put it to him), yet he was more in tune with the progressive values sweeping the country than any predecessor in memory. A change of values had already been signalled by a change in symbols, with Albanese standing in front of Aboriginal and Torres Strait Islander flags in addition to the national flag in his first press conference after his swearing-in. 'Without announcing it, we just did it,' he told us. 'And I've never been asked about it.' Times have changed. 'We've been left a bin-fire of problems to solve,' he commented as the new government took on China's assertive diplomacy in the Pacific and rising inflation at home.

'Anthony will be an even better prime minister and the rest of us a better team for having to fight and scrap so hard for it,' Chalmers told us. The strength of that team was about to face an even bigger test. Soaring gas prices and threatened blackouts ensured a short honeymoon.

While Wong showed what an asset she would be with some rapid diplomacy in the Pacific, where China was seeking to land a comprehensive trade and security deal, Albanese continued the recent tradition of new Australian prime ministers making Indonesia their first bilateral visit. There was a high-risk photo-op bicycling in the presidential grounds with President Joko Widodo. No children to barrel over in sight. He also showed that he had a great rapport with New Zealand's Jacinda Ardern, who'd had a polite — but nothing more — relationship with Morrison. Albanese received the consensus of the national cabinet for the new climate targets and for constitutional recognition of an Indigenous Voice to Parliament.

On the other side of the chamber, all the signs of political grief were there — blindness to the faults of the previous government, wishful thinking about voting trends, and internal brawling. Who you gonna call when you need to win back moderate voters? Peter Dutton, of course. If history is any guide, any notion that the Coalition needs to rediscover the centre ground is likely to fall on deaf ears. The right has become increasingly ideological rather than pragmatic and the moderates are too timid to fight back. If there was one thing that both major parties could learn from the success of the Greens and teals, it was the importance of being in touch with local communities. Major party gatekeepers will resist any reinvigoration of party democracy, though, even though the Liberals, in particular, can benefit from changes that make it easier to attract women candidates.

The ministry

No prime minister can govern effectively without a strong team around them. The incoming ministry was the most experienced in a generation. Albanese had to work with whichever names the factions threw up for the ministry, but allocating portfolios was his right as leader. There were few changes either to personnel or portfolios. In government, Albanese's game of favouring mates wasn't just about loyalty. As a prime minister modelling himself on Hawke, he would need to delegate. He needed absolute trust in his senior team. Working more closely with Chalmers during the budget and campaign achieved that in the case of treasury. He appointed the first Muslim ministers:

Minister for Industry Ed Husic to cabinet, and Anne Aly in the outer ministry. Matt Thistlethwaite was appointed Assistant Minister for the Republic, a surprise portfolio, although any action there in the first term seems unlikely. The process of telling prospective ministers which portfolios they were receiving was done mostly by face-to-face meetings, rather than by phone. The new team were in Canberra for the first caucus meeting after the election and were set to be sworn in the following day, 1 June. Ministers report Albanese had papers strewn across his desk. One reminded us of an old saying, 'If a cluttered desk is a sign of a cluttered mind, of what, then, is an empty desk a sign of?'

While there were a few surprises in the line-up, one caught particular attention. Plibersek was second only to Albanese in parliamentary experience in the cabinet, but that didn't count for much, it seemed. Despite six years as Labor's shadow education spokeswoman, the Education ministry she coveted went to Labor's new star Jason Clare, where he would work closely with Employment Minister Tony Burke. Education was to Plibersek what infrastructure had been to Albanese, but he was prepared to take it away from her anyway. Plibersek also lost out as minister for women to Katy Gallagher. Albanese wanted this role to go to one of his close supporters. Instead, Plibersek was allocated the environment and water portfolio, a very senior one, according to her supporters. With climate change stripped out, though, it was an unambiguous demotion. Besides, she has been very clear that education policy was her passion. Plibersek said she was 'delighted' to be able to show that the government values the environment and water 'after a decade of the Liberal Party not giving a stuff'. Her relationship with the Prime Minister, she said, was 'terrific'. She showed some intent in her new portfolio by ordering a review of the pre-election removal of plans for threatened species, although that is part of the genius of the move. Without Shadow Environment Minister Terri Butler's loss in Griffith, it would have been hard for Albanese to find Plibersek anything that didn't look humiliating for his rival without creating ructions elsewhere. It was also an appointment that would require the thing he most admired about her — her work ethic — especially in the water portfolio, in which she had shown little interest.

Albanese took another shot at Plibersek for good measure. Asked what he thought of Plibersek saying Dutton looks like Voldemort from the *Harry Potter* films, and that the visage of the new opposition leader would frighten children, the Prime Minister said, 'It was a mistake. It shouldn't have been said. We all make mistakes from time to time.' He wished Dutton well. 'I certainly have a good personal relationship with Peter Dutton. He has never broken a confidence or his word to me.' Plibersek soon apologised to the new Opposition Leader. Albanese's authority was clear. Now, there were no rivals.

It was a ministry brimming with talent and diversity — such a clear distinction from the outgoing tribe. They will need to use their collective experience from the failures of the Rudd and Gillard years to do better, learning to overcome the instincts of opposition — to wreck things for political advantage. Madigan thinks it is an advantage that Albanese isn't starting his prime ministership with the sky-high expectations Kevin Rudd did after the 2007 win. The fact there is no clear successor to Albanese despite the quality of the line-up should help maintain unity. Nobody knows better than him that the last two opposition leaders to win their way to the prime ministership were both rolled in their first term.

A job for a woman

Labor's gender quota was paying dividends. The proportion of women in the Senate edged towards 60 per cent, the House nearly 40 per cent. Australia zoomed past Tanzania to improve its dismal position on the global list of women in parliament, held back of course by the conservatives. A record 40 per cent of candidates were women. To illustrate the strategic stupidity of the Coalition's approach to pre-selection, as Labor campaign veteran Bob McMullan pointed out, the biggest swing towards Labor in every state was achieved by a woman. If the Liberal and National parties aren't now prepared to concede the fact that they have a gender problem, they never will. Most of the seats the Liberals lost went to women. The success of the teal independents saw six women win seats from five men and one woman. Why were the Liberal Party's safest seats occupied almost exclusively by men? An exception, Celia Hammond, losing her seat of Curtin, has deprived the Liberal Party of arguably its most highly qualified woman in parliament. Hammond was a university vice-chancellor before leaving the academy for what turned out to be a short-lived career in politics. Six well-credentialled centrist women have entered the parliament in traditionally safe Liberal seats, but they won't sit with the Coalition.

Hammond wasn't the only woman in Liberal ranks to lose her seat. Katie Allen lost Higgins, Fiona Martin was defeated in Reid, Lucy Wicks was edged out in Roberston, and Amanda Stoker wasn't returned in the Senate. In addition, retiring women such as Nicolle Flint were not replaced with women. Pre-selecting women in marginal seats is a temporary solution. Action is needed across the board. The parliamentary ranks of the Liberal Party are even weaker now when it comes to gender representation than they were before the election, despite the laughable 50 per cent women in parliament 'target' for 2025. Some teals could have been interested in a parliamentary career with the Liberal Party had that been a more attractive prospect. These women had no interest joining in the branch stacking and other games essential to landing a safe seat.

The most important take-away from polling day was that women punished the Liberal Party. The gender gap in voting was electorally catastrophic. Women delivered the election, both in the way they deserted the government in marginal seats, and the price the Coalition paid fighting a war on two fronts against the teal independents.

The gender problem is three-fold. The first is policy-based and should be the easiest to solve: stop alienating half the electorate. Yet, how does a party with so few women compared to their opponents formulate policy attractive to the whole electorate? The second is the clear need for more representation of women in winnable seats. The conservative parties used to be better at this than Labor and should be able to do it again. The third problem is that factional loyalties will always overcome the need to pre-select more women in the absence of a quota. It just won't be anyone's priority. The facade we see of the Coalition putting a disproportionate number of women on its front bench, to mask the fact the parliamentary ranks are so thin, can't continue. The party needs a critical mass of women on the back bench in order to choose the strongest shadow ministry, and the only way to quickly make that happen is to convince qualified women to run for the conservatives. Liberals need to implement some form of affirmative action to get high-calibre women into their ranks who are already fit to serve on the front bench.

Sussan Ley's elevation to deputy Liberal leader was consequential since she had advocated for quotas and promised after the election to make that argument in the party room. Ley could do a lot worse than devote herself to this between now and the next election. She was supported after the election by Linda Reynolds, who had previously been against quotas. Ley became a convert to quotas when serving on the back bench between ministries. A junior frontbencher in John Howard's final term as Prime Minister, she has been around long enough to witness first-hand how blokey the Coalition is, but she is just one woman in a depleted party room. To bring about change the blokes must get on board. The only senior male Liberal to advocate quotas is Matt Kean, the New South Wales Treasurer. That we must turn to state politics to find such an advocate shows how far the Liberals are from consensus. Raising the idea in a room full of men who have dedicated what intellectual thought they possess to finding excuses not to embrace quotas — partly a philosophical position but mostly because Labor did it first — will be pointless.

Some years ago, when Barnaby Joyce was in full flight explaining why quotas are degrading and tokenistic, he was asked why it was okay for the Nationals to have a quota for the number of front-bench positions it gets in the Coalition agreement. To Joyce's credit, he paused for thought, offering 'I'll get back to you on that; I hadn't thought about it like that' — an honest response at least. Add to this the informal quotas for the ministry based on state representation over merit and there is really no reason why gender representation shouldn't follow a similar principle. Instead, shallow arguments against quotas have triumphed: the ministerial quotas are different; the practicalities of implementing gender quotas is harder for the Coalition parties because they don't have a rigid factional system like Labor; and our favourite: women don't want quotas. Liberals need to find ways to improve their systems to entice more women into the tent, rather than relying on those exclusionary systems to justify why the teal independents were always going to be a problem.

While the Coalition parties have rustled up a pair of women to serve as deputy leaders, the number of women in the ranks of the depleted opposition are thin compared to Labor, which, courtesy of its quota system, has near-equal representation. This has been a slow and steady build for Labor, to the point where it now has ten women in the cabinet — a number certain to increase. Labor increased its representation of women despite losing Kristina Keneally and Terri Butler at the election, both shadow cabinet ministers. Morrison made much of preselecting women in New South Wales. It was an afterthought, though, to what so many see as the main game — faction is the first source of loyalty.

The ability of the Liberals to represent the broadest possible cross-section of the community is compromised in other ways. The election removed three openly gay MPs. The Nationals also became proportionately larger in opposition. They bragged about holding all their seats, but this was mostly due to the big margins run up at the previous elections. Parties happy with their electoral performance don't dump their leader. New leader David Littleproud has a different style to Barnaby Joyce but is just as conservative. He voted against the same-sex marriage legislation; Barnaby just walked out of the chamber.

Shades of blue

The next challenge facing the Liberal Party will be understanding why they lost seats to Labor, the Greens and the teals. On election night, Finance Minister Simon Birmingham said Trent Zimmerman, who lost North Sydney, was the victim of a 'contagion effect' and was being 'punished' for the views of other candidates. This tends to assume that voters didn't know exactly what they were doing in ousting the moderate MPs. Cabinet ministers such as Marise Payne did not speak up enough about the consequences of perpetual culture wars. Less noticed than moderate MPs losing to the teals were some right-wing MPs losing their seats as well. We also waved goodbye to Eric Abetz in the Senate, not returned from the number-three position on the Tasmanian ticket. It is less the numbers balance between the factions as the sheer ineffectiveness of the moderates that led to the rise of the teal independents. The moderates are too quiet internally, too timid externally, and most of them neglected the community needs of their electorates, increasing their vulnerability when challenged. The disdain for Morrison personally in these former Liberal strongholds only exacerbated a problem dating back to the 1970s.

Candidate Andrew Constance opened up after the election: 'The party has been too introverted and too focused on itself,' he said shortly before knowing the final fate of his challenge in Gilmore. He lost by 373 votes. The party needs 'broad-based appeal', not 'sectional interest', he said. 'The party exists for the community … there's no such thing as a "heartland" in Australian politics. We're a progressive country and people want change — that's what the vote was about for everybody. The party's future depends on its ability to uphold community values, and you can't lose sight of that.'

The independent insurgency was part of longer-term changes in politics, most obviously the steady decline in the vote for the major parties since the 1960s. The Labor Party dealing with the rise of the Greens has been much of the focus of this trend. Labor's declining blue-collar base and the rise of a more educated and affluent middle class is a familiar story. An important milestone came in 2001 when university-educated voters preferred Labor over the Coalition for the first time. In 2022, highly educated voters moved from the Coalition to Labor while those who hadn't finished high school were most likely to stick with the government. Two Australian National University professors, Ian McAllister and Toni Makkai, found that occupation, the main determinant of party preference for most of the twentieth century, had become 'unimportant' to it. The leftward march of the Australian Democrats obscures the fact that they were a breakaway group from the Liberal Party in the 1970s. However, the Democrats never enjoyed success in the lower house. By contrast, challengers to the Liberals and Nationals on the right have been more fragmented. A more populist approach to governing helped keep challengers on the right at bay at the cost of moderate voters in the centre, at one point condescendingly referred to by political strategists as 'doctors' wives'. It hasn't been obvious until now, though, where these voters could turn if Labor didn't appeal. The warning signs were there for the government beyond the losses in Indi and Warringah. Amid the celebrations of the 'miracle' 2019 win, there were swings against the government of between 2 and 5 per cent in North Sydney, Goldstein and Mackellar, while in Kooyong, Frydenberg received a strong challenge from lawyer Julian Burnside representing the Greens. These longer-term trends were supercharged by Morrison's failures on gender politics in 2021.

Julie Bishop, former holder of Curtin, was prepared to name names. 'Women did not see their concerns and interests reflected in a party led by Scott Morrison in coalition with Barnaby Joyce,' she said.

'You look at the values of this community,' Allegra Spender said of Sydney's Eastern Suburbs after the election. 'We are socially progressive, we are environmentally focused. They were not reflected in the parliament, and were not reflected in the Liberal Party.' Spender pointed to the same-sex marriage debate as part of the journey. 'We want our parliament to be the best of us,' she said.

Sharma said after the election, 'The teal candidates position themselves quite cleverly, I think, as a repository for an anti-government protest vote without being a Labor or Greens vote.' Voters, he thought, were not convinced the government was taking climate change seriously despite the final position they took to the election.

Seats won by independents can be hard to win back. Dutton will hardly win over the sorts of voters flocking to the teals. There is an argument that he shouldn't try — at least in the short term. This is separate from the question of the party's broad church. The party's moderate wing is hardly limited to the wealthiest suburbs of Sydney and Melbourne. While the focus on the outer suburban areas didn't produce any victories, swings to the Liberals in Lindsay and McEwen make matters more complicated. Hard-headed analysis, not ideology, might lend itself to concentrating on such seats at the next election, with a longer-term strategy to unseat the teals. Similarly, the seats won by the Greens could be hard for both major parties to win back. This will complicate any campaign in Queensland, which would need to appeal to both progressive and conservative voters.

Tim Wilson told us that none of the teal women would be prepared to go through the pre-selection processes to become a Liberal candidate in a safe seat — which is the whole point. They shouldn't be condemned for not wanting to enter a race that is stacked against professional women. For not wanting to waste their time stacking branches when their careers are clearly impressive and important.

Former prominent moderate MP Fred Chaney, backing his niece Kate in Curtin, provided a different perspective to the familiar ideological explanation for the rise of the teals: 'We've got people in parliament now whose primary interest is the business of politics and not enough interest in the business of good government.'

Fellow Fraser-era moderate (from the days when they were called 'wets') and former minister Ian Macphee described the party as beyond reform and advocated a vote for independents. Former senior moderate Peter Baume voted for Zali Steggall.

On election night, Albanese called time on the 'climate wars'. A ceasefire, at least, would help the Liberals in the teal seats. Institutional forces within the Coalition, though, may ensure that a civil war on climate continues within the Liberal and National parties. Political historian Judith Brett argues that the culture war helped perpetuate the climate war, which conservatives were destined to lose. Contrary to their longstanding political strategy, which was successful throughout the twentieth century, Australia's conservative parties continually promoted their ability to govern in the national interest, whereas Labor represented a sectional interest. On climate change and other issues, it is now the Coalition parties that represent sectional interests. The Greens, long dismissed as a narrow interest group, and the teals, captured the national interest vote on this issue. Indeed, the teal independents should be recognised as the political expression of a democratic social movement. Cathy McGowan started out as a cookie-cutter local independent in Indi seeking to raise local issues, but in forming the Community Independents Network, and passing the baton to Helen Haines, she may have changed Australian politics permanently. The teal seats could be won back by addressing, on a national basis, the policy issues they have raised — not through local pump-priming or waiting for individuals to retire. It's not clear the Liberals can do this any time soon and it's not even clear that they wish to try.

In dealing with this challenge, the Liberals don't face the mirror image of the contest between Labor and the Greens, where Labor can sit in the middle and tolerate losing some votes to their left. The poor One Nation and UAP performance in 2022 shows that the far right remains too fragmented to really challenge the Liberals and Nationals, and these parties will be even less effective with the Coalition no longer in government. The Greens taking two seats from the Liberals, and the teals six, shows that the problem for the Coalition lies in the centre. However, this simple mathematics was beyond some.

'When we go left, we lose,' Matt Canavan said, claiming that the teal seats were lost even though the moderates wrote the climate policy, which the moderates would have been surprised to hear. There are also those among the Liberals, like Queensland senator Gerard Rennick, concerned that signing up to net zero was part of the problem. 'The Liberal Party's experiment with the poison of leftism and progressivism must be over,' was the diagnosis of South Australian Senator Alex Antic. This resistance to simple facts shows that the Coalition has lost its ability for sensible debate.

The diminished number of moderates were horrified at this sentiment. 'Australians want cemented policy on climate change that is robust and actionable,' the Member for

Moncrieff, Angie Bell, said. 'They want trust restored in their democratic systems, equality and inclusion for women.' Perhaps she was angling for Climate 200 funding. Frydenberg pleaded that climate science is not a religion and governments need to find solutions 'from a perspective of engineering, economics and also environmental science'. It was ideas that need to drive politics, he said, not 'warring personalities'. Frydenberg was not a moderate but under Turnbull tried unsuccessfully to bring a rational approach to climate policy, apparently a sin in some Coalition circles.

The leader

Menzies (Kooyong), Holt (Higgins), Gorton (Higgins), McMahon (Lowe), Howard (Bennelong), Abbott (Warringah) and Turnbull (Wentworth). These Liberal Prime Ministers have one thing in common: the seats they occupied in the House of Representatives are no longer held by the Liberal Party. Some of this is explained by demographic changes and electoral redistributions. To have the seats of seven of your nine prime ministers (assuming Morrison's Cook doesn't go at a by-election before you read this) fall to the opposition or independents, though, seems careless.

What does an opposition learn from a period of government nominally successful in electoral terms but rancid in terms of policy and leadership in-fighting? Not much if the remaining personnel lack the capacity to self-reflect. Even less if the party membership that pre-selects them isn't reflective of the broader electorate that determines which party forms government.

The guile of Liberal Party campaign strategies has for years now overcome other deficiencies. Perhaps we can blame Mark Latham, who baited John Howard into changing the parliamentary superannuation scheme, for Scott Morrison staying on in Cook. Morrison would be no help whatsoever in understanding the loss. 'Sometimes people like to change the curtains because they just like to change the curtains,' he said post-election, echoing Joyce's pre-election Press Club speech.

The fact that Labor landed just one seat away from minority government obscured the fact that the Coalition is miles away from government of any sort. Yet, obituaries for the Liberal Party are nothing new, having been written while the body is still very much warm. Previous factional infighting has produced tomes by leading moderates such as *Is the Party Over?* and *What's Wrong with the Liberal Party?* Nothing that electoral success couldn't overcome, as it turned out. Your authors edited and contributed to a volume titled *Where to From Here for the Liberal Party?* after its 2007 defeat. It was easy enough to blame Morrison personally for the 2022 defeat. Incompetence, cruelty and failure to take responsibility were hallmarks of the government as a whole — not just their third prime minister. The 2022 defeat revealed structural problems papered over by narrow wins in 2016 and 2019.

Scott Morrison was fond of distancing himself from the 'Canberra bubble'. Yet, the scale of their election loss reflects the fact that so many Liberals live in a bubble of their own, created by their media consumption. Political scientist Jim Walter argues that, like the original United Australia Party before it, the contemporary Liberal Party has 'abandoned any philosophy that now equates with what majority opinion demands.' In sharp contrast to Menzies' coalition-building approach, elements of the party seem proud of their narrowness. The gaps are filled with cheap populism and cultural tropes.

'The resistance starts here,' declared Sky's Paul Murray after the election. Morrison had preferred his 'mate' Murray's cosy forum to venues such as the ABC, preaching to the converted. When polemicists like Murray declare themselves the 'resistance' to a Labor government, they are resisting majority opinion. Murray only needs tens of thousands of Australians to join his resistance to make a living. The Liberal Party needs slightly more votes to be competitive in a two-party system. It is questionable as to whether these *After Dark* performers have the institutional interests of the Liberal party at heart. They craft conflict, not policy. They're not interested in solving problems, because they thrive on them. Budding politicians are not exposed to serious scrutiny in this environment. The Foxification of the Republican Party in the United States is not a path that Australia's conservative parties can afford to follow. Due to the nature of the political system in the United States, the Republicans can win elections without a majority of the vote. Australia's preferential voting system and independent Electoral Commission make this an unviable path.

To argue that the teal independents are 'loud, rich and entitled', as former Victorian state MP Tim Smith did in *Spectator Australia*, misses the point. The London *Spectator* provides space for conservative intellectuals. The local version seems designed to show that Australian conservatives have little intellect. Smith might be right about the rich part, suggesting that the fast-growing part of the economy won't be filling the Liberal

Party's coffers if they keep their climate change scepticism. However, the teals gained a broad base of support in seats where figures on average wealth are distorted by a small number of very wealthy individuals and a majority well below that mark.

Believing their own stereotypes about the teals as Labor- or Greens-leaning all but ensures Liberals will find it hard to win back the teal seats. All they needed to know about Zoe Daniel was that she had worked for the ABC. That guaranteed she was a lefty in the eyes of the partisans. But narrowcasting what constitutes 'a Liberal' or 'right of centre' over time will shut more people out than it will include. It will further contribute to the decline of the two-party system. The rhetoric of the Liberal Party as a broad church has become less about the broad and more about the Church in recent years. The contrast with Albanese, who avoided media echo chambers as a deliberate strategy, is instructive.

Talking among themselves will also affect future strategy. The bubble will perpetuate the nonsense that the Liberals are now the party of the working class. The average income of a seat conceals a lot of variation, much of which remains when analysed at the booth level — which is what a lot of instant post-election analysis relies upon. In the teal seats, the Liberals dominated among high-income earners. As political scientist Shaun Ratcliff pointed out in a post-election piece for *The Australian*, the Liberals win outer suburban seats by winning the middle-class vote there. The wealthiest still vote Liberal, the poorest Labor. This may still point towards a strategy of winning the outer suburban seats at the next election, but there should be no illusions about which voters they need to target.

Energy policy provided a good illustration of discussing policy in a media bubble. Numerous Coalition politicians met the soaring cost of energy by promoting the most expensive form of energy in history — nuclear. The awful politics — which MPs would welcome a reactor in their seat? — on this sort of issue arise because conservative politicians can receive a round of applause for this nonsense within their own bubble, only for it to land like a dead cat in wider public debate.

Without Frydenberg, Dutton was the only candidate for Liberal leader. Borrowing a line from a former National Party senator, Ron Boswell, from when he was staving off a challenge from One Nation, Dutton said, 'I'm not the prettiest bloke on the block, but I hope I'll be pretty effective.' Like all Liberal leaders, he also acknowledged a debt to the party's founder, although the further removed we become from Menzies' leadership, the less even the Liberal Party seems to understand him. Dutton promised to reach out to 'aspirational, hardworking "forgotten people" across cities, suburbs, regions and in the bush'. Just about everybody, then, which should be the starting point. Invoking Menzies' famous line, though, was an odd move after nearly a decade in power. If they were forgotten, who forgot them? In claiming that the middle class was being left out, Menzies was not only referencing the Labor governments of the 1940s but his own United Australia Party government, which Menzies conceded favoured big business. Menzies was brutal about his party's prospects. 'The name United Australia Party has fallen into complete disregard,' he wrote. 'It no longer means anything.' The UAP was torched and the Liberal Party formed from the ashes. Something for Menzies' successors to consider?

Dutton did indeed attempt to distance the party from big business, rhetorically at least, although this was a little mystifying to the businesses that had shovelled millions of dollars to the Coalition parties over the life of the government. Fossil fuel money does tie Coalition fortunes to a declining industry, but it's not clear that's what was on Dutton's mind. He is more interested in the competing interests of small and big business. Dutton seems mindful not just of the need for a broad church of views but a more consensus-oriented leadership style. The incentive for him to demonstrate this as the first opposition leader facing a new government, though, is not strong.

On climate change, Dutton has been in the parliament long enough to know how many times Liberal leaders have been torn apart by the issue, and will be cautious. He also doesn't have Labor's rules protecting the leader in opposition. The Liberals moved to protect leaders after throwing out consecutive PMs, but only when in government. Dutton might take a leaf from the British Conservative Party's book on climate change. There is no climate war in the UK. Gone are the days when the Liberals' two factions could at least see eye to eye on economic policy. The legacy of Howard and Costello, when Dutton was a junior minister, was thoroughly trashed by the do-nothing, debt-accumulating, non-reforming government just defeated. If Dutton wants to distance himself from big business, he can start with a contrast to the tin-eared business community's attitudes to wages and labour deregulation. Some wages growth would have helped the Coalition electorally. Former Victorian deputy state director Tony Barry believes that housing affordability marks a political fault line. Attention to greater affordability will not just be popular, he believes, but will help generate a new generation of conservative Australians. Dutton could support the new government's efforts at restoring public confidence in conservative institutions such as the Australian Public Service, which American-style politics has strangled.

While Dutton almost certainly won't move on quotas for women candidates, he is at least alive to the need to pre-select more women. The problem with these types of issues in the Liberal Party is that only the parliamentary leader has the influence to make a difference and they are reluctant to expend political capital on it in the short term. Keating, channeling his mentor Jack Lang, once said, 'In the race of life always back self-interest, at least you know it's trying.' It is in Dutton's self-interest to fix the Liberal Party's women problem because, if he doesn't, he will never become prime minister.

Chapter 13

Where to from here?

Albanese has become the prime minister with the most experience in parliament prior to winning office since the Second World War. This makes him an interesting political figure — desperate to win and govern but not giving the electorate much of an idea of what to expect from a new Labor government. Even upon winning the 2022 election he was a relatively unknown quantity, despite his length of service and seniority across so many parliamentary years. That's because Albanese's role was always larger within the party and parliament than in the wider electorate. Six years as Leader of the House of Representatives managing parliamentary business during the Rudd and Gillard years didn't win him a lot of publicity. Being Opposition Leader during a pandemic gave Albanese a lower profile than would usually be the case in that role. Victory would bring the chance to change all of that. To show Australia what voters in his electorate had seen for years.

With a majority of just two, Labor can't afford to lose seats unless it's prepared to govern in minority. Relying on minor parties and independents didn't end well for Julia Gillard, despite her administration managing the parliament effectively. One of the reasons Albanese succeeded when few within his party initially thought that he would is because of long-term planning. As he likes to say, he was 'kicking with the wind in the final quarter' — but only after years of planning and careful execution. Albo might be a rugby league man at heart, not a code hopper like Scott Morrison, but that descriptor neatly encapsulates his approach. It was a deliberate contrast from Shorten's strategy to win the news cycle week to week, day to day. Having been successful, we can expect that to continue in government.

Anthony Albanese wants to change politics. There's a good chance, of course, that his diabolical political inheritance will change him. Journalist George Megalogenis wrote that every new Labor government faces 'the drumbeat of global crisis': the Great Depression for James Scullin; war for John Curtin; oil price shocks for Gough Whitlam; Kevin Rudd had his Global Financial Crisis. Bob Hawke is a partial exception, the 1982–83 recession helping his election and providing a catalyst for economic reform. If you will forgive us one last football analogy, Hawke and Keating had the wind at their backs when they set about the inclusive growth strategy Albanese admires. The danger for Albanese and Chalmers is that their inheritance is closer to Scullin's than that of Hawke: a global recession, the budget deteriorating from an already weak position, and rising inflation and interest rates. Better to face those challenges early in a parliamentary term.

When politics is as broken as it has been in Australia, a change of leadership can go a long way. Albanese was as good as his word in seeking to change the way politics works. New South Wales Liberal Premier Dominic Perrottet, himself surprising observers with his cooperation with the Andrews government in Victoria in reforming school education, was complimentary. 'I thought today's national cabinet was refreshingly collaborative,' Perrottet said in a not-so-subtle dig at Morrison after the first meeting of that forum chaired by Albanese on 17 June. The new prime minister enjoyed the praise, referencing it during our interview that same afternoon. 'This is what good government looks like,' he told us.

The combination of a consultative style and a more inclusive set of social policies was certainly noticeable in the early weeks of the government. In other policy areas, the fact that Albanese sees policy as a problem to solve rather than a target for ideology will help.

Climate change provides a good example. It was potentially divisive for Labor, but it could now become a potent political weapon with the advantage of incumbency. Finding the money to make the promised changes to childcare, aged care and health will be challenging enough. Living up to the expectation that he hinted at during the campaign, that it is Labor governments that make the big reforms, will be even harder. However, to turn Megalogenis' argument on its head, Labor takes the tough decisions because they are forced to — only winning when conservative governments are well past their use-by dates and Labor have to clean up the mess. A student of this history, Albanese knows that it wasn't the GFC that tore the Rudd government apart but Rudd's poor grasp of politics and governance. Albanese is determined to learn from the past.

Making a difference

The smart-target election strategy dovetailed with Albanese's conclusions about the failures of the Rudd government — trying to do too much too quickly and without adequate process. Unlike Rudd, Albanese is a creature of both the Labor Party and the parliament. He knows that principles are one thing, a finished Act of parliament quite another. In one respect, the discussion about the 'real Albo' was a compliment. We didn't ponder the 'real ScoMo' because we knew there was little authentic to find. Both Albanese's enemies and friends, though, imagined there was more to Albo than the risk-averse leader presented to voters. Shadow cabinet took some difficult decisions but worked by consensus — the chair's understanding of consensus, of course. That means taking up the views and ideas of colleagues and senior public servants more so than imposing them.

Albanese has firm views about public-sector reform. Morrison's department head Phil Gaetjens resigned before the first brace of ministers was sworn in. Albanese announced Glyn Davis as Gaetjens' replacement to head the Department of Prime Minister and Cabinet. It was a good appointment, coming from outside the Commonwealth public service, Davis being a former professor of public policy and vice-chancellor of the University of Melbourne, with a good Labor pedigree, having led the Department of Premier and Cabinet under two Queensland premiers. Davis won't be a yes man, which is just what Albanese needs. The government also announced the weakening of Home Affairs with the federal police moving back to the Attorney-General's Department.

Albanese told us about his priorities. 'There's been a privatisation of labour in the public service whereby you have ex-public servants working as contractors costing taxpayers more, but they're off the books. That makes no sense.' He sees the Hawke government as a model of 'good cabinet government and the way that government functions. They engaged in debate.'

Albanese spoke during the campaign about the importance of a government having 'structures in place to drive the change, the creation of Jobs and Skills Australia, the creation of the National Reconstruction Fund', and that they are properly run rather than stacked with mates. He had clearly thought deeply about such things during years of hard labour in opposition. It is an approach to government more Hawke than Rudd. Albanese did have to paper over some policy cracks, though. Asked during the campaign about the near 30 per cent gap between men's and women's super at retirement, he pointed towards his childcare policy. We should expect Labor to do something more pro-active about such issues, shouldn't we?

Not all policy change requires bucket-loads of money to illustrate the fact that a change of government would mean a change of values. There was a strong personal connection to one early change. Dropping the cashless debit card used to torture welfare recipients marked a useful divide on social policy. According to the Auditor-General, five years of trials for moving welfare recipients on to the restrictive debit card had failed to show any benefits. Growing up in a household where the disability pension was the sole source of income, Albanese despised the previous government's policy. The change would require a legislative amendment.

Earlier in the year Albanese had tweeted pictures of the food served in some aged-care residences to underline the issue of standards and enforcement. Albanese has also been a big supporter of the vibrant arts community in his electorate. Signalling something other than contempt around cultural questions would be noticeable. Indeed, Albanese will have a free hand on social and cultural issues, given the state of the parliament.

Allowing the Murugappan family to return to the Queensland town of Biloela cost little in policy or financial terms but was an important signal about Albanese's social conscience. He was moved by the commitment of the local community to the Sri Lankan family. 'We are a strong enough society to say that we should not treat people badly, in order to send a message to others,' the Prime Minister said in his first week in the job. 'And it's beyond my comprehension how this has gone on for so long, at enormous cost. We're better than that. Australia is a more generous and kind country than that.' The previous government had acknowledged the public campaign around the family by releasing them from detention but cruelly stopped short of finalising their status. Yet, immigration and asylum would inevitably cause a few headaches for the new government. Labor's adoption of boat turnbacks caused a lot of consternation on the left. Here the character of the leaders becomes important. Would Albanese use detainees as pawns, leaving documented refugees in limbo for years for purely political rather than policy reasons? Of course not.

Some policies without a high cost, such as an anti-corruption commission, allowed Labor to throw plenty of shade at the Morrison government and provided an opportunity to work constructively with the new parliament. Ending ministerial interference in painstaking research-grant processes was also a no-cost no-brainer. As was a gradual phase-out of live animal exports, having learned from the knee-jerk decision to ban cattle exports after a disturbing media report in 2011. The Federal Court later found the decision to have been unlawful (setting up conflict with the Western Australian government). All this added up to a clear demarcation from the previous government without the 'big target' some observers had demanded.

What sort of leader?

Albanese will want to manage his cabinet as Hawke did, with a consensus style of leadership. However, the modern prime ministership lends itself towards the inexorable centralisation that has taken place since the end of the Second World War. Having successfully portrayed Morrison as a shirker, the new prime minister will naturally want to take a more assertive approach to problem-solving and crisis management. The competing instincts of seeking consensus but acting as the lone wolf at times will inevitably play out in his government's approach to policy.

How does the new prime minister deal with the crossbench even though he has a majority in the lower house? He was sensible enough to know he might need them one day even though he ruled out deals during the campaign. But he did cut their staffing allocations shortly after the election, much to their collective irritation. He was always going to need the Greens in the Senate. A consensus style of leadership goes beyond the numbers in each chamber.

Albanese's rhetoric that he wants to govern for all of Australia was in part a marketing tool designed to highlight Morrison's New South Wales–centric outlook. But he will have to do just that if he wants to make gains in Queensland to offset losses elsewhere at the next election. His successful framing of Morrison as a blame shifter and someone not to be trusted paid off, as did his own positioning as a small target. But they are not among the advantages of incumbency. The next election will be fought differently, irrespective of whether Queenslander Dutton is leading the Coalition by then. New Nationals leader Littleproud is also a Queenslander. The next election will be won and lost in Queensland, with some interest in Western Australia, where losing seats like Hasluck and Tangney could cost Labor its majority. Winning four seats with the help of McGowan's popularity — and Morrison's unwise decision to take him on over COVID — feels like a one-off. Tangney would be high on the list of electorates Liberals think they can win next time. If McGowan is either retired or less popular in three years' time, federal Labor needs to prepare for the possibility that its extraordinary showing in the west in 2022 won't be replicated. Similarly, Victoria has run out of winnable seats for Labor, and Higgins may be difficult to hold, as will Bennelong in New South Wales. Even if Dee Madigan is right and the Liberal ads claiming 'it won't be easy under Albanese' missed their mark, three years from now a campaign that 'it hasn't been easy under Albanese' could resonate.

Queenslanders in the Labor caucus worry that the party elsewhere in the country will take the 2022 win for granted since it showed that Labor can win without Queensland. Discussing the many treks he made up north prior to the election, Albanese told us he was happy with what they had achieved. 'In Queensland, we didn't win the seats we wanted to win but we're now in striking distance. The margins had blown out so big. Flynn, we were targeting, was 9 per cent. We've knocked off more than half of that.' Armed with the power of incumbency, the seats that saw a lot of margins fall by half could be won next time, alongside seats perhaps only held because of popular Liberal MPs who may retire now that the Coalition is out of office. Dutton is unlikely to be as popular in southern states as he could be in his home state or in the west.

Contrasting fortunes in these states will in turn affect the way Labor approaches government. With more Western Australians than Queenslanders in the Labor caucus, the risk is that issues affecting the Sunshine State aren't adequately addressed by the new government. It will be the job of senior Queenslanders Jim Chalmers and Murray Watt to prevent that happening, keeping their leader to his word about governing for the whole nation. Placing his authority in Queensland's corner when interstate disputes over issues like GST revenue arise will matter the most. Chalmers' high profile will grow with the responsibility of running the economy. A high-profile Queensland frontbencher in cabinet could offset the lost clout of Queenslanders in the party room. It might also help come campaign time. 'Ours will be a really Queensland-focused government regardless and my job is to help ensure that,' Chalmers told us. Watt was elevated to the agriculture portfolio in cabinet after the election precisely because Albanese is aware of the importance of appealing to Queenslanders at the next election; Watt is a member of Albanese's left faction and has his leader's ear.

Leadership can be a matter of contrasts as well as style. Facing Dutton instead of Morrison, and not having to look over his shoulder for Labor leadership aspirants for some time, Albanese has to watch that the confidence that comes with an election victory does not drift towards arrogance. The policy difficulties he inherits will militate against that.

A taxing inheritance

What economic problems do the new government face? Let's hand the microphone to Jim Chalmers on the day he released Labor's election costings: 'Whoever wins the election on Saturday will inherit high and rising inflation, with interest rates rising as well. The worst real wages cut in more than twenty years, and a trillion dollars in debt with almost nothing to show for it.' These would be, he continued, 'the trickiest economic conditions inherited by an incoming government since World War II'. Arguably not, but certainly tricky for a party that wants to spend more money on core services but had been thumped by the electorate three years earlier for offering increases to taxation. The nature of the economic debate during the campaign simply didn't reflect this reality. A brutal post-election budget loomed whoever triumphed in May. Chalmers conceded this by flagging a mini-budget for the second half of the year, although he promoted this as a reorientation of spending from Coalition waste to Labor priorities. Chalmers had his inevitable 'the cupboard is bare' moment after the election in spite of the Charter of Budget Honesty. Of course, he blamed the previous government for the deficit, but that doesn't resolve the problem.

One strategy that will be more effective from government than from opposition is to change the parameters of economic debate to ground more friendly to Labor. One such issue is making the economy more resilient to climate change. In opposition, Albanese had discussed climate change as an economic as much as an environmental problem. One poll found that nearly 70 per cent of respondents believe that 'meaningful action on climate change will deliver long term economic benefits', and nearly half thought the benefits would outweigh any costs to them personally. Concentrating minds on that sort of thing during an election campaign, as opposed to what meaningful action would cost, as Labor more or less conceded with its approach to budget and climate policy, wasn't great preparation for government. Yet, a government determined to take meaningful action with a sustained argument designed to buttress these attitudes, could find itself on the right side of this issue.

Still, the same issues that had made re-election tough would make government tough: rising inflation, rising interest rates, house prices out of reach of first-time buyers, sluggish wages, low productivity growth. Having familiarised himself with the unemployment rate, Albanese can expect it to rise as international students and other sources of immigration increase, even if they don't quite return to pre-pandemic levels. There is a good chance ratings agencies will take away Australia's AAA credit rating, increasing interest payments and threatening confidence. A vote for Labor might have been a vote for doing something about all this. Yet, while Labor had, in opposition, systematically addressed these issues, their policies designed to tackle them were very broad but not very deep. 'This is an economy crying out for reform,' Albanese told the Australian Chamber of Commerce during the campaign, praising the Hawke and Keating model of 'inclusive growth'. While Labor rightly criticised the government's performance in enhancing productivity growth, Albanese offered only incremental efforts based on existing policies such as more funding for childcare to increase women's workforce participation. While we would expect Labor to be up to the challenges of governing in these circumstances, the political problem is that this will undoubtedly involve policies not flagged prior to the election. The Hawke government managed this political problem and emerged with successive election victories. New governments have a very limited window to enact reform. Hawke and Keating quickly moved to put in place the micro-economic reforms the Fraser government eschewed. The public service knew what was required. It was a thirteen-year Labor government, but the heavy lifting happened early. However, their policies on deregulation, pension asset tests and wage restraint were not popular. And Albanese is no Bob Hawke.

Similarly, John Howard and Peter Costello's first budget was a painful one. Howard's first term included industrial relations reforms, then his first re-election involved campaigning for a goods and services tax. Kevin Rudd was quickly engulfed by the Global Financial Crisis, which curtailed his capacity to pursue meaningful economic reforms. The Henry Tax Review was commissioned, but the retreat from the taxes it recommended, coupled with Rudd baulking at a double dissolution election to legislate the twice-rejected emissions reduction scheme, left him with little more than an apology to Indigenous Australians as his legacy. Abbott understood the need for a new government to act decisively, which is why Joe Hockey's first budget, in 2014, was so brutal. Unfortunately for the newly elected Coalition government, Abbott had ruled out all manner of spending cuts before polling day. A small-target strategy can have big consequences. As a result, the new parliament blocked most of Abbott's fiscal agenda, and before the federation and taxation white papers came back, leadership wrangling put an end to reformist instincts.

That task now falls to Albanese and Chalmers. They know the history. Chalmers was chief of staff to Swan. Keating wryly commented that there was an unthumbed copy of the Campbell report on financial deregulation in the Treasurer's office when he took it over from Howard in 1983. As George Megalogenis pointed out, the states seem more prepared to do some of the heavy lifting they eschewed under Whitlam and Hawke. The Henry Report recommended greater use of land taxes instead of stamp duty. Some states and territories are headed in this direction. Chalmers could facilitate this without breaking federal Labor's promise about taxes. He would just need to grease the wheels and provide some political cover to the premiers.

Treasurers always bristle about prime ministers looking over their shoulders, concerned about the political consequences of difficult economic decisions. They know they must work well together if the government is to succeed. 'It's evolved over time, had its ups and downs of course like any friendship and any working relationship,' Chalmers told us. 'We're conscious of how we work together without obsessing over it. We trust each other, support each other, and believe in each other. We've backed each other at important times, making difficult calls on policy and politics.' That included saying no to shadow ministers who wanted bigger spending commitments in their areas during the campaign. Chalmers seems as close to Albanese's inner circle as he needs to be and wants to be, without being all the way in.

Having promised to ease cost-of-living pressures, Albanese will want to ensure Labor's first budget doesn't undercut his campaign pledges. But the head of Treasury used a post-election speech to make the point that the tax system needs reforming, and spending restraint should be on the agenda. The shape of tensions between political and economic realities was established early. The times may suit the Prime Minister, though. Albanese's instinct will be to keep his spending commitment without reversing the income tax cuts he waved through in one of his first actions as opposition leader.

What will it take for the incoming government simply to restore services to an acceptable level? Economist Richard

Denniss argues that taxes and debt are already around peace-time highs. Instead of talking about small government in those circumstances, we should be making sure that our interventions in the economy are positive. Albanese was edging towards recognition of these needs. He wrote in *The Australian* after the 2022 floods in Queensland and New South Wales:

> Government can make it easier for business and communities to respond to crisis. They can provide the leadership the community is looking for. Now is the time to address the weaknesses exposed by the pandemic and, in the process, make our nation stronger and more prosperous. If we applied Morrison's approach to the post-flooding rebuild, we would rebuild our communities exactly the way they were prior to the calamity. And we would never spend a dollar in flood mitigation schemes and infrastructure upgrades that can reduce potential effects of future floods. That would be foolish.

Yet, at both state and Commonwealth level, there is a lack of perceived political benefit in properly funding existing programs. The way the Commonwealth has treated aged care provides an example. The sector has been under-funded for decades and an ageing population provides additional challenges. At any given time, the incentive for the incumbent government to provide a substantial funding boost is limited. The pandemic led to staff shortages and higher mortality rates, the former prime minister giving in to calls for the military to assist. The Aged Care Royal Commission highlighted systemic problems. Like many public institutions, aged-care facilities have drawn heavily on the goodwill of staff working in a crucial care sector. Having justifiably criticised a minister with limited ability, Labor should give the aged-care portfolio a higher profile. Yet, even without policy changes, the 2022 budget projected spending in the sector to increase nearly 10 per cent in real terms over four years.

Pollster RedBridge Group conducted research in the electorates of Corangamite, Lindsay and Banks, canvassing 1500 voters for their views on the aged-care crisis. Four out of five voters believed the Commonwealth should spend more. There was widespread agreement that the sector needed to pay more to attract workers and retain those in place. The Aged Care Royal Commission gave plenty of ammunition for an opposition keen to make an impact. An ineffective minister made this a political winner, whereas Labor's shadow aged care spokeswoman Clare O'Neil was an effective advocate for action and additional resources. The opposition parties forced the government to provide an in-principle commitment on aged-care wages but little immediate funding. For Labor's part, there was little sense that the very structure and incentives in aged care need shaking up. Albanese promoted O'Neil into cabinet, but as the Minister for Home Affairs. Anika Wells was elevated from the backbench to take over aged care, leaving the important portfolio in the outer ministry.

In some policy areas, such as foreign aid and public broadcasting, Labor had created high expectations by complaining about every cut made by the previous government, but they only guaranteed limited restoration of funding in their first term. Other policies, such as high-speed rail links between Sydney and Newcastle, come with a big price tag, and in opposition Labor promised to make a modest start, as a first step towards a larger network. Promising to restore funding to the Environmental Defender's Office, withdrawn in the first Abbott budget, is a good example of a modest policy change that was supported by the relevant interest groups during the campaign. 'We're going to start to fix things and try to turn around the decade of neglect that we've seen under this government,' Albanese said. It was a line he returned to frequently during the campaign, almost apologising for the modesty of many Labor promises.

Other policies have consequences far beyond the budget. Labor's 2030 climate commitments were consistent with two degrees of warming, compared to three degrees for the government but short of the Greens and teals target of one and a half. Positioning Labor between the government and the Greens should not have been too difficult, but Labor's ambiguous position on coal mining would become a recurring theme of the campaign. It was also tough for Labor to match the Greens' promise to join the United Nations goal to abandon coal use, and ban new coal and gas developments. A range of able Labor shadow ministers have worked on climate policy. On the other hand, providing an Indigenous Voice in the Constitution, a clear point of difference from the government, would require prime ministerial leadership.

It has been easy enough for Labor to occupy the centre ground on these issues, vacated by the Liberal Party. However, the narrow majority requires Labor to think about their relationship with the Greens. It was the retirement of Lindsay Tanner in 2010 that cleared the way for Adam Bandt to take the seat of Melbourne. Inner-Sydney seats may be up for grabs when Albanese and Plibersek retire, to add to the trend in Melbourne and Brisbane. A long-term strategy of expecting an election win over the opposition to provide majority government, with hung parliaments the rare exception, may be living in the past. However, the Greens vote may have peaked for the time being, given it has risen in the last three elections with the Coalition in power. Bandt was adamant that a vote for the Greens was a vote to throw out the government in 2022. No wonder Albanese knew he didn't need to negotiate with the Greens to form government even if his majority didn't quite eventuate. On the other hand, the total 'others' vote — all minor parties and independents — has risen steadily since 2007, and was close to Labor's in 2022.

It wasn't just Labor that benefited from the fact that the pandemic turned the economic debate in Australia upside down. Unemployment was low, but small business continued to feel the effects of shutdowns. Budget deficits dominated forward estimates, but nobody seemed to care. Focusing on the economic issues within the government's control made the Morrison government, in particular, look even worse. Similarly, the previous government pretty much waved the white flag on economic reform after Abbott and Turnbull fell afoul of the often-difficult politics involved. Sluggish wages growth and cost-of-living pressures are directly related to the lack of productivity-enhancing policy of the last decade.

The prospect of a budget surplus featured in the Coalition's 2019 election campaign advertising and was front and centre in Morrison's rhetoric, the Prime Minister occasionally tripping by referring to a surplus as though it had been already achieved rather than simply forecast. This 'surplus good, deficit bad' rhetoric reflects the low quality of economic debate in Australia, but for decades Labor has failed to unshackle itself from the parameters of that debate; indeed, Wayne Swan positively embraced an unhelpful comparison between government and household budgets.

Some of these issues are related to the small-target versus big-target debate. Public opinion does change over time, though, over whether taxation or spending is too high (or low). Similarly, the agenda in this policy area can favour one side or the other depending on the circumstances, so Albanese's priorities will be crucial. While the Morrison government could point to low unemployment, the expectation that a strong labour market would push up wages proved false. Public opinion associating Labor with stronger wages growth is, like that associating the Coalition with lower taxes, seemingly impervious to evidence. The Hawke government's Accord, for example, was designed to keep a lid on wages and therefore inflation. Indeed, discussing inflation in terms of living costs, as opposed to an economic ill affecting the allocation of resources in the economy, tended to favour Labor during the campaign but is something they will need to turn their attention to in government.

'Tonight, the Australian people have voted for change,' Anthony Albanese started his victory speech on 21 May 2022.

Elections are blunt instruments, though. Results can be over-interpreted. It is telling that all eight factors behind Labor's win listed by Erickson are about the shortcomings of the Morrison government. While the new ministry will constantly remind voters of those problems, they will never again be as potent.

The bottom line is that Labor is back in power. The optimism and common purpose of which Albanese often speaks will be important in facing the challenges left by the lost decade of divisive politics and policy paralysis. The Albanese government now has a chance to live up to the rhetoric of its leader: to shape change rather than be shaped by it; to end the climate wars; to build an economy that works for people, not the other way around; to embrace the Uluru Statement from the Heart. For Albo, whatever happens, nothing will take away from his 2022 victory.

Acknowledgements

We were both undergraduate students when Pamela Williams's *The Victory*, about the 1996 election, was published. Anyone who can make Gary Gray and Andrew Robb sound interesting is a genius. That book helped inspire our enthusiasm for writing about politics.

Thanks to the many senior Labor and Coalition figures, inside and outside of the parliament, who agreed to be interviewed, in particular Prime Minister Anthony Albanese who very generously gave us hours of valuable interview time during his busy transition to government. We contacted Scott Morrison for an interview. He never responded.

Thanks to everyone at HarperCollins for making the publication process easy. In particular Helen Littleton, Mary Rennie, Shannon Kelly and our copy-editor John Mapps. All errors are of course our own.

Peter would like to thank Ainslie, Sasha and Chloe, for always reminding him what matters.

Wayne would like to thank Cory, for bringing the light.

Finally, a special thanks to our publisher for the past 15 years, Louise Adler. This is the first book we've written without her, having followed her to three different publishing houses prior to now. Her decision to take up a new challenge in life will surely make the Adelaide Writers' Week an event not to be missed. Louise's sea change fortuitously led us to the wonderful people at HarperCollins.

Sources

Except where noted in the text, quotations are taken from the public record. As Adam Bandt said during the campaign, 'Google it, mate.' The sources listed below were used for ideas and evidence.

Bali, Meghna, 2021, 'How TikTok Could Influence Next Year's Election', *Triple J Hack*, 8 December, https://www.abc.net.au/triplej/programs/hack/how-tiktok-could-influence-2022-federal-election/13668042.

Bashford Canales, Sarah, and Dan Jarvis-Bardy, 2022, 'Is Australian Politics About to Have Its Independents Day in the 2022 Federal Election?', *The Canberra Times*, 4 April, https://www.canberratimes.com.au/story/7665996/the-teal-wave-the-new-breed-of-independents-shaking-up-australian-politics/.

Blaine, Lech, 2022, 'Teal and Loathing: On the Campaign Trail', *The Monthly*, June.

Bonham, Kevin, 2022, 'Two-Party Swing Decided This Election', *Dr Kevin Bonham*, 25 June.

Bor, Alexander, Frederik Juhl Jorgensen and Michael Bang Petersen, 2021, 'The COVID-19 Pandemic Eroded System Support but Not Social Solidarity', https://psyarxiv.com/qjmct/.

Brett, Judith, 2022, 'How the Liberals Lost the "Moral Middle Class"', *The Conversation*, 4 May, https://theconversation.com/how-the-liberals-lost-the-moral-middle-class-and-now-the-teal-independents-may-well-cash-in-182293.

———— 2022, 'Morrison's Power Without Purpose', *The Monthly*, May.

Butler, Josh, 2022, 'Who is Anthony Albanese?', *Guardian Australia*, 22 May, https://www.theguardian.com/australia-news/2022/may/22/who-is-anthony-albanese-how-a-working-class-activist-became-australias-pm.

Cooke, Richard, 2020, 'The Disappearing Man', *The Monthly*, November.

Coper, Ed, 2022, 'Secrets from the Teals' Digital War Room', *The Sunday Age*, 5 June, https://www.theage.com.au/national/secrets-from-the-teals-digital-war-room-we-created-a-direct-line-to-voters-and-now-tv-political-ads-are-dead-20220605-p5ar5j.html.

Emerson, Craig, and Jay Weatherill, 2019, *Review of Labor's 2019 Election Campaign*, Australian Labor Party, Canberra.

Errington, Wayne and Peter van Onselen, 2007, 'Managing Expectations: The Howard Government's WorkChoices Information Campaign', *Media International Australia*, 123(5).

———— 2021, *Who Dares Loses: Pariah Policies*, Monash University Press, Melbourne.

Greber, Jacob, 2022, 'New Look Albo', *AFR Magazine*, 24 February, https://www.afr.com/politics/federal/new-look-albo-i-m-comfortable-in-the-boardrooms-as-well-as-the-pub-20201217-p56ohc.

Hardaker, David, 2022, 'An Interview with Simon Holmes à Court', *Crikey*, 30 May.

Johnson, Carol, 2022, 'Why Morrison's Can-Do Capitalism and Conservative Masculinity May Not Be Cutting Through Anymore', *The Conversation*, 17 May, https://theconversation.com/why-morrisons-can-do-capitalism-and-conservative-masculinity-may-not-be-cutting-through-anymore-183118.

Kelly, Sean, 2021, *The Game: A Portrait of Scott Morrison*, Black Inc, Melbourne.

Long, Stephen, 2019, 'The Rich Listers Funding Politicians Who Back Climate Action', *ABC News*, 29 October, https://www.abc.net.au/news/2019-10-29/clean-green-rich-wealthy-donors-climate-200-politicians/11647162.

McAllister, Ian, and Toni Makkai, 2018, 'The Decline and Rise of Class Voting: From Occupation to Culture in Australia', *Journal of Sociology*, October 29.

McMullan, Bob, 2022, 'Early Lessons From the 2022 Campaign', *Pearls and Irritations*, 11 June, https://johnmenadue.com/early-lessons-from-the-2022-election/.

Megalogenis, George, 2022, 'Labor and the Curse of the Global Shocks: Can Albanese Defy History?', *The Age*, 18 June, https://www.theage.com.au/politics/federal/labor-and-the-curse-of-the-global-shocks-can-albanese-defy-history-20220617-p5auif.html.

Middleton, Karen, 2017, *Albanese: Telling It Straight*, Vintage, Sydney.

Murphy, Katharine, 2022, 'Labor's Lone Wolf: Anthony Albanese Embarks on the Fight of His Life', *The Guardian*, 29 January https://www.theguardian.com/australia-news/2022/jan/29/labors-lone-wolf-anthony-albanese-embarks-on-the-fight-of-his-life.

Palmieri, Sonia, 2022, 'Our New Parliament Will Have Record Numbers of Women', *The Conversation*, 31 May, https://theconversation.com/our-new-parliament-will-have-record-numbers-of-women-will-this-finally-make-it-a-safe-place-to-work-181598.

Parkinson, Martin, 2021, *A Decade of Drift*, Monash University Publishing, Clayton.

Raue, Ben, 2022, 'What Happened to the Chinese Australian Vote in the Big Cities?', *The Tally Room*, 24 May, https://www.tallyroom.com.au/47839.

Seccombe, Mike, 2022, 'Collapse of the Modern Liberal Party', *The Monthly*, 11–17 June.

Simons, Margaret, 2022, 'Focus on Gaffes Misses the Real Issues', *The Age*, 18 April, https://www.theage.com.au/national/focus-on-gaffes-misses-the-real-issues-20220417-p5adz1.html.

———— 2022, 'Independents and the Balance of Power', *The Monthly*, April.

Snow, Deborah, 2022, 'Reinventing Tanya: The One Discordant Note in Albanese's Reshuffle', *The Sydney Morning Herald*, 6 June, https://www.smh.com.au/politics/federal/reinventing-tanya-the-one-discordant-note-in-albanese-s-reshuffle-20220605-p5ar6y.html.

Strangio, Paul, 2022, 'If the Polls Are Right, He May Soon Be the Next Australian Prime Minister. Who Is Anthony Albanese?' *The Conversation*, 16 May, https://theconversation.com/if-the-polls-are-right-he-may-soon-be-the-next-australian-prime-minister-so-who-is-anthony-albanese-177617.

Sweet, Melissa, 2022, 'Why This Doctor Gave Up General Practice to Run For Election as an Independent Candidate', *Croakey*, 26 April, https://www.croakey.org/why-this-doctor-gave-up-general-practice-to-run-for-election-as-an-independent-candidate/.

Tranter, Bruce, 2015, 'The Impact of Political Context on the Measurement of Postmaterialist Values', *SAGE Open*, 22 June, https://journals.sagepub.com/doi/10.1177/2158244015591826.

Turner, Brook, 2021, 'Simon Holmes à Court: If It Works, The Payoff Will Be Enormous', *Good Weekend*, 30 October.

Walter, James, 2022, 'Leadership Now: What Can History Tell Us', *Australian Policy and History*, 30 May, https://aph.org.au/2022/05/leadership-now-what-can-history-tell-us/.

Index of People